Great Wars and Great Leaders

Great Wars and Great Leaders

A Libertarian Rebuttal

Ralph Raico

MISESINSTITUTE

Published 2010 by the Mises Institute and licensed under a Creative Commons Attribution-NonCommercial-NoDerivs 4.0 International License. http://creativecommons.org/licenses/by-nc-nd/4.0/

Mises Institute
518 West Magnolia Avenue
Auburn, Alabama 36832
mises.org

ISBN: 978-1-61016-096-4

Dedicated to the memory of Murray N. Rothbard

Lifelong mentor and friend

Contents

Foreword by Robert Higgs ... iii
Introduction ... vii

Essays

1 World War I: The Turning Point ... 1
2 Rethinking Churchill ... 53
3 Harry S. Truman: Advancing the Revolution ... 103
4 Marxist Dreams and Soviet Realities ... 143
5 Nazifying the Germans ... 157

Reviews

6 Trotsky: The Ignorance and the Evil ... 165
7 The Two "Testaments" of American Foreign Policy ... 177
8 The Other War that Never Ends: A Survey of Some Recent Literature on World War I ... 185
9 Starving a People into Submission ... 197
10 John T. Flynn and the Apotheosis of Franklin Roosevelt ... 207
11 On the Brink of World War II ... 219
12 The Great War Retold ... 229

Foreword

by Robert Higgs

For many years, I have described Ralph Raico as "my favorite historian." When David Theroux and I were making our plans in 1995 for the publication of a new scholarly quarterly, *The Independent Review*, and selecting the scholars we would ask to serve as associate editors, I knew that I would want one of them to be an excellent historian, and I knew also that the person I wanted most was Raico. I had complete confidence that he would bring to our project precisely the combination of personal integrity, scholarly mastery, and sound judgment I needed in an associate. In the fifteen years since then, I have never regretted that I prevailed on Ralph to serve in this capacity and that he graciously accepted my invitation. Three of the marvelous review essays that appear here were first published in *TIR*.

Much earlier I had developed a deep respect for Raico as a scholar and as a person. I insist that these two qualities cannot be separated without dire consequences. Some scholars have energy, brilliance, and mastery of their fields, but they lack personal integrity; hence they bend easily before the winds of professional fashion and social pressure. I have always admired Ralph's amazing command of the wide-ranging literature related to the topics about which he lectures and writes. But I have admired even more his courageous capacity for frankly evaluating the actors and the actions in question, not to mention the clarity and wit of his humane, level-headed judgments.

Academic historians, who long ago came to dominate the writing of serious history in the United States, have not distinguished themselves as independent thinkers. All too often, especially in the past thirty or forty years, they have surrendered their judgments and even their attention spans to a combination of hyper-sensitive multiculturalism and power worship. They tend to see society as divided between a small group of oppressors (nearly all of whom are, not coincidentally, straight white males engaged in or closely associated with corporate business) and a conglomeration of oppressed groups, among whom nonwhites, women, homosexuals, and low-wage workers receive prominent attention and solicitude. When the historians write about the economy, they usually view it though quasi-Marxist lenses, perceiving that investors and employers have been (and remain) the natural enemies of the workers, who would never have escaped destitution except for the heroic struggles waged on their behalf by labor unions and progressive politicians. When they write about international affairs, they elevate the "democratic" wartime leaders to god-like status, especially so for Abraham Lincoln, Woodrow Wilson, Winston Churchill, and Franklin D. Roosevelt—politicians whose public declarations of noble intentions the historians tend to accept at face value.

Raico, in contrast, steadfastly refuses to be sucked into this ideological mire. Having attended Ludwig von Mises's famous seminar at New York University and having completed his Ph.D. dissertation at the University of Chicago under F. A. Hayek's supervision, he understands classical liberalism as well as anyone, and his historical judgments reflect this more solid and humane grounding. For Ralph, it would be not only unseemly but foolish to quiver obsequiously in the historical presence of a Churchill, a Roosevelt, or a Truman. He knows when he has encountered a politician who lusted after power and public adulation, and he describes the man accordingly. He does not sweep under the rug the crimes committed by the most publicly revered Western political leaders. If they ordered or acceded to the commission of mass murder, he tells us, without mincing words, that they did so. The idea that the United States has invariably played the role of savior or "good guy" in its international relations Raico recognizes as state propaganda, rather than honest history.

Thus, in these pages, you will find descriptions and accounts of World War I, of the lead-up to formal U.S. belligerence in World War II, and of Churchill, Roosevelt, and Truman, among others, that bear little resemblance to what you were taught in school. Here you will encounter, perhaps for the first time, compelling evidence of how the British maneuvered U.S. leaders and tricked the American people prior to the U.S. declarations of war in 1917 and 1941. You will read about how the British undertook to starve the Germans — men, women, and children alike — not only during World War I, but for the greater part of a year after the armistice. You will be presented with descriptions of how the communists were deified and the German people demonized by historians and others who ought to have known better. You will see painted in truer shades a portrait of the epic confrontation between the great majority of Americans who wished to keep their country at peace in 1939, 1940, and 1941 and the well-placed, unscrupulous minority who sought to plunge the United States into the European maelstrom.

Raico's historical essays are not for the faint of heart or for those whose loyalty to the U.S. or British state outweighs their devotion to truth and humanity. Yet Ralph did not invent the ugly facts he recounts here, as his ample documentation attests. Indeed, many historians have known these facts, but few have been willing to step forward and defy politically popular and professionally fashionable views in the forthright, pull-no-punches way that Raico does. The historians' principal defect for the most part has not been a failure or refusal to dig out the relevant facts, but rather a tendency to go along to get along in academia and "respectable" society, a sphere in which individual honesty and courage generally count against a writer or teacher, whereas capitulation to trendy nonsense often brings great rewards and professional acclaim.

Those who have not read Raico's essays or listened to his lectures have a feast in store here. Those who have read some, but not all of the essays in this collection may rest assured that the quality remains high throughout the volume. Any one of the main essays well justifies the price of the book, and each of the review essays is a jewel of solid scholarship and excellent judgment. Moreover, in contrast to the bland, uninspired writing that most academic historians dish out, Ralph's clear, vigorous prose serves as a tasty spice for the meaty substance. *Bon appétit.*

Introduction

The King of Prussia, Frederick II ("the Great"), confessed that he had seized the province of Silesia from the Empress Maria Theresa in 1740 because, as a newcomer to the throne, he had to make a name for himself. This initiated a war with Austria that developed into a world-wide war (in North America, the French and Indian War), and went on to 1763. Of course, many tens of thousands died in that series of wars.

Frederick's admission is probably unique in the annals of leaders of states. In general, rulers have been much more circumspect about revealing the true reasons for their wars, as well as the methods by which they conduct them. Pretexts and evasions have proliferated. In today's democratic societies, these are endorsed—often invented—by compliant professors and other intellectuals.

For generations, the unmasking of such excuses for war and war-making has been the essence of *historical revisionism*, or simply *revisionism*. Revisionism and classical liberalism, today called libertarianism, have always been closely linked.

The greatest classical liberal thinker on international affairs was Richard Cobden, whose crusade for repeal of the Corn Laws triumphed in 1846, bringing free trade and prosperity to England. Cobden's two-volume *Political Writings* (reprinted by Garland Publishing in 1973) are all revisionist accounts of British foreign policy.

Cobden maintained that "The middle and industrious classes of England can have no interest apart from the preservation of peace. The honours, the fame, the emoluments of war belong not to them; the battle-plain is the harvest-field of the aristocracy, watered by the blood of the people." He looked forward to a time when the slogan *"no foreign politics"* would become the watchword of all who aspired to be representatives of a free people. Cobden went so far as to trace the calamitous English wars against revolutionary France — which went on for a generation and ended only at Waterloo — to the hostility of the British upper classes to the anti-aristocratic policies of the French.

Castigating the aristocracy for its alleged war-lust was standard for liberal writers of earlier generations. But Cobden's views began to change when he observed the intense *popular* enthusiasm for the Crimean War, against Russia and on behalf of the Ottoman Turks. His outspoken opposition to that war, seconded by his friend and co-leader of the Manchester School, John Bright, cost both of them their seats in the Commons at the next election.

Bright outlived his colleague by twenty years, witnessing the growing passion for empire in his country. In 1884, the acclaimed Liberal Prime Minister, William Gladstone, ordered the Royal Navy to bombard Alexandria to recover the debts owed by the Egyptians to British investors. Bright scornfully dismissed it as "a jobbers' war," war on behalf of a privileged class of capitalists, and resigned from the Gladstone Cabinet. But he never forgot what had started him on the road to anti-imperialism. When Bright passed with his young grandson in front of the statue in London, labeled "Crimea," the boy asked the meaning of the memorial. Bright replied, simply, "A Crime."

Herbert Spencer, the most widely read philosopher of his time, was squarely in the classical liberal tradition. His hostility to statism is exemplified by his assertion that, "Be it or be it not true that Man is shapen in iniquity and conceived in sin, it is unquestionably true that Government is begotten of aggression and by aggression."

While noting the state's inborn tendency towards "militancy" — as opposed to the peaceful intercourse of civil society — Spencer denounced the various apologias for his country's wars in his lifetime, in China, South Africa, and elsewhere.

In the United States, anarchist author Lysander Spooner was a renowned abolitionist, even conspiring with John Brown to promote a servile insurrection in the South. Yet he vociferously opposed the Civil War, arguing that it violated the right of the southern states to secede from a Union that no longer represented them. E. L. Godkin, influential editor of *The Nation* magazine, opposed U.S. imperialism to the end of his life, condemning the war against Spain. Like Godkin, William Graham Sumner was a forthright proponent of free trade and the gold standard and a foe of socialism. He held the first professorship in sociology (at Yale) and authored a great many books. But his most enduring work is his essay, "The Conquest of the United States by Spain," reprinted many times and today available online. In this ironically titled work, Sumner portrayed the savage U.S. war against the Philippines, which cost some 200,000 Filipino lives, as an American version of the imperialism and lust for colonies that had brought Spain the sorry state of his own time.

Unsurprisingly, the most thoroughgoing of the liberal revisionists was the arch-radical Gustave de Molinari, originator of what has come to be known as anarcho-capitalism. In his work on the Great Revolution of 1789, Molinari eviscerated the founding myth of the French Republic. France had been proceeding gradually and organically towards liberal reform in the later eighteenth century; the revolution put an end to that process, substituting an unprecedented expansion of state power and a generation of war. The self-proclaimed liberal parties of the nineteenth century were, in fact, machines for the exploitation of society by the now victorious predatory middle classes, who profited from tariffs, government contracts, state subsidies for railroads and other industries, state-sponsored banking, and the legion of jobs available in the ever-expanding bureaucracy.

In his last work, published a year before his death in 1912, Molinari never relented. The American Civil War had not been simply a humanitarian crusade to free the slaves. The war "ruined the conquered provinces," but the Northern plutocrats pulling the strings achieved their aim: the imposition of a vicious protectionism that led ultimately "to the regime of trusts and produced the billionaires."

Libertarian revisionism continued into the twentieth century. The First World War furnished rich pickings, among them Albert Jay Nock's *The Myth of a Guilty Nation* and H. L. Mencken's continuing, and of course witty, exposés of the lies of America's wars and war-makers. In the next generation, Frank Chodorov, the last of the Old Right greats, wrote that "Isolationism is not a political policy, it is a natural attitude of a people." Left to their own devices, the people "do not feel any call to impose their own customs and values on strangers." Declining to dodge the scare word, Chodorov urged a "return to that isolationism which for over a hundred years prospered the nation and gained for us the respect and admiration of the world." Chodorov—founder of ISI, which he named the Intercollegiate Society of Individualists, later tamed down to "the Intercollegiate Studies Institute"—broke with the "New Right," the neocons of the that era, over his opposition to the Korean War.

Murray Rothbard was the heir to this whole legacy, totally familiar with it and bringing it up-to-date. Aside from his many other, really amazing contributions, Murray and his colleague Leonard Liggio introduced historical revisionism to the burgeoning American libertarian movement (including me). This is a work now carried on with great gusto by Lew Rockwell, of the Mises Institute, and his associated accomplished scholars, particularly the indefatigable Tom Woods.

The essays and reviews I have published and now collected and mostly expanded in this volume are in the tradition of libertarian revisionism, animated by the spirit of Murray Rothbard. They expose the consecrated lies and crimes of some of our most iniquitous, and beloved, recent rulers. My hope is, in a small way, to lay bare historically the nature of the state.

Tangentially, I've also taken into account the strange phenomenon, now nearly forgotten, of the deep affection of multitudes of honored Western intellectuals in the 1930s and '40s for the great experiment in socialism taking place in Soviet Russia under Josef Stalin. Their propaganda had an impact on a number of Western leaders and on Western policy towards the Soviet Union. To my mind, this is worthy of a certain revisionism even today.

CHAPTER 1

World War I: The Turning Point

> With the World War mankind got into a crisis with which nothing that happened before in history can be compared.... In the world crisis whose beginning we are experiencing, all peoples of the world are involved.... War has become more fearful because it is waged with all the means of the highly developed technique that the free economy has created.... Never was the individual more tyrannized than since the outbreak of the World War and especially of the world revolution. One cannot escape the police and administrative technique of the present day.
>
> Ludwig von Mises (1919)[1]

The First World War is the turning point of the twentieth century. Had the war not occurred, the Prussian Hohenzollerns would most probably have remained heads of Germany, with their panoply of subordinate kings and nobility in charge of the lesser German states. Whatever gains Hitler might have scored in the Reichstag elections, could he have erected his totalitarian, exterminationist

---

This is a much expanded version of an essay that originally appeared in *The Costs of War: America's Pyrrhic Victories*, 2nd edition, John V. Denson, ed. (New Brunswick, N.J.: Transaction, 2001).

[1] Ludwig von Mises, *Nation, State, and Economy: Contributions to the Politics and History of Our Time*, Leland B. Yeager, trans. (New York: New York University Press, 1983), pp. 215–16.

dictatorship in the midst of this powerful aristocratic superstructure? Highly unlikely. In Russia, Lenin's few thousand Communist revolutionaries confronted the immense Imperial Russian Army, the largest in the world. For Lenin to have any chance to succeed, that great army had first to be pulverized, which is what the Germans did. So, a twentieth century without the Great War might well have meant a century without Nazis or Communists. Imagine that. It was also a turning point in the history of our American nation, which under the leadership of Woodrow Wilson developed into something radically different from what it had been before. Thus, the importance of the origins of that war, its course, and its aftermath.

Introduction

In 1919, when the carnage at the fronts was at long last over, the victors gathered in Paris to concoct a series of peace treaties. Eventually, these were duly signed by the representatives of four of the five vanquished nations, Germany, Austria, Hungary, and Bulgaria (the final settlement with Turkey came in 1923), each at one of the palaces in the vicinity. The signing of the most important one, the treaty with Germany, took place at the great Palace of Versailles. Article 231 of the Treaty of Versailles reads:

> The Allied and Associated Governments affirm and Germany accepts the responsibility of Germany and her allies for causing all the loss and damage to which the Allied and Associated Governments and their nationals have been subjected as a consequence of the war imposed upon them by the aggression of Germany and her allies.[2]

It was unprecedented in the history of peace negotiations that those who lost a war should have to admit their guilt for starting it.

---

[2] Alan Sharp, *The Versailles Settlement: Peacemaking in Paris, 1919* (New York: St. Martin's Press, 1991), p. 87. The Allied Covering Letter of June 16, 1919 filled in the indictment, accusing Germany of having deliberately unleashed the Great War in order to subjugate Europe, "the greatest crime" ever committed by a supposedly civilized nation. Karl Dietrich Erdmann, "War Guilt 1914 Reconsidered: A Balance of New Research," in H. W. Koch, ed., *The Origins of the First World War: Great Power Rivalries and German War Aims*, 2nd ed. (London: Macmillan, 1984), p. 342.

The fact that the "war-guilt clause" implied German liability for unstated but huge reparations added fuel to the controversy over who was to blame for the outbreak of the war. This immediately became, and has remained, one of the most disputed questions in all of historical writing. When the Bolsheviks seized power, they gleefully opened the Tsarist archives, publishing documents that included some of the secret treaties of the Entente powers to divide up the spoils after the war was over. Their purpose was to embarrass the sanctimonious "capitalist" governments, which had insisted on the virgin purity of their cause. This move contributed to other nations making public many of their own documents at an earlier point than might have been expected.

In the interwar period, a consensus developed among scholars that the war-guilt clause of the Versailles Treaty was historically worthless. Probably the most respected interpretation was that of Sidney Fay, who apportioned major responsibility among Austria, Russia, Serbia, and Germany.[3] In 1952, a committee of prominent French and German historians concluded:

> The documents do not permit any attributing, to any government or nation, a premeditated desire for European war in 1914. Distrust was at its highest, and leading groups were dominated by the thought that war was inevitable; everyone thought that the other side was contemplating aggression....[4]

This consensus was shaken in 1961 with the publication of Fritz Fischer's *Griff nach der Weltmacht* ("Grab for World Power"). In the final formulation of this interpretation, Fischer and the scholars who followed him maintained that in 1914 the German government deliberately ignited a European war in order to impose its hegemony over Europe.[5] (Would that all historians were as cynical regarding

---

[3] Sidney B. Fay, *The Origins of the World War*, 2 vols. (New York: Free Press, 1966 [1928]).

[4] Joachim Remak, *The Origins of World War I, 1871–1914*, 2nd ed. (Fort Worth, Tex.: Harcourt, Brace, 1995), p. 131.

[5] See Fritz Fischer, *Germany's Aims in the First World War* (New York: W. W. Norton, 1967 [1961]); idem, *War of Illusions: German Policies from 1911 to 1914* (New York: W. W. Norton, 1975 [1969]), Marian Jackson, trans.; Imanuel Geiss, *July 1914: The Outbreak of the First World War, Selected Documents* (New York: Charles Scribner's, 1967 [1963–64]); and idem, *German Foreign Policy, 1871–1914*

the motives of their own states.) The researches of the Fischer school forced certain minor revisions in the earlier generally accepted view.

But the historiographical pendulum has now swung much too far in the Fischer direction. Foreign historians have tended to accept his analysis wholesale, perhaps because it fit their "image of German history, determined largely by the experience of Hitler's Germany and the Second World War."[6] The editors of an American reference work on World War I, for example, state outright that "Kaiser and [the German] Foreign Office ... along with the General Staff ... purposely used the crisis [caused by the assassination of Franz Ferdinand] to bring about a general European war. Truth is simple, refreshingly simple."[7]

Well, maybe not so simple. Fritz Stern warned that while the legend propagated in the interwar period by some nationalistic German historians of their government's total innocence "has been effectively exploded, in some quarters there is a tendency to create a legend in reverse by suggesting Germany's sole guilt, and thus to perpetuate the legend in a different form."[8]

Prelude to War

The roots of the First World War reach back to the last decades of the nineteenth century.[9] After France's defeat by Prussia, the

---

(London: Routledge and Kegan Paul, 1975). The work by John W. Langdon, *July 1914: The Long Debate, 1918–1990* (New York: Berg, 1991) is a useful historiographical survey, from a Fischerite viewpoint.

[6] H. W. Koch, "Introduction," in idem, *Origins*, p. 11.

[7] Holger H. Herwig and Neil M. Heyman, eds., *Biographical Dictionary of World War I* (Westport, Conn.: Greenwood Press, 1982), p. 10.

[8] Fritz Stern, "Bethmann Hollweg and the War: The Limits of Responsibility," in Leonard Krieger and Fritz Stern, eds., *The Responsibility of Power: Historical Essays in Honor of Hajo Holborn* (Garden City, N.Y.: Doubleday, 1967), p. 254. Cf. H. W. Koch, "Introduction," p. 9: Fischer "ignores the fundamental readiness of the other European Powers to go to war, but also their excessive war aims which made any form of negotiated peace impossible. What is missing is the comparative yardstick and method." Also Laurence Lafore, *The Long Fuse: An Interpretation of the Origins of World War I*, 2nd ed. (Prospect Heights, Ill.: Waveland Press, 1971), p. 22: "Fischer's treatment is very narrowly on the German side of things, and a wider survey indicates clearly that the Germans were by no means the only people who were prepared to risk a war and who had expansionist programs in their minds."

[9] The following discussion draws on Luigi Albertini, *The Origins of the War of*

emergence in 1871 of a great German Empire dramatically altered the balance of forces in Europe. For centuries the German lands had served as a battlefield for the European powers, who exploited the disunity of the territory for their own aggrandizement. Now the political skills of the Prussian minister Otto von Bismarck and the might of the Prussian army had created what was clearly the leading continental power, extending from the French to the Russian borders and from the Baltic to the Alps.

One of the main concerns of Bismarck, who served as Prussian minister and German Chancellor for another two decades, was to preserve the new-found unity of the this, the Second Reich. Above all, war had to be avoided. The Treaty of Frankfurt ending the Franco-Prussian War compelled France to cede Alsace and half of Lorraine, a loss the French would not permanently resign themselves to. In order to isolate France, Bismarck contrived a system of defensive treaties with Russia, Austria-Hungary, and Italy, insuring that France could find no partner for an attack on Germany.

In 1890, the old Chancellor was dismissed by the new Kaiser, Wilhelm II. In the same year, Russia was suddenly freed of the connection with Germany by the expiration and non-renewal of the "Reinsurance Treaty." Diplomatic moves began in Paris to win over Russia to an alliance which could be used to further French purposes, defensive and possibly offensive as well.[10] Negotiations between the civilian and military leaders of the two countries produced, in 1894, a Franco-Russian military treaty, which remained in effect through the onset of the First World War. At this time it was understood, as General Boisdeffre told Tsar Alexander III, that "mobilization means war." Even a partial mobilization by Germany, Austria-Hungary, or Italy was to be answered by a total mobilization of France and Russia and the inauguration of hostilities against all three members of the Triple Alliance.[11]

In the years that followed, French diplomacy continued to be,

---

1914, Isabella M. Massey, trans. (Westport, Conn: Greenwood, 1980 [1952]), 3 vols.; L. C. F. Turner, *Origins of the First World War* (New York: Norton, 1970); James Joll, *The Origins of the First World War*, 2nd ed. (Longman: London, 1992); Remak, Origins; and Lafore, *The Long Fuse*, among other works.

[10] George F. Kennan, *The Fateful Alliance: France, Russia, and the Coming of the First World War* (New York: Pantheon, 1984), p. 30.

[11] Ibid., pp. 247–52.

as Laurence Lafore put it, "dazzlingly brilliant."[12] The Germans, in contrast, stumbled from one blunder to another; the worst of these was the initiation of a naval arms race with Britain. When the latter finally decided to abandon its traditional aversion to peacetime entanglements with other powers, the French devised an *Entente cordiale*, or "cordial understanding," between the two nations. In 1907, with France's friendly encouragement, England and Russia resolved various points of contention, and a Triple Entente came into existence, confronting the Triple Alliance.

The two combinations differed greatly in strength and cohesion, however. Britain, France, and Russia were world powers. But Austria and Italy were the weakest of the European powers; moreover, Italy's unreliability as an ally was notorious, while Austria-Hungary, composed of numerous feuding nationalities, was held together only by allegiance to the ancient Habsburg dynasty. In an age of rampant nationalism, this allegiance was wearing thin in places, especially among Austria's Serb subjects. Many of these felt a greater attachment to the Kingdom of Serbia, where, in turn, fervent nationalists looked forward to the creation of a Greater Serbia, or perhaps even a kingdom of all the South Slavs—a "Yugoslavia."

A series of crises in the years leading up to 1914 solidified the Triple Entente to the point where the Germans felt they faced "encirclement" by superior forces. In 1911, when France moved to complete its subjugation of Morocco, Germany forcefully objected. The ensuing crisis revealed how close together Britain and France had come, as their military chiefs discussed sending a British expeditionary force across the Channel in case of war.[13] In 1913, a secret naval agreement provided that, in the event of hostilities, the Royal Navy would assume responsibility for protecting the French Channel coast while the French stood guard in the Mediterranean. "The Anglo-French entente was now virtually a military alliance."[14] In democratic Britain, all of this took place without the knowledge of the people, Parliament, or even most of the Cabinet.

---

[12]Lafore, *The Long Fuse*, p. 134.

[13]In February, 1912, the chief of the French Army, Joffre, stated: "All the arrangements for the English landing are made, down to the smallest detail so that the English Army can take part in the first big battle." Turner, *Origins*, pp. 30–31.

[14]Ibid., p. 25.

The dispute over Morocco was settled by a transfer of African territory to Germany, demonstrating that colonial rivalries, though they produced tensions, were not central enough to lead to war among the powers. But the French move into Morocco set into motion a series of events that brought on war in the Balkans, and then the Great War. According to a previous agreement, if France took over Morocco, Italy had the right to occupy what is today Libya, at the time a possession of the Ottoman Turks. Italy declared war on Turkey, and the Italian victory roused the appetite of the small Balkan states for what remained of Turkey's European holdings.

Russia, especially after being thwarted in the Far East by Japan in the war of 1904–5, had great ambitions in the Balkans. Nicholas Hartwig, Russia's highly influential ambassador to Serbia, was an extreme Pan-Slavist, that is, an adherent of the movement to unite the Slavic peoples under Russian leadership. Hartwig orchestrated the formation of the Balkan League, and, in 1912, Serbia, Montenegro, Bulgaria, and Greece declared war on Turkey. When Bulgaria claimed the lion's share of the spoils, its erstwhile allies, joined by Romania and Turkey itself, fell upon Bulgaria the next year, in the Second Balkan War.

These wars caused great anxiety in Europe, particularly in Austria, which feared the enlargement of Serbia backed by Russia. In Vienna, the head of the army, Conrad, pushed for a preventive war, but was overruled by the old Emperor, Franz Josef. Serbia emerged from the Balkan conflicts not only with a greatly expanded territory, but also animated by a vaulting nationalism, which Russia was happy to egg on. Sazonov, the Russian Foreign Minister wrote to Hartwig: "Serbia's promised land lies in the territory of present-day Hungary," and instructed him to help prepare the Serbians for "the future inevitable struggle."[15] By the spring of 1914, the Russians were arranging for another Balkan League, under Russian direction. They received the strong support of France, whose new President, Raymond Poincaré, born in Lorraine, was himself an aggressive nationalist. It was estimated that the new league, headed by Serbia, might provide as many as a million men on Austria's southern flank, wrecking the military plans of the Central Powers.[16]

---

[15] Albertini, *Origins*, vol. 1, p. 486.
[16] Egmont Zechlin, "July 1914: Reply to a Polemic," in Koch, *Origins*, p. 372.

Russia's military buildup was commensurate with its ambitions. Norman Stone has written, of Russia on the eve of the Great War:

> The army contained 114½ infantry divisions to Germany's 96, and contained 6,720 mobile guns to the Germans' 6,004. Strategic railway-building was such that by 1917 Russia would be able to send nearly a hundred divisions for war with the Central Powers within eighteen days of mobilization—only three days behind Germany in overall readiness. Similarly, Russia became, once more, an important naval power ... by 1913–14 she was spending £24,000,000 to the Germans' £23,000,000.[17]

And this is not even to count France.

The Russian program underway called for even more imposing forces by 1917, when they might well be needed: "Plans were going ahead for seizure by naval coup of Constantinople and the Straits, and a naval convention with Great Britain allowed for co-operation in the Baltic against Germany."[18]

Russia regarded Germany as an inevitable enemy, because Germany would never consent to Russian seizure of the Straits or to the Russian-led creation of a Balkans front whose object was the demise of Austria-Hungary. The Habsburg monarchy was Germany's last dependable ally, and its disintegration into a collection of small, mostly Slavic states would open up Germany's southern front to attack. Germany would be placed in a militarily impossible situation, at the mercy of its continental foes. Austria-Hungary had to be preserved at all costs.

Things had come to such a pass that Colonel Edward House, Woodrow Wilson's confidant, traveling in Europe to gather information for the President, reported in May, 1914:

---

[17] Hew Strachan, *The First World War*, vol. 1, *To Arms* (Oxford: Oxford University Press, 2001), pp. 30, 63: "In the summer [of 1913] the French government intervened in Russian negotiations on the French stock market for a loan to finance railway construction. The French objective was to bring pressure to bear on the speed of Russian mobilization, so as to coordinate mutually supporting attacks on Germany from east and west...." "By 1914, French loans had enabled the construction of strategic railways so that Russian mobilization could be accelerated and the first troops be into battle within fifteen days."

[18] Norman Stone, *The Eastern Front, 1914–1917* (New York: Charles Scribner's Sons, 1975), p. 18.

> The situation is extraordinary. It is militarism run stark mad....
> There is too much hatred, too many jealousies. Whenever
> England consents, France and Russia will close in on Germany
> and Austria.[19]

And the War Came

The immediate origins of the 1914 war lie in the twisted politics of the Kingdom of Serbia.[20] In June, 1903, Serbian army officers murdered their king and queen in the palace and threw their bodies out a window, at the same time massacring various royal relations, cabinet ministers, and members of the palace guards. It was an act that horrified and disgusted many in the civilized world. The military clique replaced the pro-Austrian Obrenović dynasty with the anti-Austrian Karageorgevices. The new government pursued a pro-Russian, Pan-Slavist policy, and a network of secret societies sprang up, closely linked to the government, whose goal was the "liberation" of the Serb subjects of Austria (and Turkey), and perhaps the other South Slavs as well.

The man who became Prime Minister, Nicolas Pašić, aimed at the creation of a Greater Serbia, necessarily at the expense of Austria-Hungary. The Austrians felt, correctly, that the cession of their Serb-inhabited lands, and maybe even the lands inhabited by the other South Slavs, would set off the unraveling of the great multinational Empire. For Austria-Hungary, Serbian designs posed a mortal danger.

The Russian ambassador Hartwig worked closely with Pašić and cultivated connections with some of the secret societies. The upshot of the two Balkan Wars which he promoted was that Serbia more than doubled in size and threatened Austria-Hungary not only politically but militarily as well. Sazonov, the Russian Foreign Minister, wrote to Hartwig: "Serbia has only gone through the first stage of her historic road and for the attainment of her goal must still endure a terrible struggle in which her whole existence may be at stake."

---

[19] Charles Seymour, ed., *The Intimate Papers of Colonel House* (Boston: Houghton Mifflin, 1926), vol. 1, p. 249.

[20] For this discussion, see especially Albertini, *Origins*, vol. 2, pp. 1–119 and Joachim Remak, *Sarajevo: The Story of a Political Murder* (New York: Criterion, 1959), pp. 43–78 and *passim*.

Sazonov went on, as indicated above, to direct Serbian expansion to the lands of Austria-Hungary, for which Serbia would have to wage "the future inevitable struggle."[21]

The nationalist societies stepped up their activities, not only within Serbia, but also in the Austrian provinces of Bosnia and Hercegovina. The most radical of these groups was Union or Death, popularly known as the Black Hand. It was led by Colonel Dragutin Dimitriević, called Apis, who also happened to be the head of Royal Serbian Military Intelligence. Apis was a veteran of the slaughter of his own king and queen in 1903, as well as of a number of other political murder plots. "He was quite possibly the foremost European expert in regicide of his time."[22] One of his close contacts was Colonel Artamonov, the Russian military attaché in Belgrade.

The venerable Emperor of Austria and King of Hungary, Franz Josef, who had come to the throne in 1848, clearly had not much longer to live. His nephew and heir, Franz Ferdinand, was profoundly concerned by the wrenching ethnic problems of the Empire and sought their solution in some great structural reform, either in the direction of federalism for the various national groups, or else "trialism," the creation of a third, Slavic component of the Empire, along side the Germans and the Magyars. Since such a concession would mean the ruin of any program for a Greater Serbia, Franz Ferdinand was a natural target for assassination by the Black Hand.[23]

In the spring of 1914, Serbian nationals who were agents of the Black Hand recruited a team of young Bosnian fanatics for the job. The youths were trained in Belgrade and provided with guns, bombs, guides (also Serbian nationals) to help them cross the border, and cyanide for after their mission was accomplished. Prime Minister Pašić learned of the plot, informed his Cabinet, and made ineffectual attempts to halt it, including conveying a veiled, virtually meaningless warning to an Austrian official in Vienna. (It is also likely that the Russian attaché Artamonov knew of the plot.[24]) No clear message of the sort that might have prevented the

---

[21] Albertini, *Origins*, vol. 1, p. 486.

[22] Remak, *Sarajevo*, p. 50.

[23] Albertini, *Origins*, vol. 2, p. 17: "among Serb nationalists and the Southern Slavs who drew their inspiration from Belgrade he was regarded as their worst enemy."

[24] Ibid., vol. 2, p. 86.

assassination was forwarded to the Austrians. On June 28, 1914, the plot proved a brilliant success, as 19 year old Gavrilo Princip shot and killed Franz Ferdinand and his wife Sophie in the streets of Sarajevo.

In Serbia, Princip was instantly hailed as a hero, as he was also in post-World War I Yugoslavia, where the anniversary of the murders was celebrated as a national and religious holiday. A marble tablet was dedicated at the house in front of which the killings took place. It was inscribed: "On this historic spot, on 28 June 1914, Gavrilo Princip proclaimed freedom."[25] In his history of the First World War, Winston Churchill wrote of Princip that "he died in prison, and a monument erected in recent years by his fellow-countrymen records his infamy, and their own."[26]

In Vienna, in that summer of 1914, the prevalent mood was much less Belgrade's celebration of the deed than Churchill's angry contempt. This atrocity was the sixth in less than four years and strong evidence of the worsening Serbian danger, leading the Austrians to conclude that the continued existence of an expansionist Serbia posed an unacceptable threat to the Habsburg monarchy. An ultimatum would be drawn up containing demands that Serbia would be compelled to reject, giving Austria an excuse to attack. In the end, Serbia would be destroyed, probably divided up among its neighbors (Austria, which did not care to have more disaffected South Slavs as subjects, would most likely abstain from the partition). Obviously, Russia might choose to intervene. However, this was a risk the Austrians were prepared to take, especially after they received a "blank check" from Kaiser Wilhelm to proceed with whatever measures they thought necessary. In the past, German support of Austria had forced the Russians to back down.

Scholars have now available to them the diary of Kurt Riezler, private secretary to the German Chancellor Bethmann Hollweg. From this and other documents it becomes clear that Bethmann Hollweg's position in the July crisis was a complex one. If Austria

---

[25] Ibid., vol. 2, p. 47 n. 2. A Yugoslav historian of the crime, Vladimir Dedijer, strongly sympathized with the assassins, who in his view committed an act of "tyrannicide," "for the common good, on the basis of the teachings of natural law." See his *The Road to Sarajevo* (New York: Simon & Schuster, 1966), p. 446.

[26] Winston S. Churchill, *The World Crisis*, vol. 6 (New York: Charles Scribner's Sons, 1932), p. 54.

were to vanish as a power, Germany would be threatened by rampant Pan-Slavism supported by growing Russian power in the east and by French revanchism in the west. By prompting the Austrians to attack Serbia immediately, he hoped that the conflict would be localized and the Serbian menace nullified. The Chancellor, too, understood that the Central Powers were risking a continental war. But he believed that if Austria acted swiftly presenting Europe with "a rapid *fait accompli*," the war could be confined to the Balkans, and "the intervention of third parties [avoided] as much as possible." In this way, the German–Austrian alliance could emerge with a stunning political victory that might split the Entente and crack Germany's "encirclement."[27]

But the Austrians procrastinated, and the ultimatum was delivered to Serbia only on July 23. When Sazonov, in St. Petersburg, read it, he burst out: *"C'est la guerre européenne!"* — "It is the European war!" The Russians felt they could not leave Serbia once again in the lurch, after having failed to prevent the Austrian annexation of Bosnia-Hercegovina or to obtain a seaport for Serbia after the Second Balkan War. Sazonov told a cabinet meeting on July 24 that abandoning Serbia would mean betraying Russia's "historic mission" as the protector of the South Slavs, and also reduce Russia to the rank of a second-rate power.[28]

On July 25, the Russian leaders decided to institute what was known in their plans as "The period preparatory to war," the prelude to all-out mobilization. Directed against both of the Central Powers, this "set in train a whole succession of military measures along the Austrian and German frontiers."[29] Back in the 1920s, Sidney Fay had already cited the testimony of a Serbian military officer, who, in traveling from Germany to Russia on July 28, found no military measures underway on the German side of the border, while in Russian Poland "mobilization steps [were] being taken on a grand

---

[27]Konrad H. Jarausch, "The Illusion of Limited War: Chancellor Bethmann Hollweg's Calculated Risk, July 1914," *Central European History*, vol. 2, no. 1 (March 1969), pp. 60–61; Turner, *Origins*, p. 98; also Lafore, *The Long Fuse*, p. 217: "it was hoped and expected that no general European complications would follow, but if they did, Germany was prepared to face them."

[28]Remak, *Origins*, p. 135.

[29]L. C. F. Turner, "The Russian Mobilization in 1914," *Journal of Contemporary History*, vol. 3, no. 1 (January 1968), pp. 75–76.

scale." "These secret 'preparatory measures,'" commented Fay, "enabled Russia, when war came, to surprise the world by the rapidity with which she poured her troops into East Prussia and Galicia."[30] In Paris, too, the military chiefs began taking preliminary steps to general mobilization as early as July 25.[31]

On July 28, Austria declared war on Serbia. The French ambassador in St. Petersburg, Maurice Paléologue, most likely with the support of Poincaré, urged the Russians on to intransigence and general mobilization. In any case, Poincaré had given the Russians their own "blank check" in 1912, when he assured them that "if Germany supported Austria [in the Balkans], France would march."[32] Following the (rather ineffectual) Austrian bombardment of Belgrade, the Tsar was finally persuaded on July 30 to authorize general mobilization, to the delight of the Russian generals (the decree was momentarily reversed, but then confirmed, finally). Nicholas II had no doubt as to what that meant: "Think of what awful responsibility you are advising me to take! Think of the thousands and thousands of men who will be sent to their deaths!"[33] In a very few years the Tsar himself, his family, and his servants would be shot to death by the Bolsheviks.

What had gone wrong? James Joll wrote: "The Austrians had believed that vigorous action against Serbia and a promise of German support would deter Russia; the Russians had believed that a show of strength against Austria would both check the Austrians and deter Germany. In both cases, the bluff had been called."[34] Russia—and, through its support of Russia, France—as well as Austria and Germany, was quite willing to risk war in July, 1914.

As the conflict appeared more and more inevitable, in all the capitals the generals clamored for their contingency plans to be

---

[30] Fay, *Origins*, vol. 2, p. 321 n. 98.

[31] Turner, "Russian Mobilization," p. 82. By 1914 the French general staff had grown optimistic sbout the outcome of a war with Germany. With the French army strengthened and Russian support guaranteed, in French military circles, as in German, "there was a sense that if war was to come to Europe, better now ... than later." Strachan, *The First World War. To Arms*, p. 93.

[32] Albertini, *Origins*, vol. 2, pp. 587–89, vol. 3, pp. 80–85; Turner, *Origins*, p. 41.

[33] Turner, "Russian Mobilization," pp. 85–86, Turner described this as "perhaps the most important decision taken in the history of Imperial Russia."

[34] Joll, *Origins*, p. 23, also pp. 125–26.

put into play. The best-known was the Schlieffen Plan, drawn up some years before, which governed German strategy in case of a two-front war. It called for concentrating forces against France for a quick victory in the west, and then transporting the bulk of the army to the eastern front via the excellent German railway system, to meet and vanquish the slow-moving (it was assumed) Russians. Faced with Russian mobilization and the evident intention of attacking Austria, the Germans activated the Schlieffen Plan. It was, as Sazonov had cried out, the European War.[35]

On July 31, the French cabinet, acceding to the demand of the head of the army, General Joffre, authorized general mobilization. The next day, the German ambassador to St. Petersburg, Portalès, called on the Russian Foreign Minister. After asking him four times whether Russia would cancel mobilization and receiving each time a negative reply, Portalès presented Sazonov with Germany's declaration of war. The German ultimatum to France was a formality. On August 3, Germany declared war on France as well.[36]

The question of "war-guilt" has been endlessly agitated.[37] It can be stated with assurance that Fischer and his followers have in no way proven their case. That, for instance, Helmut Moltke, head of the German Army, like Conrad, his counterpart in Vienna, pressed for a preventive war has long been known. But both military chieftains were kept in check by their superiors. In any case, there is no evidence whatsoever that Germany in 1914 deliberately unleashed a European war which it had been preparing for years—no evidence in the diplomatic and internal political documents, in the military planning, in the activities of the intelligence agencies, or in the relations between the German and Austrian General Staffs.[38]

---

[35] L. C. F. Turner, "The Significance of the Schlieffen Plan," in Paul M. Kennedy, ed., *The War Plans of the Great Powers, 1880–1914* (London: George Allen and Unwin, 1979), pp. 199–221.

[36] S. L. A. Marshall, *World War I* (Boston: Houghton Mifflin, 1964), pp. 39–42

[37] See Remak, *Origins*, pp. 132–41 for a fairly persuasive allocation of "national responsibility."

[38] Egmont Zechlin, "July 1914: Reply to a Polemic," pp. 371–85. Geiss, for instance, in *German Foreign Policy*, pp. 142–45, wildly misinterpreted the meaning of the German "war council" of December 8, 1912, when he painted it as the initiation of the "plan" that was finally realized with Germany's "unleashing" of war in

Karl Dietrich Erdmann, put the issue well:

> Peace could have been preserved in 1914, had Berchtold, Sazonov, Bethmann-Hollweg, Poincaré, [British Foreign Secretary] Grey, or one of the governments concerned, so sincerely wanted it that they were willing to sacrifice certain political ideas, traditions, and conceptions, which were not their own personal ones, but those of their peoples and their times.[39]

This sober judgment throws light on the faulty assumptions of sympathizers with the Fischer approach. John W. Langdon, for instance, concedes that any Russian mobilization "would have required an escalatory response from Germany." He adds, however, that to expect Russia *not* to mobilize "when faced with an apparent Austrian determination to undermine Serbian sovereignty and alter the Balkan power balance was to expect the impossible." Thus, Langdon exculpates Russia because Austria "seemed bent on a course of action clearly opposed to Russian interests in eastern Europe."[40] True enough—but Russia "seemed bent" on using Serbia to oppose Austrian interests (the Austrian interest in survival), and France "seemed bent" on giving full support to Russia, and so on. This is what historians meant when they spoke of shared responsibility for the onset of the First World War.

Britain still has to be accounted for. With the climax of the crisis, Prime Minister Asquith and Foreign Secretary Edward Grey were in a quandary. While the *Entente cordiale* was not a formal

---

1914. See Erwin Hölzle, *Die Entmachtung Europas: Das Experiment des Friedens vor und im Ersten Weltkrieg* (Göttingen: Musterschmidt, 1975), pp. 178–83; also Koch, "Introduction," pp. 12–13; and Turner, *Origins*, p. 49. See also the important article by Ulrich Trumpener, "War Premeditated? German Intelligence Operations in July 1914," *Central European History*, vol. 9, no. 1 (March 1976), pp. 58–85. Among Trumpener's findings are that there is no evidence of "any significant changes in the sleepy routine" of the German General Staff even after the German "blank check" to Austria, and that the actions of the German military chiefs until the last week of July suggest that, though war with Russia was considered a possibility, it was regarded as "not really all that likely" (Moltke, as well as the head of military intelligence, did not return to Berlin from their vacations until July 25).

[39] Karl Dietrich Erdmann, "War Guilt 1914 Reconsidered," p. 369.

[40] Langdon, *July 1914*, p. 181, emphasis in original.

alliance, secret military conversations between the general staffs of the two nations had created certain expectations and even definite obligations. Yet, aside from high military circles and, of course, the First Lord of the Admiralty, Winston Churchill, no one in Britain was rabid for war. Luckily for the British leaders, the Germans came to their rescue. The success of the attack on France that was the linchpin of the Schlieffen Plan depended above all on speed. This could only be achieved, it was thought, by infringing the neutrality of Belgium. "The obligation to defend Belgian neutrality was incumbent on all the signatories to the 1839 treaty *acting collectively*, and this had been the view adopted by the [British] cabinet only a few days previously. But now Britain presented itself as Belgium's *sole* guarantor" (emphasis added).[41] Ignoring (or perhaps ignorant of) the crucial precondition of collective action among the guarantors, and with the felicity of expression customary among German statesmen of his time, Bethmann Hollweg labeled the Belgian neutrality treaty "a scrap of paper."[42] Grey, addressing the House of Commons, referred to the invasion of Belgium as "the direst crime that ever stained the pages of history."[43]

The violation of non-belligerent Belgium's territory, though deplorable, was scarcely unprecedented in the annals of great powers. In 1807, units of the British navy entered Copenhagen harbor, bombarded the city, and seized the Danish fleet. At the time, Britain was at peace with Denmark, which was a neutral in the Napoleonic wars. The British claimed that Napoleon was about to invade Denmark and seize the fleet himself. As they explained in a manifesto to the people of Copenhagen, Britain was acting not only for its own survival but for the freedom of all peoples.

As the German navy grew in strength, calls were heard in Britain "to Copenhagen" the German fleet, from Sir John Fischer, First Sea Lord, and even from Arthur Lee, First Lord of the Admiralty. They

---

[41] Strachan, *The First World War. To Arms*, p. 97.

[42] What Bethmann Hollweg actually told the British ambassador was somewhat less shocking: "Can this neutrality which we violate only out of necessity, fighting for our very existence ... really provide the reason for a world war? Compared to the disaster of such a holocaust does not the significance of this neutrality dwindle into a scrap of paper?" Jarausch, "The Illusion of Limited War," p. 71.

[43] Marshall, *World War I*, p. 52.

were rejected, and England took the path of outbuilding the Germans in the naval arms race. But the willingness of high British authorities to act without scruple on behalf of perceived vital national interests did not go unnoticed in Germany.[44] When the time came, the Germans acted harshly towards neutral Belgium, though sparing the Belgians lectures on the freedom of mankind. Ironically, by 1916, the King of Greece was protesting the seizure of Greek territories by the Allies; like Belgium, the neutrality of Corfu had been guaranteed by the powers. His protests went unheeded.[45]

The invasion of Belgium was merely a pretext for London.[46] This was clear to John Morley, as he witnessed the machinations of Grey and the war party in the Cabinet. In the last act of authentic English liberalism, Lord Morley, biographer of Cobden and Gladstone and author of the tract, *On Compromise*, upholding moral principles in politics, handed in his resignation.[47]

Britain's entry into the war was crucial. In more ways than one, it sealed the fate of the Central Powers. Without Britain in the war, the United States would never have gone in.

Woodrow Wilson and his "Second Personality"

Wherever blame for the war might lie, for the immense majority of Americans in 1914 it was just another of the European horrors from which our policy of neutrality, set forth by the Founding Fathers of the Republic, had kept us free. Pašić, Sazonov, Conrad, Poincaré, Moltke, Edward Grey, and the rest—these were the men our Fathers

---

[44] Jonathan Steinberg, "The Copenhagen Complex," *Journal of Contemporary History*, vol. 1, no. 3 (July 1966), pp. 23–46.

[45] H. C. Peterson, *Propaganda for War: The Campaign against American Neutrality, 1914–1917* (Norman, Okla.: University of Oklahoma Press, 1939), pp. 45–46.

[46] Joll, *Origins*, p. 115, attributed Grey's lying to the public and to Parliament to the British democratic system, which "forces ministers to be devious and disingenuous." Joll added that more recent examples were Franklin Roosevelt in 1939–41 and Lyndon Johnson in the Vietnam War. A democratic leader "who is himself convinced that circumstances demand entry into a war, often has to conceal what he is doing from those who have elected him."

[47] John Morley, *Memorandum on Resignation* (New York: Macmillan, 1928). In the discussions before the fateful decision was taken, Lord Morley challenged the Cabinet: "Have you ever thought what will happen if Russia wins?" Tsarist Russia "will emerge pre-eminent in Europe." Lloyd George admitted that he had never thought of that.

had warned us against. No conceivable outcome of the war could threaten an invasion of our vast and solid continental base. We should thank a merciful Providence, which gave us this blessed land and impregnable fortress, that America, at least, would not be drawn into the senseless butchery of the Old World. That was unthinkable.

However, in 1914 the President of the United States was Thomas Woodrow Wilson.

The term most frequently applied to Woodrow Wilson nowadays is "idealist." In contrast, the expression "power-hungry" is rarely used. Yet a scholar not unfriendly to him has written of Wilson that "he loved, craved, and in a sense glorified power." Musing on the character of the U.S. government while he was still an academic, Wilson wrote: "I cannot imagine power as a thing negative and not positive."[48] Even before he entered politics, he was fascinated by the power of the Presidency and how it could be augmented by meddling in foreign affairs and dominating overseas territories. The war with Spain and the American acquisition of colonies in the Caribbean and across the Pacific were welcomed by Wilson as productive of salutary changes in our federal system. "The plunge into international politics and into the administration of distant dependencies" had already resulted in "the greatly increased power and opportunity for constructive statesmanship given the President."

> When foreign affairs play a prominent part in the politics and policy of a nation, its Executive must of necessity be its guide: must utter every initial judgment, take every first step of action, supply the information upon which it is to act, suggest and in large measure control its conduct. The President of the United States is now [in 1900], as of course, at the front of affairs.... There is no trouble now about getting the President's speeches printed and read, every word.... The government of dependencies must be largely in his hands. Interesting things may come of this singular change.

---

[48] Walter A. McDougall, *Promised Land, Crusader State: The American Encounter with the World since 1776* (Boston/New York: Houghton Mifflin, 1997), pp. 126, 128.

Wilson looked forward to an enduring "new leadership of the Executive," with even the heads of Cabinet departments exercising "a new influence upon the action of Congress."[49]

In large part Wilson's reputation as an idealist is traceable to his incessantly professed love of peace. Yet as soon as he became President, prior to leading the country into the First World War, his actions in Latin America were anything but pacific. Even Arthur S. Link (whom Walter Karp referred to as the keeper of the Wilsonian flame) wrote, of Mexico, Central America, and the Caribbean: "the years from 1913 to 1921 [Wilson's years in office] witnessed intervention by the State Department and the navy on a scale that had never before been contemplated, even by such alleged imperialists as Theodore Roosevelt and William Howard Taft." The protectorate extended over Nicaragua, the military occupation of the Dominican Republic, the invasion and subjugation of Haiti (which cost the lives of some 2,000 Haitians) were landmarks of Wilson's policy.[50] All was enveloped in the haze of his patented rhetoric of freedom, democracy, and the rights of small nations. The Pan-American Pact which Wilson proposed to our southern neighbors guaranteed the "territorial integrity and political independence" of all the signatories. Considering Wilson's persistent interference in the affairs of Mexico and other Latin states, this was hypocrisy in the grand style.[51]

The most egregious example of Wilson's bellicose interventionism before the European war was in Mexico. Here his attempt to manipulate the course of a civil war lead to the fiascoes of Tampico and Vera Cruz.

In April, 1914, a group of American sailors landed their ship in Tampico without permission of the authorities and were arrested. As soon as the Mexican commander heard of the incident, he had

---

[49]Woodrow Wilson, *Congressional Government: A Study in American Politics* (Gloucester, Mass.: Peter Smith, 1973 [1885]), pp. 22–23. These statements date from 1900. Wilson also assailed the Constitutional system of checks and balances as interfering with effective government, pp. 186–87.

[50]Arthur S. Link, *Woodrow Wilson and the Progressive Era, 1910–1917* (New York: Harper and Brothers, 1954), pp. 92–106.

[51]Even Link, *Woodrow Wilson*, p. 106, stated that Wilson and his colleagues were only paying "lip service" to the principle they put forward, and were not prepared to abide by it.

the Americans released and sent a personal apology. That would have been the end of the affair "had not the Washington administration been looking for an excuse to provoke a fight," in order to benefit the side Wilson favored in the civil war. The American admiral in charge demanded from the Mexicans a twenty-one gun salute to the American flag; Washington backed him up, issuing an ultimatum insisting on the salute, on pain of dire consequences. Naval units were ordered to seize Vera Cruz. The Mexicans resisted, 126 Mexicans were killed, close to 200 wounded (according to the U.S. figures), and, on the American side, 19 were killed and 71 wounded. In Washington, plans were being made for a full-scale war against Mexico, where in the meantime *both* sides in the civil war denounced *Yanqui* aggression. Finally, mediation was accepted; in the end, Wilson lost his bid to control Mexican politics.[52]

Two weeks before the assassination of the Archduke, Wilson delivered an address on Flag Day. His remarks did not bode well for American abstention in the coming war. Asking what the flag would stand for in the future, Wilson replied: "for the just use of undisputed national power ... for self-possession, for dignity, for the assertion of the right of one nation to serve the other nations of the world." As President, he would "assert the rights of mankind wherever this flag is unfurled."[53]

Wilson's alter ego, a major figure in bringing the United States into the European War, was Edward Mandell House. House, who bore the honorific title of "Colonel," was regarded as something of a "Man of Mystery" by his contemporaries. Never elected to public office, he nonetheless became the second most powerful man in the country in domestic and especially foreign affairs until virtually the end of Wilson's administration. House began as a businessman in Texas, rose to leadership in the Democratic politics of that state, and then on the national stage. In 1911, he attached himself to Wilson,

---

[52] Link, *Woodrow Wilson*, pp. 122–28; and Michael C. Meyer and William L. Sherman, *The Course of Mexican History*, 5th ed. (New York: Oxford University Press, 1995), pp. 531–34.

[53] *The Papers of Woodrow Wilson*, Arthur S. Link, ed. (Princeton, N.J.: Princeton University Press, 1979), vol. 30, pp. 184–86. Wilson's gift of self-deception was already evident. "I sometimes wonder why men even now take this flag and flaunt it. If I am respected, I do not have to demand respect," he declared. Apparently the Tampico incident of two months earlier had vanished from his mind.

then Governor of New Jersey and an aspiring candidate for President. The two became the closest of collaborators, Wilson going so far as to make the bizarre public statement that: "Mr. House is my second personality. He is my independent self. His thoughts and mine are one."[54]

Light is cast on the mentality of this "man of mystery" by a futuristic political novel House published in 1912, *Philip Dru: Administrator*. It is a work that contains odd anticipations of the role the Colonel would help Wilson play.[55] In this peculiar production, the title hero leads a crusade to overthrow the reactionary and oppressive money-power that rules the United States. Dru is a veritable messiah-figure: "He comes panoplied in justice and with the light of reason in his eyes. He comes as the advocate of equal opportunity and he comes with the power to enforce his will." Assembling a great army, Dru confronts the massed forces of evil in a titanic battle (close to Buffalo, New York): "human liberty has never more surely hung upon the outcome of any conflict than it does upon this." Naturally, Dru triumphs, and becomes "the Administrator of the Republic," assuming "the powers of a dictator." So unquestionably pure is his cause that any attempt to "foster" the reactionary policies of the previous government "would be considered seditious and would be punished by death." Besides fashioning a new Constitution for the United States and creating a welfare state, Dru joins with leaders of the other great powers to remake the world order, bringing freedom, peace, and justice to all mankind.[56] A peculiar production, suggestive of a very peculiar man, the second most important man in the country.

Wilson utilized House as his personal confidant, advisor, and emissary, bypassing his own appointed and congressionally scrutinized officials. It was somewhat similar to the position that Harry Hopkins would fill for Franklin Roosevelt some twenty years later.

When the war broke out, Wilson implored his fellow-citizens to remain neutral even in word and thought. This was somewhat disingenuous, considering that his whole administration, except for

---

[54] Seymour, *The Intimate Papers of Colonel House*, vol. 1, pp. 6, 114.

[55] Edward M. House, *Philip Dru: Administrator. A Story of Tomorrow, 1920–1935* (New York: B. W. Huebsch, 1920 [1912]).

[56] Ibid., pp. 93, 130, 150, 152, and *passim*.

the poor baffled Secretary of State, William Jennings Bryan, was pro-Allied from the start. The President and most of his chief subordinates were dyed-in-the-wool Anglophiles. Love of England and all things English was an intrinsic part of their sense of identity. With England threatened, even the Chief Justice of the United States Supreme Court, Edward D. White, voiced the impulse to leave for Canada to volunteer for the British armed forces. By September 1914, the British ambassador in Washington, Cecil Spring-Rice, was able to assure Edward Grey, that Wilson had an "understanding heart" for England's problems and difficult position.[57]

This ingrained bias of the American political class and social elite was galvanized by British propaganda. On August 5, 1914, the Royal Navy cut the cables linking the United States and Germany. Now news for America had to be funneled through London, where the censors shaped and trimmed reports for the benefit of their government. Eventually, the British propaganda apparatus in the First World War became the greatest the world had seen to that time; later it was a model for the Nazi Propaganda Minster Josef Goebbels. Philip Knightley noted:

> British efforts to bring the United States into the war on the Allied side penetrated every phase of American life.... It was one of the major propaganda efforts of history, and it was conducted so well and so secretly that little about it emerged until the eve of the Second World War, and the full story is yet to be told.

Already in the first weeks of the war, stories were spread of the ghastly "atrocities" the Germans were committing in Belgium.[58] But

---

[57] Charles Callan Tansill, *America Goes to War* (Gloucester, Mass.: Peter Smith, 1963 [1938]), pp. 26–28. Cf. the comment by Peterson, *Propaganda for War*, p. 10: "The American aristocracy was distinctly Anglophile."

[58] Philip Knightley, *The First Casualty* (New York: Harcourt Brace Jovanovich, 1975), pp. 82, 120–21; Peterson, *Propaganda for War*; John Morgan Read, *Atrocity Propaganda, 1914–1919* (New Haven, Conn.: Yale University Press, 1941); and the classic by Arthur Ponsonby, *Falsehood in Wartime* (New York: E. P. Dutton, 1928). That unflagging apologist for global interventionism, Robert H. Ferrell, in *American Diplomacy: A History*, 3rd ed. (New York: W. W. Norton, 1975), pp. 470–71, could find nothing to object to in the secret propaganda effort to embroil the United States in a world war. It was simply part of "the arts of

the Hun, in the view of American supporters of England's cause, was to show his most hideous face at sea.

America Goes to War

With the onset of war in Europe, hostilities began in the North Atlantic which eventually provided the context—or rather, pretext—for America's participation. Immediately, questions of the rights of neutrals and belligerents leapt to the fore.

In 1909, an international conference had produced the Declaration of London, a statement of international law as it applied to war at sea. Since it was not ratified by all the signatories, the Declaration never came into effect. However, once war started the United States inquired whether the belligerents were willing to abide by its stipulations. The Central Powers agreed, providing the Entente did the same. The British agreed, with certain modifications, which effectively negated the Declaration.[59] British "modifications" included adding a large number of previously "free" items to the "conditional" contraband list and changing the status of key raw materials—most important of all, food—to "absolute" contraband, allegedly because they could be used by the German army.

The traditional understanding of international law on this point was expounded a decade and a half earlier by the British Prime Minister, Lord Salisbury:

> Foodstuffs, with a hostile destination, can be considered contraband of war only if they are supplies for the enemy's forces. It is not sufficient that they are capable of being so used; it must be shown that this was in fact their destination at the time of the seizure.[60]

That had also been the historical position of the U.S. government. But in 1914 the British claimed the right to capture food as well as other previously "conditional contraband" destined not only for hostile but even for *neutral* ports, on the pretense that they would

---

peaceful persuasion," of "Public Relations," he claimed to believe, since "there is nothing wrong with one country representing its cause to another country." One wonders what Ferrell would have said to a similar campaign by Nazi Germany or the Soviet Union.

[59] Tansill, *America Goes to War*, pp. 135–62.
[60] Ibid., p. 148.

ultimately reach Germany and thus the German army. In reality, the aim was, as Churchill, First Lord of the Admiralty candidly admitted, to "starve the whole population—men, women, and children, old and young, wounded and sound—into submission."[61]

Britain now assumed "practically complete control over all neutral trade," in "flat violation of international laws."[62] A strong protest was prepared by State Department lawyers but never sent. Instead, Colonel House and Spring-Rice, the British Ambassador, conferred and came up with an alternative. Denying that the new note was even a "formal protest," the United States politely requested that London reconsider its policy. The British expressed their appreciation for the American viewpoint, and quietly resolved to continue with their violations.[63]

In November, 1914, the British Admiralty announced, supposedly in response to the discovery of a German ship unloading mines off the English coast, that henceforth the whole of the North Sea was a "military area," or war zone, which would be mined, and into which neutral ships proceeded "at their own risk." The British action was in blatant contravention of international law—including the Declaration of Paris, of 1856, which Britain had signed—among other reasons, because it conspicuously failed to meet the criteria for a legal blockade.[64]

---

[61]Cited in Peterson, *Propaganda for War*, p. 83. As Lord Devlin put it, the Admiralty's orders "were clear enough. All food consigned to Germany through neutral ports was to be captured, and all food consigned to Rotterdam was to be presumed consigned to Germany.... The British were determined on the starvation policy, whether or not it was lawful." Patrick Devlin, *Too Proud to Fight: Woodrow Wilson's Neutrality* (New York: Oxford University Press, 1975), pp. 193, 195.

[62]Edwin Borchard and William Pooter Lage, *Neutrality for the United States* (New Haven, Conn.: Yale University Press, 1937), p. 61.

[63]Borchard and Lage, *Neutrality*, pp. 62–72. The U.S. ambassador in London, Walter Hines Page, was already showing his colors. In October, he sent a telegram to the State Department, denouncing any American protests against British interference with neutral rights. "This is not a war in the sense we have hitherto used the word. It is a world-clash of systems of government, a struggle to the extermination of English civilization or of Prussian military autocracy. Precedents have gone to the scrap heap."

[64]See Ralph Raico, "The Politics of Hunger: A Review," in *Review of Austrian Economics*, vol. 3 (1989), p. 254, and the sources cited. The article is included in the present volume.

The British moves meant that American commerce with Germany was effectively ended, as the United States became the arsenal of the Entente. Bound now by financial as well as sentimental ties to England, much of American big business worked in one way or another for the Allied cause. The House of J. P. Morgan, which volunteered itself as coordinator of supplies for Britain, consulted regularly with the Wilson administration in its financial operations for the Entente. The *Wall Street Journal* and other organs of the business elite were noisily pro-British at every turn, until we were finally brought into the European fray.[65]

The United States refused to join the Scandinavian neutrals in objecting to the closing of the North Sea, nor did it send a protest of its own.[66] However, when, in February, 1915, Germany declared the waters around the British Isles a war zone, in which enemy merchant ships were liable to be destroyed, Berlin was put on notice: if any American vessels or American lives should be lost through U-boat action, Germany would be held to a "strict accountability."[67]

In March, a British steamship, *Falaba*, carrying munitions and passengers, was torpedoed, resulting in the death of one American, among others. The ensuing note to Berlin entrenched Wilson's preposterous doctrine—that the United States had the right and duty to protect Americans sailing on ships flying a *belligerent* flag. Later, John Bassett Moore, for over thirty years professor of international law at Columbia, long-time member of the Hague Tribunal, and, after the war, a judge at the International Court of Justice, stated of this and of an equally absurd Wilsonian principle:

> what most decisively contributed to the involvement of the United States in the war was the assertion of a right to protect belligerent ships on which Americans saw fit to travel and the treatment of armed belligerent merchantmen as peaceful

---

[65] Tansill, *America Goes to War*, pp. 132–33: "The Wall Street Journal was never troubled by a policy of 'editorial neutrality,' and as the war progressed it lost no opportunity to condemn the Central Powers in the most unmeasured terms."

[66] Ibid., pp. 177–78.

[67] Robert M. La Follete, the progressive senator from Wisconsin, scathingly exposed Wilson's double standard in a speech on the Senate floor two days after Wilson's call for war. It is reprinted in the vital collection, Murray Polner and Thomas E. Woods, Jr., eds., *We Who Dared to Say No to War: American Antiwar Writing from 1812 to Now* (New York: Basic Books, 2008), pp. 123–32.

vessels. Both assumptions were contrary to reason and to settled law, and no other professed neutral advanced them.[68]

Wilson had placed America on a direct collision course with Germany.

On May 7, 1915, came the most famous incident in the North Atlantic war. The British liner *Lusitania* was sunk, with the loss of 1,195 lives, including 124 Americans, by far the largest number of American victims of German submarines before our entry into the war.[69] There was outrage in the eastern seaboard press and throughout the American social elite and political class. Wilson was livid. A note was fired off to Berlin, reiterating the principle of "strict accountability," and concluding, ominously, that Germany

> will not expect the Government of the United States to omit any word or any act necessary to the performance of its sacred duty of maintaining the rights of the United States and its citizens and of safeguarding their free exercise and enjoyment.[70]

At this time, the British released the Bryce Report on Belgian atrocities. A work of raw Entente propaganda, though profiting from the name of the distinguished English writer, the Report underscored the true nature of the unspeakable Hun.[71] Anglophiles everywhere were enraged. The Republican Party establishment raised the ante on Wilson, demanding firmer action. The great majority of

---

[68]Peterson, *Propaganda for War*, p. 112. Cf. Borchard and Lage, *Neutrality*, p. 136 (emphasis in original): "there was no precedent or legal warrant for a neutral to protect a *belligerent* ship from attack by its enemy because it happened to have on board American citizens. The exclusive jurisdiction of the country of the vessel's flag, to which all on board are subject, is an unchallengeable rule of law."

[69]On the possible involvement of Winston Churchill, First Lord of the Admiralty, in the genesis of this disaster, see "Rethinking Churchill," in the present volume.

[70]Thomas G. Paterson, ed., *Major Problems in American Foreign Policy. Documents and Essays*, vol. 2, *Since 1914*, 2nd ed. (Lexington, Mass.: D. C. Heath, 1978), pp. 30–32.

[71]On the fraudulence of the Bryce Report, see Read, *Atrocity Propaganda*, pp. 201–08; Peterson, *Propaganda for War*, pp. 51–70; and Knightley, *The First Casualty*, pp. 83–84, 107.

Americans, who devoutly wished to avoid war, had no spokesmen within the leadership of either of the major parties. America was beginning to reap the benefits of our divinely appointed "bipartisan foreign policy."

In their reply to the State Department note, the Germans observed that submarine warfare was a reprisal for the illegal hunger blockade; that the *Lusitania* was carrying munitions of war; that it was registered as an auxiliary cruiser of the British Navy; that British merchant ships had been directed to ram or fire upon surfacing U-boats; and that the *Lusitania* had been armed.[72]

Wilson's Secretary of State, William Jennings Bryan, tried to reason with the President: "Germany has a right to prevent contraband going to the Allies, and a ship carrying contraband should not rely upon passengers to protect her from attack—it would be like putting women and children in front of an army." He reminded Wilson that a proposed American compromise, whereby Britain would allow food into Germany and the Germans would abandon submarine attacks on merchant ships, had been welcomed by Germany but rejected by England. Finally, Bryan blurted out: "Why be shocked by the drowning of a few people, if there is to be no objection to starving a nation?"[73] In June, convinced that the Administration was headed for war, Bryan resigned.[74]

The British blockade was taking a heavy toll, and in February, 1916, Germany announced that enemy merchant ships, except passenger liners, would be treated as auxiliary cruisers, liable to be attacked without warning. The State Department countered with a declaration that, in the absence of "conclusive evidence of aggressive purpose" in each individual case, armed belligerent merchant

---

[72]Tansill, *America Goes to War*, p. 323. The German captain of the U-boat that sank the *Lusitania* afterwards pointed out that British captains of merchant ships had already been decorated or given bounties for ramming or attempting to ram surfaced submarines; see also Peterson, *Propaganda for War*, p. 114.

[73]William Jennings Bryan and Mary Baird Bryan, *The Memoirs of William Jennings Bryan* (Philadelphia: John C. Winston, 1925), pp. 397–99; Tansill, *America Goes to War*, pp. 258–59.

[74]To my mind, Bryan's antiwar position and principled resignation more than make up for his views on evolution, despite H. L. Mencken's attempted demolition of Bryan in a well-known essay.

ships enjoyed all the immunities of peaceful vessels.[75] Wilson rejected Congressional calls at least to issue a warning to Americans traveling on armed merchant ships that they did so at their own risk. During the Mexican civil war, he had cautioned Americans against traveling in Mexico.[76] But now Wilson stubbornly refused.

Attention shifted to the sea war once more when a French passenger ship, the *Sussex*, bearing no flag or markings, was sunk by a U-boat, and several Americans injured. A harsh American protest elicited the so-called *Sussex* pledge from a German government anxious to avoid a break: Germany would cease attacking without warning enemy merchant ships found in the war zone. This was made explicitly conditioned, however, on the presumption that "the Government of the United States will now demand and insist that the British Government shall forthwith observe the rules of international law." In turn, Washington curtly informed the Germans that their own responsibility was "absolute," in no way contingent on the conduct of any other power.[77] As Borchard and Lage commented:

> This persistent refusal of President Wilson to see that there was a relation between the British irregularities and the German submarine warfare is probably the crux of the American involvement. The position taken is obviously unsustainable, for it is a neutral's duty to hold the scales even and to favor neither side.[78]

But in reality, the American leaders were anything but neutral.

Anglophile does not begin to describe our ambassador to London, Walter Hines Page, who, in his abject eagerness to please his

---

[75] Borchard and Lage, *Neutrality*, pp. 122–24. John Bassett Moore was scathing in his denunciation of Wilson's new doctrine, that an armed merchant ship enjoyed all the rights of an unarmed one. Citing precedents going back to Supreme Court Justice John Marshall, Moore stated that: "By the position actually taken, the United States was committed, while professing to be a neutral, to maintain a belligerent position." Alex Mathews Arnett, *Claude Kitchin and the Wilson War Policies* (New York: Russell and Russell, 1971 [1937]), pp. 157–58.

[76] In fact, during the Mexican conflict, Wilson had prohibited outright the shipment of arms to Mexico. As late as August, 1913, he declared: "I shall follow the best practice of nations in this matter of neutrality by forbidding the exportation of arms or munitions of war of any kind from the United States to any part of the Republic of Mexico." Tansill, *America Goes to War*, p. 64.

[77] Ibid., pp. 511–15.

[78] Borchard and Lage, *Neutrality*, p. 168.

hosts, displayed all the qualities of a good English spaniel. Afterwards, Edward Grey wrote of Page: "From the first he considered that the United States could be brought into the war early on the side of the Allies if the issue were rightly presented to it and a great appeal made by the President." "Page's advice and suggestion were of the greatest value in warning us when to be careful or encouraging us when we could safely be firm." Grey recalled in particular one incident, when Washington contested the right of the Royal Navy to stop American shipments to neutral ports. Page came to him with the message. " 'I am instructed,' he said, 'to read this despatch to you.' He read and I listened. He then added: 'I have now read the despatch, but I do not agree with it; let us consider how it should be answered.' " Grey, of course, regarded Page's conduct as "the highest type of patriotism."[79]

Page's attitude was not out of place among his superiors in Washington. In his memoirs, Bryan's successor as Secretary of State, Robert Lansing, described how, after the *Lusitania* episode, Britain "continued her policy of tightening the blockade and closing every possible channel by which articles could find their way to Germany," committing ever more flagrant violations of our neutral rights. In response to State Department notes questioning these policies, the British never gave the slightest satisfaction. They knew they didn't have to. For, as Lansing confessed:

> in dealing with the British Government there was always in my mind the conviction that we would ultimately become an ally of Great Britain and that it would not do, therefore, to let our controversies reach a point where diplomatic correspondence gave place to action.

Once joining the British, "we would presumably wish to adopt some of the policies and practices, which the British adopted," for then we, too, would be aiming to "destroy the morale of the German people by an economic isolation, which would cause them to lack the very necessaries of life." With astounding candor, Lansing disclosed that the years-long exchange of notes with Britain had been a sham:

---

[79]Edward Grey, Viscount Grey of Fallodon, *Twenty-Five Years. 1892–1916* (New York: Frederick A. Stokes, 1925), pp. 101–02, 108–11.

everything was submerged in verbiage. It was done with deliberate purpose. It insured the continuance of the controversies and left the questions unsettled, which was necessary in order to leave this country free to act and even act illegally when it entered the war.[80]

Colonel House, too, was distinctly unneutral. Breaking with all previous American practice, as well as with international law, House maintained that it was the *character* of the foreign government that must decide which belligerent a "neutral" United States should favor. When in September, 1914, the Austrian ambassador complained to House about the British attempt to starve the peoples of Central Europe — "Germany faces famine if the war continues" — House smugly reported the interview to Wilson: "He forgot to add that England is not exercising her power in an objectionable way, for it is controlled by a democracy."[81]

In their President, Page, Lansing, and House found a man whose heart beat as theirs. Wilson confided to his private secretary his deep belief: "England is fighting our fight and you may well understand that I shall not, in the present state of the world's affairs, place obstacles in her way.... I will not take any action to embarrass England when she is fighting for her life and the life of the world."[82]

---

[80] Robert Lansing, *War Memoirs* (Indianapolis: Bobbs–Merrill, 1935), pp. 127–28.

[81] Seymour, *The Intimate Papers of Colonel House*, vol. 1, p. 323.

[82] Joseph P. Tumulty, *Woodrow Wilson as I Know Him* (New York: Doubleday, Page, 1921), p. 231. Proofs such as these that our leaders had shamelessly lied in their protestations of neutrality were published in the 1920s and '30s. This explains the passion of the anti-war movement before the Second World War much better than the imaginary "Nazi sympathies" or "anti-Semitism" nowadays invoked by ignorant interventionist writers. As Susan A. Brewer writes in *Why America Fights: Patriotism and War Propaganda from the Philippines to Iraq* (New York: Oxford University Press 2009), p. 280, "The Committee on Public Information presented the war as a noble crusade fought for democracy against demonized Germans. Such a portrayal was overturned by unfulfilled war aims overseas, the abuse of civil liberties at home, and revelations of false atrocity propaganda. In the years that followed Americans expressed distrust of government propaganda and military intervention in what they considered to be other people's wars." This helps account for the appearance from time to time of debunking works of popular revisionism by authors infuriated by the facts they discovered, such as C. Hartley Grattan, *Why We Fought* (Indianapolis: Bobbs–Merrill, 1969 [1929]); Walter Millis, *Road to War: America 1914–1917* (Boston: Houghton Mifflin, 1935); and later Charles L. Mee, Jr.,

Meanwhile, Colonel House had discovered a means to put the impending American entry into war to good use—by furthering the cause of democracy and "turning the world into the right paths." The author of *Philip Dru: Administrator* revealed his vision to the President who "knew that God had chosen him to do great things."[83] The ordeal by fire would be a hard one, but "no matter what sacrifices we make, the end will justify them." After this final battle against the forces of reaction, the United States would join with other democracies to uphold the peace of the world and freedom on both land and sea, forever. To Wilson, House spoke words of seduction: "This is the part I think you are destined to play in this world tragedy, and it is the noblest part that has ever come to a son of man. This country will follow you along such a path, no matter what the cost may be."[84]

As the British leaders had planned and hoped, the Germans were starving. On January 31, 1917, Germany announced that the next day it would begin unrestricted submarine warfare. Wilson was stunned, but it is difficult to see why. This is what the Germans had been implicitly threatening for years, if nothing was done to end the illegal British blockade.

The United States severed diplomatic relations with Berlin. The President decided that American merchant ships were to be armed and defended by American sailors, thus placing munitions and other contraband sailing to Britain under the protection of the U.S. Navy. When eleven Senators, headed by Robert La Follette, filibustered the authorization bill, a livid Wilson denounced them: "A little group of willful men, representing no opinion but their own, have rendered the great Government of the United States helpless and contemptible." Wilson hesitated to act, however, well aware that the defiant Senators represented far more than just themselves.

There were troubling reports—from the standpoint of the war party in Washington—like that from William Durant, head of General Motors. Durant telephoned Colonel House, entreating him to stop the rush to war; he had just returned from the West and met

---

The End of Order: Versailles 1919 (New York: E. P. Dutton, 1980); and Walter Karp's invaluable, *The Politics of War: The Story of Two Wars which Altered Forever the Political Life of the American Republic (1890–1920)* (New York: Harper and Row, 1979).

[83] McDougall, *Promised Land*, p. 127.

[84] Seymour, *The Intimate Papers of Colonel House*, vol. 1, p. 470; vol. 2, p. 92.

only one man between New York and California who wanted war.[85] But opinion began to shift and gave Wilson the opening he needed. A telegram, sent by Alfred Zimmermann of the German Foreign Office to the Mexican government, had been intercepted by British intelligence and forwarded to Washington. Zimmermann proposed a military alliance with Mexico *in case* war broke out between the United States and Germany. Mexico was promised the American Southwest, including Texas. The telegram was released to the press.

For the first time backed by popular feeling, Wilson authorized the arming of American merchant ships. In mid-March, a number of freighters entering the declared submarine zone were sunk, and the President called Congress into special session for April 2.

Given his war speech, Woodrow Wilson may be seen as the anti-Washington. George Washington, in his Farewell Address, advised that "the great rule of conduct for us in regard to foreign nations is, in extending our commercial relations, to have with them as little *political* connection as possible" (emphasis in original). Wilson was also the anti-John Quincy Adams. Adams, author of the Monroe Doctrine, declared that the United States of America "does not go abroad in search of monsters to destroy." Discarding this whole tradition, Wilson put forward the vision of an America that was entangled in countless political connections with foreign powers and on perpetual patrol for monsters to destroy. Our purpose in going to war was

> to fight thus for the ultimate peace of the world and for the liberation of its peoples, the German people included: for the rights of nations great and small and the privilege of men everywhere to choose their way of life and of obedience. The world must be made safe for democracy ... [we fight] for a universal dominion of right by such a concert of free peoples as shall bring peace and safety to all nations and make the world at last free.[86]

Wilson was answered in the Senate by Robert La Follette, and

---

[85] Seymour, *The Intimate Papers of Colonel House*, vol. 2, p. 448.

[86] *The Papers of Woodrow Wilson, January 24–April 6, 1917*, Arthur S. Link, ed. (Princeton, N.J.: Princeton University Press, 1983), vol. 41, pp. 525–27.

in the House by the Democratic leader Claude Kitchin, to no avail.[87] In Congress, near-hysteria reigned, as both chambers approved the declaration of war by wide margins. The political class and its associates in the press, the universities, and the pulpits ardently seconded the plunge into world war and the abandonment of the America that was. As for the population at large, it acquiesced, as one historian has remarked, out of general boredom with peace, the habit of obedience to its rulers, and a highly unrealistic notion of the consequences of America's taking up arms.[88]

Three times in his war message, Wilson referred to the need to fight without passion or vindictiveness—rather a professor's idea of what waging war entailed. The reality for America would be quite different.

The War on the Home Front

The changes wrought in America during the First World War were so profound that one scholar has referred to "the Wilsonian Revolution in government."[89] Like other revolutions, it was preceded by an intellectual transformation, as the philosophy of progressivism came to dominate political discourse.[90] Progressive notions—of the obsolescence of laissez-faire and of constitutionally limited government, the urgent need to "organize" society "scientifically," and the superiority of the collective over the individual—were propagated by the most influential sector of the intelligentsia and began to make inroads in the nation's political life.

---

[87]See Robert M. La Follette, "Speech on the Declaration of War against Germany," in Arthur A. Ekirch, Jr., ed., *Voices in Dissent: An Anthology of Individualist Thought in the United States* (New York: Citadel Press, 1964), pp. 211–22; and Arnett, *Claude Kitchin*, pp. 227–35.

[88]Otis L. Graham, Jr., *The Great Campaigns: Reform and War in America, 1900–1928* (Malabar, Fla.: Robert E. Krieger, 1987), p. 89.

[89]Bruce D. Porter, *War and the Rise of the State: The Military Foundations of Modern Politics* (New York: Free Press, 1993), p. 269.

[90]Arthur A. Ekirch, Jr., *Progressivism in America: A Study of the Era from Theodore Roosevelt to Woodrow Wilson* (New York: New Viewpoints, 1974); and Robert Higgs, *Crisis and Leviathan: Critical Episodes in the Growth of American Government* (New York: Oxford University Press, 1987), pp. 113–16. See also Murray N. Rothbard's essay on "World War I as Fulfillment: Power and the Intellectuals," in John V. Denson, ed., *The Costs of War*, pp. 249–99.

As the war furnished Lenin with otherwise unavailable opportunities for realizing his program, so too, on a more modest level, it opened up prospects for American progressives that could never have existed in peacetime. The coterie of intellectuals around *The New Republic* discovered a heaven-sent chance to advance their agenda. John Dewey praised the "immense impetus to reorganization afforded by this war," while Walter Lippmann wrote: "We can dare to hope for things which we never dared to hope for in the past." The magazine itself rejoiced in the war's possibilities for broadening "social control ... subordinating the individual to the group and the group to society," and advocated that the war be used "as a pretext to foist innovations upon the country."[91]

Woodrow Wilson's readiness to cast off traditional restraints on government power greatly facilitated the "foisting" of such "innovations." The result was a shrinking of American freedoms unrivaled since at least the War Between the States.

It is customary to distinguish "economic liberties" from "civil liberties." But since all rights are rooted in the right to property, starting with the basic right to self-ownership, this distinction is in the last analysis an artificial one.[92] It is maintained here, however, for purposes of exposition.

As regards the economy, Robert Higgs, in his seminal work, *Crisis and Leviathan*, demonstrated the unprecedented changes in this period, amounting to an American version of Imperial Germany's *Kriegssozialismus*. Even before we entered the war, Congress passed the National Defense Act. It gave the President the authority, in time of war "or when war is imminent," to place orders with private firms which would "take precedence over all other orders and contracts." If the manufacturer refused to fill the order at a "reasonable price as determined by the Secretary of War," the government was "authorized to take immediate possession of any such plant [and] ... to manufacture therein ... such product or material as may be required"; the private owner, meanwhile, would be "deemed guilty of a felony."[93]

---

[91] David M. Kennedy, *Over There: The First World War and American Society* (New York: Oxford University Press, 1980), pp. 39–40, 44, 246; Ekirch, *Decline of American Liberalism*, p. 205.

[92] See Murray N. Rothbard, *The Ethics of Liberty* (New York: New York University Press, 1998 [1982]).

[93] Higgs, *Crisis and Leviathan*, pp. 128–29.

Once war was declared, state power grew at a dizzying pace. The Lever Act alone put Washington in charge of the production and distribution of all food and fuel in the United States.

> By the time of the armistice, the government had taken over the ocean-shipping, railroad, telephone, and telegraph industries; commandeered hundreds of manufacturing plants; entered into massive enterprises on its own account in such varied departments as shipbuilding, wheat trading, and building construction; undertaken to lend huge sums to business directly or indirectly and to regulate the private issuance of securities; established official priorities for the use of transportation facilities, food, fuel, and many raw materials; fixed the prices of dozens of important commodities; intervened in hundreds of labor disputes; and conscripted millions of men for service in the armed forces.

Fatuously, Wilson conceded that the powers granted him "are very great, indeed, but they are no greater than it has proved necessary to lodge in the other Governments which are conducting this momentous war."[94] So, according to the President, the United States was simply following the lead of the Old World nations in leaping into war socialism.

Throngs of novice bureaucrats eager to staff the new agencies overran Washington. Many of them came from the progressive intelligentsia. "Never before had so many intellectuals and academicians swarmed into government to help plan, regulate, and mobilize the economic system" — among them Rexford Tugwell, later the key figure in the New Deal Brain Trust.[95] Others who volunteered from the business sector harbored views no different from the statism of the professors. Bernard Baruch, Wall Street financier and now head of the War Industries Board, held that the free market was characterized by anarchy, confusion, and wild fluctuations. Baruch stressed the crucial distinction between consumer *wants* and consumer *needs*, making it clear who was authorized to decide which

---

[94] Higgs, *Crisis and Leviathan*, pp. 123, 135.
[95] Murray N. Rothbard, "War Collectivism in World War I," in Ronald Radosh and Murray N. Rothbard, eds., *A New History of Leviathan: Essays on the Rise of the American Corporate State* (New York: E. P. Dutton, 1972), pp. 97–98. Tugwell lamented, in Rothbard's words, that "only the Armistice prevented a great experiment in control of production, control of price, and control of consumption."

was which. When price controls in agriculture produced their inevitable distortions, Herbert Hoover, formerly a successful engineer and now food administrator of the United States, urged Wilson to institute *overall* price controls: "The only acceptable remedy [is] a general price-fixing power in yourself or in the Federal Trade Commission." Wilson submitted the appropriate legislation to Congress, which, however, rejected it.[96]

Ratification of the Income Tax Amendment in 1913 paved the way for a massive increase in taxation once America entered the war. Taxes for the lowest bracket tripled, from 2 to 6 per cent, while for the highest bracket they went from a maximum of 13 per cent to 77 per cent. In 1916, less than half a million tax returns had been filed; in 1917, the number was nearly three and half million, a figure which doubled by 1920. This was in addition to increases in other federal taxes. Federal tax receipts "would never again be less than a sum five times greater than prewar levels."[97]

But even huge tax increases were not nearly enough to cover the costs of the war. Through the recently established Federal Reserve system, the government created new money to finance its stunning deficits, which by 1918 reached a billion dollars a month—more than the total *annual* federal budget before the war. The debt, which had been less than $1 billion in 1915, rose to $25 billion in 1919. The number of civilian federal employees more than doubled, from 1916 to 1918, to 450,000. After the war, two-thirds of the new jobs were eliminated, leaving a "permanent net gain of 141,000 employees—a 30 per cent 'rachet' effect.'"[98]

---

[96]Kennedy, *Over There*, pp. 139–41, 243. Kennedy concluded, p. 141: "under the active prodding of war administrators like Hoover and Baruch, there occurred a marked shift toward corporatism in the nation's business affairs. Entire industries, even entire economic sectors, as in the case of agriculture, were organized and disciplined as never before, and brought into close and regular relations with counterpart congressional committees, cabinet departments, and Executive agencies." On Hoover, see Murray N. Rothbard, "Herbert Clark Hoover: A Reconsideration," *New Individualist Review* (Indianapolis, Ind.: Liberty Press, 1981), pp. 689–98, reprinted from *New Individualist Review*, vol. 4, no. 2 (Winter 1966), pp. 1–12.

[97]Kennedy, *Over There*, p. 112. Porter, *War and the Rise of the State*, p. 270.

[98]Jonathan Hughes, *The Governmental Habit: Economic Controls from Colonial Times to the Present* (New York: Basic Books, 1977), p. 135; Kennedy, *Over There*, pp. 103–13; Porter, *War and the Rise of the State*, p. 271.

Readers who might expect that such a colossal extension of state control provoked a fierce resistance from heroic leaders of big business will be sorely disappointed. Instead, businessmen welcomed government intrusions, which brought them guaranteed profits, a "riskless capitalism." Many were particularly happy with the War Finance Corporation, which provided loans for businesses deemed essential to the war effort. On the labor front, the government threw its weight behind union organizing and compulsory collective bargaining. In part, this was a reward to Samuel Gompers for his territorial fight against the nefarious IWW, the Industrial Workers of the World, which had ventured to condemn the war on behalf of the working people of the country.[99]

Of the First World War, Murray Rothbard wrote that it was "the critical watershed for the American business system ... [a war-collectivism was established] which served as the model, the precedent, and the inspiration for state corporate capitalism for the remainder of the century."[100] Many of the administrators and principal functionaries of the new agencies and bureaus reappeared a decade and a half latter, when another crisis evoked another great surge of government activism. It should also not be forgotten that Franklin Roosevelt himself was present in Washington, as Assistant Secretary of the Navy, an eager participant in the Wilsonian revolution.

The permanent effect of the war on the mentality of the American people, once famous for their devotion to private enterprise, was summed up by Jonathan Hughes:

> The direct legacy of war—the dead, the debt, the inflation, the change in economic and social structure that comes from

---

[99] Kennedy, *Over There*, pp. 253–58; Hughes, *The Governmental Habit*, p. 141. Hughes noted that the War Finance Corporation was a permanent residue of the war, continuing under different names to the present day. Moreover, "subsequent administrations of both political parties owed Wilson a great debt for his pioneering ventures into the pseudo-capitalism of the government corporation. It enabled collective enterprise as 'socialist' as any Soviet economic enterprise, to remain cloaked in the robes of private enterprise." Rothbard, "War Collectivism in World War I," p. 90, observed that the railroad owners were not at all averse to the government takeover, since they were guaranteed the same level of profits as in 1916–17, two particularly good years for the industry.

[100] Rothbard, "War Collectivism in World War I," p. 66.

immense transfers of resources by taxation and money creation—these things are all obvious. What has not been so obvious has been the pervasive yet subtle change in our increasing acceptance of federal nonmarket control, and even our enthusiasm for it, as a result of the experience of war.[101]

Civil liberties fared no better in this war to make the world safe for democracy. In fact, "democracy" was already beginning to mean what it means today—the right of a government legitimized by formal majoritarian processes to dispose at will of the lives, liberty, and property of its subjects. Wilson sounded the keynote for the ruthless suppression of anyone who interfered with his war effort: "Woe be to the man or group of men that seeks to stand in our way in this day of high resolution." His Attorney General Thomas W. Gregory seconded the President, stating, of opponents of the war: "May God have mercy on them, for they need expect none from an outraged people and an avenging government."[102]

The Espionage Act of 1917, amended the next year by the addition of the Sedition Act, went far beyond punishing spies. Its real target was opinion. It was deployed particularly against socialists and critics of conscription.[103] People were jailed for questioning the constitutionality of the draft and arrested for criticizing the Red Cross. A woman was prosecuted and convicted for telling a women's group that "the government is for the profiteers." A movie producer was sentenced to three years in prison for a film, *The Spirit of '76*, which was deemed anti-British. Eugene V. Debs, who had polled 900,000 votes in 1912 as presidential candidate of the Socialist Party, was sentenced to ten years in prison for criticizing the war at a rally of his party. Vigilantes attacked and on at least one occasion lynched anti-war dissenters. Citizens of German descent and even Lutheran ministers were harassed and spied on by their neighbors as well as by government agents.

The *New York Times*, then as now the mouthpiece of the powers that be, goaded the authorities to "make short work" of IWW

---

[101] Hughes, *The Governmental Habit*, p. 137. See also Higgs, *Crisis and Leviathan*, pp. 150–56.

[102] Quotations from Wilson and Gregory in H. C. Peterson and Gilbert C. Fite, *Opponents of War, 1917–1918* (Seattle, Wash.: University of Washington Press, 1968 [1957]), p. 14.

[103] Ibid., pp. 30–60, 157–66, and *passim*.

"conspirators" who opposed the war, just as the same paper applauded Nicholas Murray Butler, president of Columbia, for "doing his duty" in dismissing faculty members who opposed conscription. The public schools and the universities were turned into conduits for the government line. Postmaster General Albert Burleson censored and prohibited the circulation of newspapers critical of Wilson, the conduct of the war, or the Allies.[104] The nation-wide campaign of repression was spurred on by the Committee on Public Information, headed by George Creel, the U.S. government's first propaganda agency.

In the cases that reached the Supreme Court the prosecution of dissenters was upheld. It was the great liberal, Justice Oliver Wendell Holmes, Jr., who wrote the majority decision confirming the conviction of a man who had questioned the constitutionality of the draft, as he did also in 1919, in the case of Debs, for his anti-war speech.[105] In the Second World War, the Supreme Court of the United States could not, for the life of it, discover anything in the Constitution that might prohibit the rounding up, transportation to the interior, and incarceration of American citizens simply because they were of Japanese descent. In the same way, the Justices, with Holmes leading the pack, now delivered up the civil liberties of the American people to Wilson and his lieutenants.[106] Again,

---

[104] Ekirch, *Decline of American Liberalism*, pp. 217–18; Porter, *War and the Rise of the State*, pp. 272–74; Kennedy, *Over There*, pp. 54, 73–78. Kennedy comments, p. 89, that the point was reached where "to criticize the course of the war, or to question American or Allied peace aims, was to risk outright prosecution for treason."

[105] Ray Ginger, *The Bending Cross: A Biography of Eugene Victor Debs* (New Brunswick, N.J.: Rutgers University Press, 1949), pp. 383–84. Justice Holmes complained of the "stupid letters of protest" he received following his judgment on Debs: "there was a lot of jaw about free speech," the Justice said. See also Kennedy, *Over There*, pp. 84–86.

[106] See the brilliant essay by H. L. Mencken, "Mr. Justice Holmes," in idem, *A Mencken Chrestomathy* (New York: Vintage, 1982 [1949]), pp. 258–65. Mencken concluded: "To call him a Liberal is to make the word meaningless." Kennedy, *Over There*, pp. 178–79 pointed out Holmes's mad statements glorifying war. It was only in war that men could pursue "the divine folly of honor." While the experience of combat might be horrible, afterwards "you see that its message was divine." This is reminiscent less of liberalism as traditionally understood than of the world-view of Benito Mussolini.

precedents were established that would further undermine the people's rights in the future. In the words of Bruce Porter: "Though much of the apparatus of wartime repression was dismantled after 1918, World War I left an altered balance of power between state and society that made future assertions of state sovereignty more feasible—beginning with the New Deal."[107]

We have all been made very familiar with the episode known as "McCarthyism," which, however, affected relatively few persons, many of whom were, in fact, Stalinists. Still, this alleged time of terror is endlessly rehashed in schools and media. In contrast, few even among educated Americans have ever heard of the shredding of civil liberties under Wilson's regime, which was far more intense and affected tens of thousands.

The worst and most obvious infringement of individual rights was conscription. Some wondered why, in the grand crusade against militarism, we were adopting the very emblem of militarism. The Speaker of the House Champ Clark (D–Mo.) remarked that "in the estimation of Missourians there is precious little difference between a conscript and a convict." The problem was that, while Congress had voted for Wilson's war, young American males voted with their feet against it. In the first ten days after the war declaration, only 4,355 men enlisted; in the next weeks, the War Department procured only one-sixth of the men required. Yet Wilson's program demanded that we ship a great army to France, so that American troops were sufficiently "blooded." Otherwise, at the end the President would lack the credentials to play his providential role among the victorious leaders. Ever the deceiver and self-deceiver, Wilson declared that the draft was "in no sense a conscription of the unwilling; it is, rather, selection from a nation which has volunteered in mass."[108]

Wilson, lover of peace and enemy of militarism and autocracy, had no intention of relinquishing the gains in state power once the war was over. He proposed post-war military training for all 18 and

---

[107] Porter, *War and the Rise of the State*, p. 274. On the roots of the national-security state in the World War I period, see Leonard P. Liggio, "American Foreign Policy and National-Security Management," in Radosh and Rothbard, *A New History of Leviathan*, pp. 224–59.

[108] Peterson and Fite, *Opponents of War*, p. 22; Kennedy, *Over There*, p. 94; Higgs, *Crisis and Leviathan*, pp. 131–32. See also the essay by Robert Higgs, "War and Levithan in Twentieth Century America: Conscription as the Keystone," in Denson, ed., *The Costs of War*, pp. 375–88.

19 year old males and the creation of a great army and a navy equal to Britain's, and called for a *peacetime* sedition act.[109]

Two final episodes, one foreign and one domestic, epitomize the statecraft of Woodrow Wilson.

At the new League of Nations, there was pressure for a U.S. "mandate" (colony) in Armenia, in the Caucasus. The idea appealed to Wilson; Armenia was exactly the sort of "distant dependency" which he had prized twenty years earlier, as conducive to "the greatly increased power" of the President. He sent a secret military mission to scout out the territory. But its report was equivocal, warning that such a mandate would place us in the middle of a centuries-old battleground of imperialism and war, and lead to serious complications with the new regime in Russia. The report was not released. Instead, in May 1920, Wilson requested authority from Congress to establish the mandate, but was turned down.[110] It is interesting to contemplate the likely consequences of our Armenian mandate, comparable to the joy Britain had from its mandate in Palestine, only with constant friction and probable war with Soviet Russia thrown in.

In 1920, the United States—Wilson's United States—was the only nation involved in the World War that still refused a general amnesty to political prisoners.[111] The most famous political prisoner in the country was the Socialist leader Eugene Debs. In June, 1918, Debs had addressed a Socialist gathering in Canton, Ohio, where he pilloried the war and the U.S. government. There was no call to violence, nor did any violence ensue. A government stenographer took down the speech, and turned in a report to the federal authorities in Cleveland. Debs was indicted under the Sedition Act, tried, and condemned to ten years in federal prison.

In January, 1921, Debs was ailing and many feared for his life. Amazingly, it was Wilson's rampaging Attorney General A. Mitchell Palmer himself who urged the President to commute Debs's sentence. Wilson wrote across the recommendation the single word, "Denied." He claimed that "while the flower of American youth was pouring out its blood to vindicate the cause of civilization, this man,

---

[109] Kennedy, *Over There*, p. 87; Ekirch, *Decline of American Liberalism*, pp. 223–26.

[110] Carl Brent Swisher, *American Constitutional Development*, 2nd ed. (Cambridge, Mass.: Houghton Mifflin, 1954), pp. 681–82.

[111] Ekirch, *Decline of American Liberalism*, p. 234.

Debs, stood behind the lines, sniping, attacking, and denouncing them ... he will never be pardoned during my administration."[112] Actually, Debs had denounced not "the flower of American youth" but Wilson and the other war-makers who sent them to their deaths in France. It took Warren Harding, one of the "worst" American Presidents according to numerous polls of history professors, to pardon Debs, when Wilson, a "Near-Great," would have let him die a prisoner. Debs and twenty-three other jailed dissidents were freed on Christmas Day, 1921. To those who praised him for his clemency, Harding replied: "I couldn't do anything else.... Those fellows didn't mean any harm. It was a cruel punishment."[113]

An enduring aura of saintliness surrounds Woodrow Wilson, largely generated in the immediate post-World War II period, when his "martyrdom" was used as a club to beat any lingering isolationists. But even setting aside his role in bringing war to America, and his foolish and pathetic floundering at the peace conference— Wilson's crusade against freedom of speech and the market economy alone should be enough to condemn him in the eyes of any authentic liberal. Yet his incessant invocation of terms like "freedom" and "democracy" continues to mislead those who choose to listen to self-serving words rather than look to actions. What the peoples of the world had in store for them under the reign of Wilsonian "idealism" can best be judged by Wilson's conduct at home.

Walter Karp, a wise and well-versed student of American history, though not a professor, understood the deep meaning of the regime of Woodrow Wilson:

> Today American children are taught in our schools that Wilson was one of our greatest Presidents. That is proof in itself that the American Republic has never recovered from the blow he inflicted on it.[114]

THE ROAD TO WORLD WAR II

The war's direct costs to the United States were: 130,000 combat deaths; 35,000 men permanently disabled; $33.5 billion (plus another $13 billion in veterans' benefits and interest on the war debt, as of

---

[112]Ginger, *The Bending Cross*, pp. 356–59, 362–76, 405–06.

[113]Peterson and Fite, *Opponents of War*, p. 279.

[114]Karp, *The Politics of War*, p. 340.

1931, all in the dollars of those years); perhaps also some portion of the 500,000 influenza deaths among American civilians from the virus the men brought home from France.[115] The indirect costs, in the battering of American freedoms and the erosion of attachment to libertarian values, were probably much greater. But as Colonel House had assured Wilson, no matter what sacrifices the war exacted, "the end will justify them"—the end of creating a world order of freedom, justice, and everlasting peace.

The process of meeting that rather formidable challenge began in Paris, in January, 1919, where the leaders of "the Allied and Associated Powers" gathered to decide on the terms of peace and write the Covenant of the League of Nations.[116]

A major complication was the fact that Germany had not surrendered unconditionally, but under certain definite conditions respecting the nature of the final settlement. The State Department note of November 5, 1918 informed Germany that the United States and the Allied governments consented to the German proposal. The basis of the final treaties would be "the terms of peace laid down in the President's address to Congress of January, 1918 [the Fourteen Points speech], and the principles of settlement enunciated in his subsequent addresses."[117]

---

[115] Graham, *The Great Campaigns*, p. 91. On the influenza epidemic, see T. Hunt Tooley, "Some Costs of the Great War: Nationalizing Private Life," *The Independent Review* (Fall, 2009), p. 166 n. 1 and the sources cited there. Tooley's essay is an original, thought-provoking treatment of some of the war's "hidden costs."

[116] The following discussion draws on John Maynard Keynes, *The Economic Consequences of the Peace* (New York: Harcourt, Brace and Howe, 1920); Alcide Ebray, *La paix malpropre: Versailles* (Milan: Unitas, 1924); Sally Marks, *The Illusion of Peace: International Relations in Europe, 1918–1933* (New York: St. Martin's Press, 1976), pp. 1–25; Eugene Davidson, *The Making of Adolf Hitler: The Birth and Rise of Nazism* (Columbia, Mo.: University of Missouri Press, 1997 [1977]); Roy Denman, *Missed Chances: Britain and Europe in the Twentieth Century* (London: Cassell, 1996), pp. 29–49; and Alan Sharp, *The Versailles Settlement: Peacemaking in Paris, 1919* (New York: St. Martin's, 1991), among other works.

[117] James Brown Scott, ed., *Official Statements of War Aims and Peace Proposals, December 1916 to November 1918* (Washington, D.C.: Carnegie Endowment for International Peace, 1921), p. 457. The two modifications proposed by the Allied governments and accepted by the United States and Germany concerned freedom of the seas and the compensation owed by Germany for the damage done to the civilian populations of the Allied nations. For earlier notes exchanged between Germany and the United States regarding the terms of surrender, see pp. 415, 419, 420–21, 430–31, 434–35, 455.

The essence of these pronouncements was that the peace treaties must be animated by a sense of justice and fairness to all nations. Vengeance and national greed would have no place in the new scheme of things. In his "Four Principles" speech one month after the Fourteen Points address, Wilson stated:

> There shall be no contributions, no punitive damages. People are not to be handed about from one sovereignty to another by an international conference.... National aspirations must be respected; peoples may now be dominated and governed only by their own consent. "Self-determination" is not a mere phrase.... All the parties to this war must join in the settlement of every issue anywhere involved in it ... every territorial settlement involved in this war must be made in the interest and for the benefit of the populations concerned, and not as a part of any mere adjustment or compromise of claims amongst rival states....[118]

During the pre-armistice negotiations, Wilson insisted that the conditions of any armistice had to be such "as to make a renewal of hostilities on the part of Germany impossible." Accordingly, the Germans surrendered their battle fleet and submarines, some 1,700 airplanes, 5,000 artillery, 30,000 machine guns, and other materiel, while the Allies occupied the Rhineland and the Rhine bridgeheads.[119] Germany was now defenseless, dependant on Wilson and the Allies keeping their word.

Yet the hunger blockade continued, and was even expanded, as the Allies gained control of the German Baltic coast and banned even fishing boats. The point was reached where the commander of the British army of occupation demanded of London that food be sent to the famished Germans. His troops could no longer stand the sight of hungry German children rummaging in the rubbish bins of the British camps for food. (See also "Starving a People into

---

[118] *The Papers of Woodrow Wilson, January 16–March 12, 1918*, Arthur S. Link, ed. (Princeton, N.J.: Princeton University Press, 1984), vol. 46, pp. 321–23. For the Fourteen Points speech of January 8, 1918, see *The Papers of Woodrow Wilson, November 11, 1917–January 15, 1918*, Arthur S. Link, ed. (Princeton, N.J.: Princeton University Press, 1984), vol. 45, pp. 534–39.

[119] Scott, *Official Statements*, p. 435; Davidson, *The Making of Adolf Hitler*, p. 112; and Denman, *Missed Chances*, p. 33.

Submission, in the present volume.)[120] Still, food was only allowed to enter Germany in March, 1919, and the blockade of raw materials continued until the Germans signed the Treaty.

Early on in Paris, there were disquieting signs that the Allies were violating the terms of surrender. The German delegation was permitted to take no part in the deliberations. The Treaty, negotiated among the bickering victors—Wilson was so angry at one point that he temporarily withdrew—was drawn up and handed to the German delegates. Despite their outraged protests, they were finally forced to sign it, in a humiliating ceremony at the Palace of Versailles, under threat of the invasion of a now helpless Germany.

This wobbly start to the era of international reconciliation and eternal peace was made far worse by the provisions of the Treaty itself.

Germany was allowed an army of no more than 100,000 men, no planes, tanks, or submarines, while the whole left bank of the Rhine was permanently demilitarized. But this was a *unilateral* disarmament. No provision was made for the *general* disarmament (Point 4 of the Fourteen Points) of which this was supposed to be the first step and which, in fact, never occurred. There was no "free, open-minded and absolutely impartial adjustment of all colonial claims" (Point 5). Instead, Germany was stripped of its colonies in Africa and the Pacific, which were parceled out among the winners of the war. In that age of high imperialism, colonies were greatly, if mistakenly, valued, as indicated by the brutality with which Britain and France as well as Germany repressed revolts by the native peoples. Thus, the transfer of the German colonies was another source of grievance. In place of a peace with "no contributions or punitive damages," the Treaty called for an unspecified amount in reparations. These were to cover the costs not only of damage to civilians but also of pensions and other military expenses. The sum eventually proposed was said to amount to more than the

---

[120]Denman, *Missed Chances*, pp. 33–34; and Vincent, *The Politics of Hunger*, pp. 110 and 76–123. That the hunger blockade had a part in fueling later Nazi fanaticism seems undeniable. See Theodore Abel, *The Nazi Movement: Why Hitler Came to Power* (New York: Atherton, 1960 [1938]) and Peter Lowenberg, "The Psychohistorical Origins of the Nazi Youth Cohorts," *American Historical Review*, vol. 76, no. 3 (December 1971), discussed in "Starving a People into Submission," a review of Vincent's book, reprinted in this volume.

entire wealth of Germany, and the Germans were expected to keep on paying for many decades to come.[121]

Most bitterly resented, however, were the territorial changes in Europe.

Wilson had promised, and the Allies had agreed, that "self-determination" would serve as the cornerstone of the new world order of justice and peace. It was this prospect that had produced a surge of hope throughout the Western world as the Peace Conference began. Yet, there was no agreement among the victors on the desirability of self-determination, or even its meaning. Georges Clemenceau, the French Premier, rejected it as applied to the Germans, and aimed to set up the Rhineland as a separate state. The British were embarrassed by the principle, since they had no intention of applying it to Cyprus, India, Egypt—or Ireland. Even Wilson's Secretary of State could not abide it; Lansing pointed out that both the United States and Canada had flagrantly violated the sanctity of self-determination, in regard to the Confederacy and Quebec, respectively.[122]

Wilson himself had little understanding of what his doctrine implied. As the conference progressed, the President, buffeted by the grimly determined Clemenceau and the clever British Prime Minister David Lloyd George, acquiesced in a series of contraventions of self-determination that in the end made a farce of his own lofty if ambiguous principle.

Wilson had declared that national groups must be given "the utmost satisfaction that can be accorded them without introducing new, or perpetuating old, elements of discord and antagonism." At Paris, Italy was given the Brenner pass as its northern frontier, placing nearly a quarter of a million Austrian Germans in the South Tyrol under Italian control. The German city of Memel was given to Lithuania, and the creation of the Polish Corridor to the Baltic and of the "Free City" of Danzig (under Polish control) affected another 1.5 million Germans. The Saar region was handed over to France

---

[121] Charles Callan Tansill, "The United States and the Road to War in Europe," in Harry Elmer Barnes, ed., *Perpetual War for Perpetual Peace* (Caldwell, Id.: Caxton, 1953), pp. 83–88; Denman, *Missed Chances*, pp. 32, 57–59; Davidson, *The Making of Adolf Hitler*, p. 155.

[122] Alfred Cobban, *The Nation State and National Self-Determination* (New York: Thomas Y. Crowell, 1970), pp. 61–62. On the scorn with which the Anglophile Wilson treated the request of the Irish for independence, see p. 66.

for at least 15 years. Altogether some 13.5 million Germans were separated from the Reich.[123] The worst cases of all were Austria and the Sudetenland.

In Austria, when the war ended, the Constituent Assembly that replaced the Habsburg monarchy voted unanimously for *Anschluss*, or union with Germany; in plebiscites, the provinces of Salzburg and the Tyrol voted the same way, by 98 per cent and 95 per cent, respectively. But *Anschluss* was forbidden by the terms of the Treaty (as was the use of "German-Austria" as the name of the new country).[124] The only grounds for this shameless violation of self-determination was that it would strengthen Germany—hardly what the victors had in mind.[125]

The Peace Conference established an entity called "Czechoslovakia," a state that in the interwar period enjoyed the reputation of a gallant little democracy in the dark heart of Europe. In reality, it was another "prison-house of nations."[126] The Slovaks had been deceived into joining by promises of complete autonomy; even so, Czechs and Slovaks together represented only 65% of the population. In fact, the second largest national group was the Germans.[127]

---

[123] R. W. Seton-Watson, *Britain and the Dictators: A Survey of Post-War British Policy* (New York: Macmillan, 1938), p. 324.

[124] Davidson, *The Making of Adolf Hitler*, pp. 115–16. Even Charles Homer Haskins, head of the western Europe division of the American delegation, considered the prohibition of the Austrian–German union an injustice; see Charles Homer Haskins and Robert Howard Lord, *Some Problems of the Peace Conference* (Cambridge, Mass.: Harvard University Press, 1920), pp. 226–28.

[125] The story of Reinhard Spitzy, *So Haben Wir das Reich Verspielt: Bekenntnisse eines Illegalen* (Munich: Langen Müller, 1986) is instructive in this regard. As a young Austrian, Spitzy was incensed at the treatment of his own country and of Germans in general at the Paris Conference and afterwards. The killing of 54 Sudeten German protestors by Czech police on March 4, 1919 particularly appalled Spitzy. He joined the Austrian Nazi Party and the SS. Later, Spitzy, who had never favored German expansionism, became a caustic critic of Ribbentrop and a member of the anti-Hitler resistance.

[126] On the Czech question at the Peace Conference and the First Czechoslovak Republic, see Kurt Glaser, *Czecho-Slovakia: A Critical History* (Caldwell, Id.: Caxton, 1962), pp. 13–47.

[127] This is the breakdown of the population, according the census of 1926: Czechs 6.5 million; Germans 3.3 million; Slovaks 2.5 million; Hungarians 800 thousand; Ruthenians 400 thousand; Poles 100 thousand. John Scott Keltie, ed., *The Statesman's Yearbook, 1926* (London: Macmillan, 1926), p. 768; and Glaser, *Czecho-Slovakia*, p. 6.

Germans had inhabited the Sudetenland, a compact territory adjacent to Germany and Austria, since the Middle Ages. With the disintegration of Austria-Hungary they wished to join what remained of Austria, or even Germany itself. This was vehemently opposed by Thomas Masaryk and Eduard Beneš, leaders of the well-organized Czech contingent at the Conference and liberal darlings of the Allies. Evidently, though the Czechs had the right to secede from Austria-Hungary, the Germans had no right to secede from Czechoslovakia. Instead, the incorporation of the Sudetenland was dictated by economic and strategic considerations—and historical ones, as well. It seems that the integrity of the lands of the Crown of St. Wenceslaus—Bohemia, Moravia, and Austrian Silesia—had to be preserved. No such concern, however, was shown at Paris for the integrity of the lands of the Crown of St. Stephen, the ancient Kingdom of Hungary.[128] Finally, Masaryk and Beneš assured their patrons that the Sudeten Germans yearned to join the new west Slavic state. As Alfred Cobban commented wryly: "To avoid doubt, however, their views were not ascertained."[129]

---

[128] The Germans were by no means the only people whose "right to self-determination" was manifestly infringed. Millions of Ukrainians and White Russians were included in the new Poland. As for the Hungarians, the attitude that prevailed towards them in Paris is epitomized by the statement of Harold Nicholson, one of the British negotiators: "I confess that I regarded, and still regard, that Turanian tribe with acute distaste. Like their cousins the Turks, they had destroyed much and created nothing." The new borders of Hungary were drawn in such a way that one-third of the Magyars were assigned to neighboring states. See Stephen Borsody, "State- and Nation-Building in Central Europe: The Origins of the Hungarian Problem," in idem, ed., *The Hungarians: A Divided Nation* (New Haven, Conn.: Yale Center for International and Area Studies, 1988), pp. 3–31 and especially in the same volume Zsuzsa L. Nagy, "Peacemaking after World War I: The Western Democracies and the Hungarian Question," pp. 32–52. Among the states that inherited territories from Germany and Austria-Hungary, the minority components were as follows: Czechoslovakia: (not counting Slovaks) 34.7 per cent; Poland 30.4 per cent; Romania 25 per cent; Yugoslavia (not counting Croats and Slovenes) 17.2 per cent. Seton-Watson, *Britain and the Dictators*, pp. 322–23.

[129] Cobban, *The Nation State*, p. 68. C. A. Macartney, *National States and National Minorities* (New York: Russell and Russell, 1968 [1934]), pp. 413–15, noted that by official decree Czech was the language of state, to be used exclusively in all major departments of government and as a rule with the general public. This led to German complaints that the aim was "to get the whole administration of the country, as far as possible, into Czechoslovak hands." Macartney maintained, nonetheless, that the Sudeten Germans were "not, fundamentally, irredentist." Of course, as Cobban observed, they had not been asked.

This is in no way surprising. The instrument of the plebiscite was employed when it could harm Germany. Thus, plebiscites were held to divide up areas that, if taken as a whole, might vote for union with Germany, e.g., Silesia. But the German request for a plebiscite in Alsace-Lorraine, which many French had left and many Germans entered after 1871, was turned down.[130]

In the new Czechoslovakia, Germans suffered government-sponsored discrimination in the ways typical of the statist order of Central Europe. They were disadvantaged in "land reform," economic policy, the civil service, and education. The civil liberties of minority groups, including the Slovaks, were violated by laws criminalizing peaceful propaganda against the tightly centralized structure of the new state. Charges by the Germans that their rights under the minority-treaty were being infringed brought no relief.[131]

The protests of Germans within the boundaries of the new Poland resembled those in Czechoslovakia, except that the former were subjected to frequent mob violence.[132] The Polish authorities, who looked on the German minority as potentially treasonous, proposed to eliminate it either through assimilation (unlikely) or coerced emigration. As one scholar has concluded: "Germans in Poland had ample justification for their complaints; their prospects for even medium-term survival were bleak."[133]

At the end of the twentieth century, we are accustomed to viewing certain groups as eternally oppressed victims and other groups as eternal oppressors. But this ideological stratagem did not begin with the now pervasive demonization of the white race. There was

---

[130] Cobban, *The Nation State*, p. 72. Even Marks, *The Illusion of Peace*, p. 11, who was generally supportive of the Versailles Treaty, stated that Alsace-Lorraine was returned to France "to the considerable displeasure of many of its inhabitants."

[131] Glaser, *Czecho-Slovakia*, pp. 13–33.

[132] Unlike the Sudeten Germans, however, who mainly lived in a great compact area adjacent to Germany and Austria, most of the Germans in Poland (but not Danzig) could only have been united with their mother country by bringing in many non-Germans as well. But even some areas with a clear German majority that were contiguous to Germany were awarded to Poland. In Upper Silesia, the industrial centers of Kattowitz and Königshütte, which voted in plebiscites for Germany by majorities of 65% and 75% respectively, were given to Poland. Richard Blanke, *Orphans of Versailles: The Germans in Western Poland 1918–1939* (Lexington, Ky.: 1993), pp. 21, 29.

[133] Ibid., pp. 236–37. See also Tansill, "The United States and the Road to War in Europe," pp. 88–93.

an earlier mythology, which held that the Germans were always in the wrong vis-à-vis their Slavic neighbors. Heavily reinforced by Nazi atrocities, this legend is now deeply entrenched. The idea that at certain times Poles and Czechs victimized *Germans* cannot be mapped on our conceptual grid. Yet it was often the case in the interwar period.[134]

The German leaders, of course, had been anything but angels preceding and during the war. But, if a lasting peace was the purpose of the Versailles Treaty, it was a bad idea to plant time bombs in Europe's future. Of Germany's border with Poland, Lloyd George himself predicted that it "must in my judgment lead sooner or later to a new war in the east of Europe."[135] Wilson's pretense that all injustices would be rectified in time — "It will be the business of the League to set such matters right" — was another of his complacent delusions. The League's Covenant stipulated unanimity in such questions and thus "rendered the League an instrument of the *status quo*."[136]

Vengeance continued to be the order of the day, as France invaded the Ruhr in 1923, supposedly because reparations payments were in arrears (Britain and Italy, equal partners in supervision of reparations, disagreed). The French also stepped up their futile efforts to establish a separatist state in the Rhineland. There, as in the Ruhr, they ostentatiously deployed native colonial troops, who delighted in the novelty of their superior status to Europeans. This was felt to be a further indignity by many Germans.[137]

---

[134] In 1919, Ludwig von Mises wrote: "The unfortunate outcome of the war [i.e., increased statism and injustice] brings hundreds of thousands, even millions, of Germans under foreign rule and imposes tribute payments of unheard-of size on the rest of Germany." Mises, *Nation, State, and Ecomomy*, p. 217. Still, Mises admonished the Germans to eschew the path of imperialism and follow economic liberalism instead. See also the comment of Hew Strachan, *The First World War. To Arms*, p. 2: "the injustices done to Germans residing in the successor states of the Austro-Hungarian empire came to be widely recognized."

[135] "By the early spring of 1922, Lloyd George came to the conclusion that the Treaty of Versailles had been an awful mistake and that it was in no small way responsible for the economic crisis in which both Great Britain and the Continental European nations now found themselves." Richard M. Watt, *The Kings Depart: The Tragedy of Versailles and the German Revolution* (New York: Simon and Schuster, 1968), p. 513.

[136] Denman, *Missed Chances*, pp. 42, 45; Marks, *The Illusion of Peace*, p. 14.

[137] Tansill, "The United States and the Road to War in Europe," pp. 94–95;

The problems dragged on through the 1920s and early '30s. The territorial settlement was bitterly opposed by every political party in Germany, from the far left to the far right, through to the end of the Weimar Republic. In the past, treaties had often been gradually and peacefully revised through changes enacted by one party which the other parties declined to challenge.[138] Yet even with the Nazi threat looming over Weimar Germany, France refused to give an inch. In 1931, Chancellor Heinrich Brüning arranged for a customs union with Austria, which would have amounted to a great patriotic triumph for the fledging democracy. It was vetoed by France. Vansittart, at the British Foreign Office, no lover of Germany, warned that "Brüning's Government is the best we can hope for; its disappearance would be followed by a Nazi avalanche."[139]

In the east, France's allies, Poland and Czechoslovakia, similarly refused any concessions. They had been obliged to sign agreements guaranteeing certain rights to their ethnic minorities. Protests to the League from the German minorities got nowhere: League mediators "almost always recommended accepting the promises of member governments to mend their ways.... Even when the League found fault with a policy that had led to a minority complaint, it was almost never able to get a member state to act accordingly." In any case, the Polish position was that "minority peoples needed no protection from their own government and that it was 'disloyal' for minority organizations to seek redress before the League."[140]

When Germany became a League member, evidence of terrorism against the German minority in Poland carried more weight. In 1931, the League Council unanimously accepted a report "essentially substantiating the charges against the Poles." But again no effective action was taken. The British delegates had "frankly adopted the view that where German minorities were concerned, it was for the German Government to look after their interests."[141]

Denman, *Missed Chances*, pp. 51–52.

[138] Ebray, *La paix malpropre*, pp. 341–43.

[139] Denman, *Missed Chances*, p. 53.

[140] Blanke, *Orphans of Versailles*, pp. 132, 136–37.

[141] Davidson, *The Making of Adolf Hitler* (the best work on the role of the Versailles Treaty in assisting the rise of Nazism), p. 289; and Cobban, *The Nation State*, p. 89.

After 1933, a German government chose to do exactly that, in its own savage way.[142]

Back in January, 1917, Wilson had addressed Congress on the nature of the settlement, once the terrible war was over:

> it must be a peace without victory.... Victory would mean peace forced upon the loser, a victor's terms imposed upon the vanquished. It would be accepted in humiliation, under duress, at an intolerable sacrifice, and would leave a sting, a resentment, a bitter memory upon which terms of peace would rest, not permanently, but only as upon quicksand.[143]

A prescient warning indeed. Woodrow Wilson's own foolish, blatant disregard of it helped bring about a tragedy for Europe and the world that surpassed even the First World War.

---

[142] The idea that an Anglo-American guarantee to France against German "aggression" would have availed to freeze the constellation of forces as of 1919 *ad infinitum* was a fantasy. Already in 1922, Weimar Germany reached a *rapprochement* with Soviet Russia, at Rapallo.

[143] *The Papers of Woodrow Wilson, November 20, 1916–January 23, 1917*, Arthur S. Link, ed. (Princeton, N.J.: Princeton University Press, 1982), vol. 40, p. 536.

CHAPTER 2

Rethinking Churchill

CHURCHILL AS ICON

When, in a very few years, the pundits start to pontificate on the great question: "Who was the Man of the Century?" there is little doubt that they will reach virtually instant consensus. Inevitably, the answer will be: Winston Churchill. Indeed, Professor Harry Jaffa has already informed us that Churchill was not only the Man of the Twentieth Century, but the Man of Many Centuries.[1]

In a way, Churchill as Man of the Century will be appropriate. This has been the century of the State—of the rise and hypertrophic growth of the welfare-warfare state—and Churchill was from first to last a Man of the State, of the welfare state and of the warfare state. War, of course, was his lifelong passion; and, as an admiring

---

This is an expanded version of an essay that first appeared in *The Costs of War: America's Pyrrhic Victories*, John V. Denson, ed. (New Brunswick, N.J.: Transaction, 1997).

[1] Harry V. Jaffa, "In Defense of Churchill," *Modern Age* 34, no. 3 (Spring 1992), p. 281. For what it might be worth, Henry Kissinger, "With Faint Praise," *New York Times Book Review*, July 16, 1995, has gone so far as to call Churchill "the quintessential hero."

historian has written: "Among his other claims to fame, Winston Churchill ranks as one of the founders of the welfare state."[2] Thus, while Churchill never had a principle he did not in the end betray,[3] this does not mean that there was no slant to his actions, no systematic bias. There was, and that bias was towards lowering the barriers to state power.

To gain any understanding of Churchill, we must go beyond the heroic images propagated for over half a century. The conventional picture of Churchill, especially of his role in World War II, was first of all the work of Churchill himself, through the distorted histories he composed and rushed into print as soon as the war was over.[4] In more recent decades, the Churchill legend has been adopted by an international establishment for which it furnishes the perfect symbol and an inexhaustible vein of high-toned blather. Churchill has become, in Christopher Hitchens's phrase, a "totem" of the American establishment, not only the scions of the New Deal, but the neo-conservative apparatus as well—politicians like Newt Gingrich and Dan Quayle, corporate "knights" and other denizens of the Reagan and Bush Cabinets, the editors and writers of the *Wall Street Journal*, and a legion of "conservative" columnists led by William Safire and William Buckley. Churchill was, as Hitchens writes, "the human bridge across which the transition was made"

---

[2]Paul Addison, "Churchill and Social Reform," in *Churchill*, Robert Blake and William Roger Louis, eds. (New York: Norton, 1993), p. 57.

[3]A sympathetic historian, Paul Addison, *Churchill on the Home Front 1900–1955* (London: Pimlico, 1993), p. 438, phrases the same point this way: "Since [Churchill] never allowed himself to be hampered by a fixed programme or a rigid ideology, his ideas evolved as he adapted himself to the times." Oddly enough, Churchill himself confessed, in 1898: "I do not care so much for the principles I advocate as for the impression which my words produce and the reputation they give me." Clive Ponting, *Churchill* (London: Sinclair–Stevenson, 1994), p. 32.

[4]For some of Churchill's distortions, see Tuvia Ben-Moshe, *Churchill: Strategy and History* (Boulder, Colo.: Lynne Rienner, 1992), pp. 329–33; Dietrich Aigner, "Winston Churchill (1874–1965)," in *Politiker des 20. Jahrhunderts*, 1, *Die Epoche der Weltkriege*, Rolf K. Hocevar, et al., eds. (Munich: Beck, 1970), p. 318, states that Churchill, in his works on World War II, "laid the foundation of a legend that is nothing less than a straightforward travesty of the historical truth.... But the Churchill version of World War II and its prehistory remains unshaken, the power of his eloquence extends beyond the grave." Aigner, incidentally, is an informed, scholarly critic of Churchill and by no means a "right-wing radical."

between a non-interventionist and a globalist America.[5] In the next century, it is not impossible that his bulldog likeness will feature in the logo of the New World Order.

Let it be freely conceded that in 1940 Churchill played his role superbly. As the military historian, Major-General J. F. C. Fuller, a sharp critic of Churchill's wartime policies, wrote: "Churchill was a man cast in the heroic mould, a berserker ever ready to lead a forlorn hope or storm a breach, and at his best when things were at their worst. His glamorous rhetoric, his pugnacity, and his insistence on annihilating the enemy appealed to human instincts, and made him an outstanding war leader."[6] History outdid herself when she cast Churchill as the adversary in the duel with Hitler. It matters little that in his most famous speech—"we shall fight them on the beaches ... we shall fight them in the fields and in the streets"—he plagiarized Clemenceau at the time of the Ludendorff offensive in the Great War, that there was little real threat of a German invasion or, that, perhaps, there was no reason for the duel to have occurred in the first place. For a few months in 1940, Churchill played his part magnificently and unforgettably.[7]

Opportunism and Rhetoric

Yet before 1940, the word most closely associated with Churchill was "opportunist."[8] He had twice changed his party affiliation—from Conservative to Liberal, and then back again. His move to the Liberals was allegedly on the issue of free trade. But in 1930, he sold out on free trade as well, even tariffs on food, and proclaimed that he had cast off "Cobdenism" forever.[9] As head of the Board of Trade before World War I, he opposed increased armaments; after he became First Lord of the Admiralty in 1911, he pushed for bigger and bigger budgets,

---

[5] Christopher Hitchens, *Blood, Class, and Nostalgia: Anglo-American Ironies* (New York: Farrar, Straus, and Giroux, 1990), p. 186.

[6] J. F. C. Fuller, *The Conduct of War 1789–1961* (London: Eyre and Spottiswoode, 1961), p. 253.

[7] For a skeptical account of Churchill in this period, see Clive Ponting, *1940: Myth and Reality* (Chicago: Ivan R. Dee, 1991).

[8] Cf. A. J. P. Taylor, "The Statesman," in idem, et al., *Churchill Revised: A Critical Assessment* (New York: Dial Press, 1969), p. 26.

[9] Henry Pelling, *Winston Churchill* (New York: Dutton, 1974), pp. 347–48, 355; and Paul Addison, *Churchill on the Home Front*, pp. 296–99.

spreading wild rumors of the growing strength of the German navy, just as he did in the 1930s about the buildup of the German Air Force.[10] He attacked socialism before and after World War I, while during the War he promoted war socialism, calling for nationalization of the railroads, and declaring in a speech: "Our whole nation must be organized, must be socialized if you like the word."[11] Churchill's opportunism continued to the end. In the 1945 election, he briefly latched on to Hayek's *The Road to Serfdom* and tried to paint the Labour Party as totalitarian, while it was Churchill himself who, in 1943, had accepted the Beveridge plans for the post-war welfare state and Keynesian management of the economy. Throughout his career his one guiding rule was to climb to power and stay there.[12]

There *were* two principles that for a long while seemed dear to Churchill's heart. One was anti-Communism: he was an early and fervent opponent of Bolshevism. For years, he—very correctly—decried the "bloody baboons" and "foul murderers of Moscow." His deep early admiration of Benito Mussolini was rooted in his shrewd appreciation of what Mussolini had accomplished (or so Churchill thought). In an Italy teetering on the brink of Leninist revolution, Il Duce had discovered the one formula that could counteract the Leninist appeal: hypernationalism with a social slant. Churchill lauded "Fascismo's triumphant struggle against the bestial appetites and passions of Leninism," claiming that "it proved the necessary antidote to the Communist poison."[13]

---

[10]Taylor, "The Statesman," p. 31; Robert Rhodes James, "Churchill the Politician," in A. J. P. Taylor, et al., *Churchill Revised,* p. 115, writes of "Churchill's extremely exaggerated claims of German air power."

[11]Emrys Hughes, *Winston Churchill: British Bulldog* (New York: Exposition, 1955), p. 104.

[12]Cf. Simon Jenkins, (*Sunday Times,* August 26, 2007): "As for [Gertrude] Himmelfarb's apotheosis of the ever-devious Churchill, this is now historical anachronism. True, Churchill's political perception was sometimes right, but it was more often wrong and had little moral compass beyond his own eccentricities. As ideologues, both he and Disraeli might be termed Blairites, seizing the catch phrases of the moment for their political or literary convenience and changing sides when it suited them."

[13]"Churchill Extols Fascismo for Italy" *New York Times,* January 21, 1927. Churchill's praise of Mussolini continued for another decade, even after the brutal Italian conquest of Ethiopia. In 1937, he wrote of "the amazing qualities of courage, comprehension, self-contol and perservence which he exemplifies." Nicholson Baker, *Human Smoke. The Beginnings of World War II, and the End of*

Yet the time came when Churchill made his peace with Communism. In 1941, he gave unconditional support to Stalin, welcomed him as an ally, embraced him as a friend. Churchill, as well as Roosevelt, used the affectionate nickname, "Uncle Joe"; as late as the Potsdam conference, he repeatedly announced, of Stalin: "I like that man."[14] In suppressing the evidence that the Polish officers at Katyn had been murdered by the Soviets, he remarked: "There is no use prowling round the three year old graves of Smolensk."[15] Obsessed not only with defeating Hitler, but with destroying Germany, Churchill was oblivious to the danger of a Soviet inundation of Europe until it was far too late. The symbolic climax of his infatuation came at the November, 1943, Tehran conference, when Churchill presented Stalin with a Crusader's sword.[16] Those concerned to define the word "obscenity" may wish to ponder that episode.

Finally, there was what appeared to be the abiding love of his life: the British Empire. If Churchill stood *for anything at all*, it was the Empire; he famously said that he had not become Prime Minister in order to preside over its liquidation. But that, of course, is precisely what he did, selling out the Empire and everything else for the sake of total victory over Germany.

Besides his opportunism, Churchill was noted for his remarkable rhetorical skill. This talent helped him wield power over men, but it pointed to a fateful failing as well. Throughout his life, many who observed Churchill closely noted a peculiar trait. In 1917, Lord Esher described it in this way:

> He handles great subjects in rhythmical language, and becomes quickly enslaved to his own phrases. He deceives himself into

---

Civilization (New York: Simon & Schuster, 2008), p. 73. Churchill even had admiring words for Hitler; as late as 1937, he wrote: "one may dislike Hitler's system and yet admire his patriotic achievement. If our country were defeated, I hope we should find a champion as indomitable to restore our courage and lead us back to our place among the nations." James, "Churchill the Politician," p. 118. On the conditions of the Fascist takeover in Italy, see Ralph Raico, "Mises on Fascism and Democracy," *Journal of Libertarian Studies*, vol. 12, no. 1 (Spring 1996), pp. 1–27.

[14]Robin Edmonds, "Churchill and Stalin," in *Churchill*, Blake and Louis, eds., p. 326.

[15]Norman Rose, *Churchill: The Unruly Giant* (New York: Free Press, 1994), p. 378.

[16]J. F. C. Fuller, *The Second World War 1939–45: A Strategical and Tactical History* (London: Eyre and Spottiswoode, 1954), p. 218.

the belief that he takes broad views, when his mind is fixed upon one comparatively small aspect of the question.[17]

During World War II, Robert Menzies, Prime Minister of Australia, said of Churchill: "His real tyrant is the glittering phrase—so attractive to his mind that awkward facts have to give way."[18] Another associate wrote: "He is ... the slave of the words which his mind forms about ideas.... And he can convince himself of almost every truth if it is once allowed thus to start on its wild career through his rhetorical machinery."[19]

But while Winston had no principles, there *was* one constant in his life: the love of war. It began early. As a child, he had a huge collection of toy soldiers, 1500 of them, and he played with them for many years after most boys turn to other things. They were "all British," he tells us, and he fought battles with his brother Jack, who "was only allowed to have colored troops; and they were not allowed to have artillery."[20] He attended Sandhurst, the military academy, instead of the universities, and "from the moment that Churchill left Sandhurst ... he did his utmost to get into a fight, wherever a war was going on."[21] All his life he was most excited — on the evidence, only really excited — by war. He loved war as few modern men ever have[22] — he even "loved the bangs," as he called them, and he was very brave under fire.[23]

---

[17] James, "Churchill the Politician," p. 79. The same quotation from Esher is cited and endorsed by Basil Liddell Hart, "The Military Strategist," in A. J. P. Taylor, et al., *Churchill Revised*, p. 221.

[18] David Irving, *Churchill's War*, vol. 1, *The Struggle for Power* (Bullsbrook, Western Australia: Veritas, 1987), p. 517.

[19] Charles Masterman, cited in James, "Churchill the Politician," p. 71.

[20] Hart, "The Military Strategist," pp. 173–74.

[21] Ibid., p. 174.

[22] Churchill told Asquith's daughter in 1915: "I know this war is smashing and shattering the lives of thousands every moment—and yet—I cannot help it—I love every second I live." Michael Howard, "Churchill and the First World War," in *Churchill*, Blake and Louis, eds., p. 129.

[23] In his last years, during the Cold War, Churchill made a feeble attempt to effect a reconciliation between Russia and the Western powers. The solution to this puzzling about face lies in the fact that now Churchill was genuinely scared. By then the Soviet Union possessed nuclear weapons, and it was reckoned that it would take no more than seven or eight H-bombs to reduce that "realm of kings," that "scepter'd isle" to a heap of ashes.

RETHINKING CHURCHILL

In 1925, Churchill wrote: "The story of the human race is war."[24] This, however, is untrue; potentially, it is disastrously untrue. Churchill lacked any grasp of the fundamentals of the social philosophy of classical liberalism. In particular, he never understood that, as Ludwig von Mises explained, the true story of the human race is the extension of social cooperation and the division of labor. Peace, not war, is the father of all things.[25] For Churchill, the years without war offered nothing to him but "the bland skies of peace and platitude." This was a man, as we shall see, who wished for more wars than *actually happened*.

When he was posted to India and began to read avidly to make up for lost time, Churchill was profoundly impressed by Darwinism. He lost whatever religious faith he may have had — through reading Gibbon, he said — and took a particular dislike, for some reason, to the Catholic Church, as well as Christian missions. He became, in his own words, "a materialist — to the tips of my fingers," and he fervently upheld the worldview that human life is a struggle for existence, with the outcome the survival of the fittest.[26] This philosophy of life and history Churchill expressed in his one novel, *Savrola*.[27] That Churchill was a racist goes without saying, yet his racism went deeper than with most of his contemporaries.[28] It is curious how, with his stark Darwinian outlook, his elevation of war to the central place in human history, and his racism, as well as his fixation on "great leaders," Churchill's worldview resembled that of his antagonist, Hitler.[29]

---

[24] Maurice Ashley, *Churchill as Historian* (New York: Scribner's, 1968), p. 228.

[25] Ludwig von Mises, *Liberalism: A Socio-Economic Exposition*, Ralph Raico, trans. (Kansas City: Sheed Andrews and McMeel, [1927] 1985), pp. 23–27.

[26] Ponting, *Churchill*, p. 23; Dietrich Aigner, *Winston Churchill: Ruhm und Legende* (Göttingen: Musterschmidt, 1975), p. 31.

[27] Ibid., pp. 40–44.

[28] Andrew Roberts, *Eminent Churchillians* (New York: Simon and Schuster, 1994), pp. 211–15. Roberts finds it ironic that, given Churchill's views on race, it was "he of all Prime Ministers [who] allowed Britain to start to become a multiracial society" through Commonwealth immigration during his last "Indian Summer" administration, 1951–55.

[29] That Churchill's racism could be lethal is demonstrated in the recent book by the historian Madhusree Mukerjee, *Churchill's Secret War: The British Empire and the Ravishing of India during World War II* (New York: Basic Books, 2010). During the 1943 famine in Bengal, Churchill refused to supply the Bengalis with

When Churchill was not actually engaged in war, he was reporting on it. He early made a reputation for himself as a war correspondent, in Kitchener's campaign in the Sudan and in the Boer War. In December, 1900, a dinner was given at the Waldorf-Astoria in honor of the young journalist, recently returned from his well-publicized adventures in South Africa. Mark Twain, who introduced him, had already, it seems, caught on to Churchill. In a brief satirical speech, Twain slyly intimated that, with his English father and American mother, Churchill was the perfect representative of Anglo-American cant.[30]

Churchill and the "New Liberalism"

In 1900 Churchill began the career he was evidently fated for. His background—the grandson of a duke and son of a famous Tory politician—got him into the House of Commons as a Conservative. At first he seemed to be distinguished only by his restless ambition, remarkable even in parliamentary ranks. But in 1904, he crossed the floor to the Liberals, supposedly on account of his free-trade convictions. However, Robert Rhodes James, one of Churchill's admirers, wrote: "It was believed [at the time], probably rightly, that if Arthur Balfour had given him office in 1902, Churchill would not have developed such a burning interest in free trade and joined the Liberals." Clive Ponting notes that: "as he had already admitted to Rosebery, he was looking for an excuse to defect from a party that seemed reluctant to recognise his talents," and the Liberals would not accept a protectionist.[31]

---

food, instead shipping wheat from Australia to Italy and England, countries not suffering from starvation. He even refused an American offer to send food to Bengal in American ships. Churchill viewed the Bengalis, and Indians in general, as less than fully human, an opinion shared by his scientific advisor, Professor Lindemann, who advanced "eugenic" and "Malthusian" reasons for the policy. Probably 1.5 to 2 million or more Bengalis died in the wartime famine.

[30] Mark Twain, *Mark Twain's Weapons of Satire: Anti-Imperialist Writings on the Philippine-American War*, Jim Zwick, ed. (Syracuse, N.Y.: Syracuse University Press, 1992), pp. 9–11.

[31] Robert Rhodes James, "Churchill the Parliamentarian, Orator, and Statesman," in *Churchill*, Blake and Louis, eds., p. 510; Ponting, *Churchill*, p. 49.

RETHINKING CHURCHILL

Tossed by the tides of faddish opinion,[32] with no principles of his own and hungry for power, Churchill soon became an adherent of the "New Liberalism," an updated version of his father's "Tory Democracy." The "new" liberalism differed from the "old" only in the small matter of substituting incessant state activism for laissez-faire.

Although his conservative idolaters seem blithely unaware of the fact—for them it is always 1940—Churchill was one of the chief pioneers of the welfare state in Britain. The modern welfare state, successor to the welfare state of eighteenth-century absolutism, began in the 1880s in Germany, under Bismarck.[33] In England, the legislative turning point came when Asquith succeeded Campbell-Bannerman as Prime Minister in 1908; his reorganized cabinet included David Lloyd George at the Exchequer and Churchill at the Board of Trade.

Of course, "the electoral dimension of social policy was well to the fore in Churchill's thinking," writes a sympathetic historian—meaning that Churchill understood it as the way to win votes.[34] He wrote to a friend:

> No legislation at present in view interests the democracy. All their minds are turning more and more to the social and economic issue. This revolution is irresistible. They will not tolerate the existing system by which wealth is acquired, shared and employed.... They will set their faces like flint against the money power—heir of all other powers and tyrannies overthrown—and its obvious injustices. And this theoretical repulsion will ultimately extend to any party associated in maintaining the status quo.... Minimum standards of wages and comfort, insurance in some effective form or other against sickness, unemployment, old age, these are the questions and the only questions by which parties are going to live in the future. Woe to Liberalism, if they slip through its fingers.[35]

---

[32] Churchill at this time even spoke out in favor of state-enforced temperance, an amusing bit of hypocrisy in a man whose lifelong love of drink was legendary.

[33] On the history of the German welfare state, absolutist and modern, see Gerd Habermann, *Der Wohlfahrtsstaat: Geschichte eines Irrwegs* (Berlin: Propyläen, 1994).

[34] Addison, "Churchill and Social Reform," p. 60.

[35] Addison, *Churchill on the Home Front, 1900–1955*, p. 59.

Churchill "had already announced his conversion to a collectivist social policy" before his move to the Board of Trade.[36] His constant theme became "the just precedence" of public over private interests. He took up the fashionable social-engineering clichés of the time, asserting that "Science, physical and political alike, revolts at the disorganisation which glares at us in so many aspects of modern life," and that "the nation demands the application of drastic corrective and curative processes." The state was to acquire canals and railroads, develop certain national industries, provide vastly augmented education, introduce the eight-hour work day, levy progressive taxes, and guarantee a national minimum living standard. It is no wonder that Beatrice Webb noted that Winston was "definitely casting in his lot with the constructive state action."[37]

Following a visit to Germany, Lloyd George and Churchill were both converted to the Bismarckian model of social insurance schemes.[38] As Churchill told his constituents: "My heart was filled with admiration of the patient genius which had added these social bulwarks to the many glories of the German race."[39] He set out, in his words, to "thrust a big slice of Bismarckianism over the whole underside of our industrial system."[40] In 1908, Churchill announced in a speech in Dundee: "I am on the side of those who think that a greater collective sentiment should be introduced into the State and the municipalities. I should like to see the State undertaking new functions." Still, individualism must be respected: "No man can be a collectivist alone or an individualist alone. He must be both an individualist and a collectivist. The nature of man is a dual nature. The character of the organisation of human society is dual."[41] This, by the way, is a good sample of Churchill as political philosopher:

---

[36] Ibid, p. 51.

[37] W. H. Greenleaf, *The British Political Tradition*, vol. 2, *The Ideological Heritage* (London: Methuen, 1983), pp. 151–54.

[38] E. P. Hennock, *British Social Reform and German Precedents: The Case of Social Insurance 1880–1914* (Oxford: Clarendon, 1987), pp. 168–69.

[39] Gordon A. Craig, "Churchill and Germany," in *Churchill*, Blake and Louis, eds., p. 24.

[40] E. P. Hennock, "The Origins of British National Insurance and the German Precedent 1880–1914," in *The Emergence of the Welfare State in Britain and Germany*, W. J. Mommsen and Wolfgang Mock, eds. (London: Croom Helm, 1981), p. 88.

[41] Winston Churchill, *Complete Speeches 1897–1963*, vol. 1, *1897–1908*, Robert Rhodes James, ed. (New York: Chelsea House, 1974), pp. 1029–30, 1032.

it never gets much better.

But while both "collective organisation" and "individual incentive" must be given their due, Churchill was certain which had gained the upper hand:

> The whole tendency of civilisation is, however, towards the multiplication of the collective functions of society. The ever-growing complications of civilisation create for us new services which have to be undertaken by the State, and create for us an expansion of existing services.... There is a pretty steady determination ... to intercept all future unearned increment which may arise from the increase in the speculative value of the land. There will be an ever-widening area of municipal enterprise.

The statist trend met with Churchill's complete approval. As he added:

> I go farther; I should like to see the State embark on various novel and adventurous experiments.... I am very sorry we have not got the railways of this country in our hands. We may do something better with the canals.[42]

This grandson of a duke and glorifier of his ancestor, the arch-corruptionist Marlborough, was not above pandering to lower-class resentments. Churchill claimed that "the cause of the Liberal Party is the cause of the left-out millions," while he attacked the Conservatives as "the Party of the rich against the poor, the classes and their dependents against the masses, of the lucky, the wealthy, the happy, and the strong, against the left-out and the shut-out millions of the weak and poor."[43]

Churchill became the perfect hustling political entrepreneur, eager to politicize one area of social life after the other. He berated the Conservatives for lacking even a "single plan of social reform or reconstruction," while boasting that he and his associates intended to propose "a wide, comprehensive, interdependent scheme of social organisation," incorporated in "a massive series of legislative proposals and administrative acts."[44]

---

[42] Winston Churchill, *Liberalism and the Social Problem* (London: Hodder and Stoughton, 1909), pp. 80–81.

[43] Ibid., pp. 78, 226.

[44] Ibid., p. 227.

At this time, Churchill fell under the influence of Beatrice and Sidney Webb, the leaders of the Fabian Society. At one of her famous strategic dinner parties, Beatrice Webb introduced Churchill to a young protégé, William—later Lord—Beveridge. Churchill brought Beveridge into the Board of Trade as his advisor on social questions, thus starting him on his illustrious career.[45] Besides pushing for a variety of social insurance schemes, Churchill created the system of national labor exchanges: he wrote to Prime Minister Asquith of the need to "spread ... a sort of Germanized network of state intervention and regulation" over the British labor market.[46] But Churchill entertained much more ambitious goals for the Board of Trade. He proposed a plan whereby

> The Board of Trade was to act as the "intelligence department" of the Government, forecasting trade and employment in the regions so that the Government could allocate contracts to the most deserving areas. At the summit ... would be a Committee of National Organisation, chaired by the Chancellor of the Exchequer to supervise the economy.[47]

Finally, well aware of the electoral potential of organized labor, Churchill became a champion of the labor unions. He was a leading supporter, for instance, of the Trades Disputes Act of 1906.[48] This Act reversed the Taff Vale and other judicial decisions, which had held unions responsible for torts and wrongs committed on their behalf by their agents. The Act outraged the great liberal legal historian and theorist of the rule of law, A. V. Dicey, who charged that it

> confers upon a trade union a freedom from civil liability for the commission of even the most heinous wrong by the union or its servants, and in short confers upon every trade union a privilege and protection not possessed by any other person or body of persons, whether corporate or unincorporate, throughout the United Kingdom.... It makes a trade union a privileged body exempted from the ordinary law of the land.

---

[45] Hennock, *British Social Reform*, pp. 157–60.
[46] Ibid., p. 161.
[47] Ponting, *Churchill*, p. 83.
[48] See, for instance, Churchill, *Liberalism and the Social Problem*, pp. 74–75.

No such privileged body has ever before been deliberately created by an English Parliament.[49]

It is ironic that the immense power of the British labor unions, the *bête noire* of Margaret Thatcher, was brought into being with the enthusiastic help of her great hero, Winston Churchill.

World War I

In 1911, Churchill became First Lord of the Admiralty and now was truly in his element. Naturally, he quickly allied himself with the war party, and, during the crises that followed, fanned the flames of war. When the final crisis came, in the summer of 1914, Churchill was the only member of the cabinet who backed war from the start, with all of his accustomed energy. Asquith, his own Prime Minister, wrote of him: "Winston very bellicose and demanding immediate mobilization.... Winston, who has got all his war paint on, is longing for a sea fight in the early hours of the morning to result in the sinking of the [German warship] *Goeben*. The whole thing fills me with sadness."[50]

On July 27, a week before the German invasion of Belgium, he mobilized the British Home Fleet, the greatest assemblage of naval power in the history of the world to that time. As Sidney Fay wrote, Churchill ordered that:

> The fleet was to proceed during the night at high speed and without lights through the Straits of Dover from Portland to its fighting base at Scapa Flow. Fearing to bring this order before the Cabinet, lest it should be considered a provocative action likely to damage the chances of peace, Mr. Churchill had only informed Mr. Asquith, who at once gave his approval.[51]

No wonder that, when war with Germany broke out, Churchill, in

---

[49] A. V. Dicey, *Lectures on the Relation Between Law and Public Opinion in England during the Nineteenth Century*, 2nd ed. (London: Macmillan, [1914] 1963), pp. xlv–xlvi.

[50] Herbert Henry Asquith, *Memories and Reflections 1852–1927* (London: Cassell, 1928), vol. 2, pp. 7, 21.

[51] Sidney Fay, *Origins of the World War*, 2nd rev. ed. (New York: Free Press, [1930] 1966), p. 495.

contrast even to the other chiefs of the war party, was all smiles, filled with a "glowing zest."[52]

From the outset of hostilities, Churchill, as head of the Admiralty, was instrumental in establishing the hunger blockade of Germany. This was probably the most effective weapon employed on either side in the whole conflict. The only problem was that, according to everyone's interpretation of international law except Britain's, it was illegal. The blockade was not "close-in," but depended on scattering mines, and many of the goods deemed contraband—for instance, food for civilians—had never been so classified before.[53] But, throughout his career, international law and the conventions by which men have tried to limit the horrors of war meant nothing to Churchill. As a German historian has dryly commented, Churchill was ready to break the rules whenever the very existence of his country was at stake, and "for him this was very often the case."[54]

The hunger blockade had some rather unpleasant consequences.[55] About 750,000 German civilians succumbed to hunger and diseases caused by malnutrition. The effect on those who survived was perhaps just as frightful in its own way. A historian of the blockade concluded: "the victimized youth [of World War I] were to become the most radical adherents of National Socialism."[56] It was also complications arising from the British blockade that eventually provided the pretext for Wilson's decision to go to war in 1917.

Whether Churchill actually arranged for the sinking of the *Lusitania* on May 7, 1915, is still unclear.[57] A week before the disaster,

---

[52]Lady Violet Asquith, cited in Hart, "The Military Strategist," p. 182.

[53]C. Paul Vincent, *The Politics of Hunger: The Allied Blockade of Germany, 1915–1919* (Athens: Ohio University Press, 1985). See also Ralph Raico, "The Politics of Hunger: A Review," *Review of Austrian Economics* 3 (1988), pp. 253–59, reprinted in this volume under the title, "Starving a People into Submission."

[54]Aigner, *Winston Churchill (1874–1965)*, pp. 63–64.

[55]In World War II Arthur ("Bomber") Harris defended the massacre from the air of German civilians he directed by invoking the hunger blockade of the Great War. Quoted in A. C. Grayling, *Among the Dead Cities: The History and Moral Legacy of the WWII Bombing of Civilians in Germany and Japan* (New York: Walker, 2006), p. 247.

[56]Vincent, *Politics of Hunger*, p. 162. For further details on the point see the review of Vincent's book in the present volume.

[57]See Colin Simpson, *The Lusitania* (London: Penguin, [1972] 1983), who

he wrote to Walter Runciman, president of the Board of Trade that it was "most important to attract neutral shipping to our shores, in the hopes especially of embroiling the United States with Germany."[58] Many highly-placed persons in Britain and America believed that the German sinking of the *Lusitania* would bring the United States into the war.

The most recent student of the subject is Patrick Beesly, whose *Room 40* is a history of British Naval Intelligence in World War I. Beesly's careful account is all the more persuasive for going against the grain of his own sentiments. He points out that the British Admiralty was aware that German U-boat Command had informed U-boat captains at sea of the sailings of the *Lusitania*, and that the U-boat responsible for the sinking of two ships in recent days was present in the vicinity of Queenstown, off the south coast of Ireland, in the path the *Lusitania* was scheduled to take. There is no surviving record of any specific warning to the *Lusitania*. No destroyer escort was sent to accompany the ship to port, nor were any of the readily available destroyers instructed to hunt for the submarine. In fact, "no effective steps were taken to protect the *Lusitania*." Beesly concludes:

> unless and until fresh information comes to light, I am reluctantly driven to the conclusion that there was a conspiracy deliberately to put the *Lusitania* at risk in the hope that even an abortive attack on her would bring the United States into the war. Such a conspiracy could not have been put into effect without Winston Churchill's express permission and approval.[59]

In any case, what is certain is that Churchill's policies made the sinking very likely. The *Lusitania* was a passenger liner loaded with munitions of war; Churchill had given orders to the captains of merchant ships, including liners, to ram German submarines if they encountered them and the Germans were aware of this. And, as Churchill

---

presents the case for Churchill's guilt; and Thomas A. Bailey and Paul B. Ryan, *The Lusitania Disaster: An Episode in Modern Warfare and Diplomacy* (New York: Free Press, 1975), who attempt to exculpate him. See also Hitchens, *Blood, Class, and Nostalgia*, pp. 189–90.

[58] Patrick Beesly, *Room 40: British Naval Intelligence 1914–18* (San Diego: Harcourt, Brace, Jovanovich, 1982), p. 90.

[59] Ibid., p. 122.

stressed in his memoirs of World War I, embroiling neutral countries in hostilities with the enemy was a crucial part of warfare: "There are many kinds of maneuvres in war, some only of which take place on the battlefield.... The maneuvre which brings an ally into the field is as serviceable as that which wins a great battle."[60]

In the midst of bloody conflict, Churchill was energy personified, the source of one brainstorm after another. Sometimes his hunches worked out well—he was the chief promoter of the tank in World War I—sometimes not so well, as at Gallipoli. The notoriety of that disaster, which blackened his name for years, caused him to be temporarily dropped from the Cabinet in 1915.[61] His reaction was typical: To one visitor, he said, pointing to the maps on the wall: "This is what I live for.... Yes, I am finished in respect of all I care for—the waging of war, the defeat of the Germans."[62]

Between the Wars

For the next few years, Churchill was shuttled from one ministerial post to another. As minister for War—of Churchill in this position one may say what the revisionist historian Charles Tansill said of Henry Stimson as Secretary of War: no one ever deserved the title more—Churchill promoted a crusade to crush Bolshevism in Russia.[63] As Colonial Secretary, he was ready to involve Britain in

---

[60] Winston Churchill, *The World Crisis* (New York: Scribner's, 1931), p. 300.

[61] On the Dardanelles campaign, cf. Taylor, "The Statesman," pp. 21–22: "Once Churchill took up the idea, he exaggerated both the ease with which it could be carried through and the rewards it would bring. There was no enquiry into the means available. Churchill merely assumed that battleships could force the Straits unaided. When this failed, he assumed that there was a powerful army available for Gallipoli and assumed also that this inhospitable peninsula presented no formidable military obstacles. Beyond this, he assumed also that the fall of Constantinople would inflict a mortal blow on Germany. All these assumptions were wrong."

[62] Hughes, *Winston Churchill: British Bulldog*, p. 78.

[63] While Churchill opposed British occupation of Iraq except for Basra and the south, he was unbending against Iraqi insurgents who objected to the invasion of their country. "The first to use aircraft, machine guns, and bombs to put down unruly Iraqis were the British, in 1920, when Winston Churchill was British Secretary of State for War." He also suggested that the use of mustard gas should be explored, in his words, "which would inflict punishment on recalcitrant natives without inflicting grave injury upon them." Barry M. Lando, *Web of Deceit* (New York: Other Press, 2007), pp. 3, 12.

war with Turkey over the Chanak incident, but the British envoy to Turkey did not deliver Churchill's ultimatum, and in the end cooler heads prevailed.[64]

In 1924, Churchill rejoined the Conservatives and was made Chancellor of the Exchequer. His father, in the same office, was noted for having been puzzled by the decimals: what were "those damned dots"? Winston's most famous act was to return Britain to the gold standard at the unrealistic pre-war parity, thus severely damaging the export trade and ruining the good name of gold, as Murray N. Rothbard pointed out.[65] Hardly anyone today would disagree with the judgment of A. J. P. Taylor: Churchill "did not grasp the economic arguments one way or the other. What determined him was again a devotion to British greatness. The pound would once more 'look the dollar in the face'; the days of Queen Victoria would be restored."[66]

So far Churchill had been engaged in politics for 30 years, with not much to show for it except a certain notoriety. His great claim to fame in the modern mythology begins with his hard line against Hitler in the 1930s. But it is important to realize that Churchill had maintained a hard line against Weimar Germany, as well. He denounced all calls for Allied disarmament, even before Hitler came to power.[67] Like other Allied leaders, Churchill was living a protracted fantasy: that Germany would submit forever to what it viewed as the shackles of Versailles. In the end, what Britain and France refused to grant to a democratic Germany they were forced to concede to Hitler. Moreover, if most did not bother to listen when Churchill fulminated on the impending German threat, they had good reason. He had tried to whip up hysteria too often before: for a crusade against Bolshevik Russia, during the General Strike of 1926, on the mortal dangers of Indian independence, in the royal abdication crisis. Why pay any heed to his latest delusion?[68]

---

[64] James, "Churchill the Politician," p. 93

[65] Murray N. Rothbard, *America's Great Depression* (Princeton, N.J.: Van Nostrand, 1963), pp. 131–37.

[66] Taylor, "The Statesman," p. 27.

[67] Aigner, *Winston Churchill (1874–1965)*, pp. 100–03. In connection with the Geneva disarmament conference 1931–32, Churchill expressed the same anti-German position as later: Germany would rise again. Aigner sees this as stemming from Churchill's Social Darwinist philosophy.

[68] Goronwy Rees, "Churchill in der Revision," *Der Monat*, Nr. 207 (Fall 1965), p. 12.

Churchill had been a strong Zionist practically from the start, holding that Zionism would deflect European Jews from social revolution to partnership with European imperialism in the Arab world.[69] Now, in 1936, he forged links with the informal London pressure group known as The Focus, whose purpose was to open the eyes of the British public to the one great menace, Nazi Germany. "The great bulk of its finance came from Jewish businessmen such as Sir Robert Mond (a director of several chemical firms) and Sir Robert Waley-Cohn, the managing director of Shell, the latter contributing £50,000." The Focus was to be useful in expanding Churchill's network of contacts and in pushing for his entry into the Cabinet.[70]

Though a Conservative MP, Churchill began berating the Conservative governments, first Baldwin's and then Chamberlain's, for their alleged blindness to the Nazi threat. He exaggerated the extent of German rearmament, formidable as it was, and distorted its purpose by harping on German production of heavy bombers. This was never a German priority, and Churchill's fabrications were meant to demonstrate a German design to attack Britain, which was never Hitler's intention until after the war began. At this time, Churchill busily promoted the Grand Alliance[71] that was to include

---

[69] E.g., in Churchill's essay of February, 1921, "Zionism vs. Bolshevism"; see Aigner, *Winston Churchill (1874–1965)*, p. 79. See also Oskar K. Rabinowicz, *Winston Churchill on Jewish Problems: A Half Century Survey*, published by the World Jewish Congress, British Section (London: Lincolns–Prager, 1956); and N. A. Rose, *The Gentile Zionists: A Study in Anglo-Zionist Diplomacy, 1929–1939* (London: Cass, 1973). Early on, Churchill had shared the view current among many right-wingers of the time, of Bolshevism as a "Jewish" phenomenon: he referred to the Red leaders as "these Semitic conspirators" and "Jew Commissars." Norman Rose, *Churchill: The Unruly Giant*, p. 180.

[70] John Charmley, *Chamberlain and the Lost Peace* (London: Hodder and Stoughton, 1989), p. 55. The group's full name was the Focus for the Defence of Freedom and Peace. For a history, see Eugen Spier, *Focus. A Footnote to the History of the Thirties* (London: Oswald Wolff, 1963). In March, 1937, after a luncheon meeting with Churchill, Spier came to the conclusion that "destiny had marked him out to become the destroyer of Hitlerism." (Ibid., p. 112) On The Focus as well as other factors influencing British public opinion in regard to Germany in the 1930s, see Dietrich Aigner, *Das Ringen um England. Das deutsch-britische Verhältnis. Die öffentliche Meinung 1933–1939, Tragödie zweier Völker* (Munich/Esslingen: Bechtle, 1969).

[71] Aigner, *Winston Churchill (1874–1965)*, p. 105–06; see also Irving, *Churchill's War*, pp. 38–40, 44–45, 78–79.

Britain, France, Russia, Poland, and Czechoslovakia. Since the Poles, having nearly been conquered by the Red Army in 1920, rejected any coalition with the Soviet Union, and since the Soviets' only access to Germany (except for East Prussia) was through Poland, Churchill's plan was worthless.

Ironically—considering that it was a pillar of his future fame—his drumbeating about the German danger was yet another position Churchill reneged on. In the fall of 1937, he stated:

> Three or four years ago I was myself a loud alarmist.... In spite of the risks which wait on prophecy, I declare my belief that a major war is not imminent, and I still believe that there is a good chance of no major war taking place in our lifetime.... I will not pretend that, if I had to choose between Communism and Nazism, I would choose Communism.[72]

For all the claptrap about Churchill's "farsightedness" during the '30s in opposing the "appeasers," in the end the policy of the Chamberlain government—to rearm as quickly as possible, while testing the chances for peace with Germany—was more realistic than Churchill's.

The common mythology is so far from historical truth that even an ardent Churchill sympathizer, Gordon Craig, feels obliged to write:

> The time is long past when it was possible to see the protracted debate over British foreign policy in the 1930s as a struggle between Churchill, an angel of light, fighting against the velleities of uncomprehending and feeble men in high places. It is reasonably well-known today that Churchill was often ill-informed, that his claims about German strength were exaggerated and his prescriptions impractical, that his emphasis on air power was misplaced.[73]

Moreover, as a British historian has recently noted: "For the record, it is worth recalling that in the 1930s Churchill did not oppose the appeasement of either Italy or Japan."[74] It is also worth

---

[72] Hart, "The Military Strategist," p. 204.

[73] Craig, "Churchill and Germany," p. 35.

[74] Donald Cameron Watt, "Churchill and Appeasement," in *Churchill*, Blake and Louis, eds., p. 214.

recalling that it was the pre-Churchill British governments that furnished the materiel with which Churchill was able to win the Battle of Britain. Clive Ponting has observed:

> the Baldwin and Chamberlain Governments ... had ensured that Britain was the first country in the world to deploy a fully integrated system of air defence based on radar detection of incoming aircraft and ground control of fighters ... Churchill's contribution had been to pour scorn on radar when he was in opposition in the 1930s.[75]

Embroiling America in World War—Again

In September, 1939, Britain went to war with Germany, pursuant to the guarantee which Chamberlain had been panicked into extending to Poland in March. Lloyd George had termed the guarantee "hare-brained," while Churchill had supported it. Nonetheless, in his history of the war Churchill wrote: "Here was decision at last, taken at the worst possible moment and on the least satisfactory ground which must surely lead to the slaughter of tens of millions of people."[76] With the war on, Winston was recalled to his old job as First Lord of the Admiralty.

Then, in the first month of the war, an astonishing thing happened: the President of the United States initiated a personal correspondence not with the Prime Minister of Great Britain, but with the head of the British Admiralty, bypassing all the normal diplomatic channels.[77]

The messages that passed between the President and the First Lord were surrounded by a frantic secrecy, culminating in the affair of Tyler Kent, the American cipher clerk at the U.S. London embassy who was tried and imprisoned by the British authorities.

---

[75] Ponting, *Churchill*, p. 464.

[76] Winston Churchill, *The Gathering Storm*, vol. 1, *The Second World War* (Boston: Houghton Mifflin, 1948), p. 347. Churchill commented that the guarantee was extended to a Poland "which with hyena appetite had only six months before joined in the pillage and destruction of the Czechoslovak State." He was referring to the annexation of the Teschen district, by which Poland reclaimed the ethnically Polish areas of the fabrication Churchill was pleased to dignify as "the Czechoslovak State."

[77] Irving, *Churchill's War*, pp. 193–96.

The problem was that some of the messages contained allusions to Roosevelt's agreement—even before the war began—to a blatantly unneutral cooperation with a belligerent Britain.[78]

On June 10, 1939, George VI and his wife, Queen Elizabeth, visited the Roosevelts at Hyde Park. In private conversations with the King, Roosevelt promised full support for Britain in case of war. He intended to set up a zone in the Atlantic to be patrolled by the U.S. Navy, and, according to the King's notes, the President stated that "if he saw a U boat he would sink her at once & wait for the consequences." The biographer of George VI, Wheeler-Bennett, considered that these conversations "contained the germ of the future Bases-for-Destroyers deal, and also of the Lend-Lease Agreement itself."[79] In communicating with the First Lord of the Admiralty, Roosevelt was aware that he was in touch with the one member of Chamberlain's cabinet whose belligerence matched his own.

In 1940 Churchill at last became Prime Minister, ironically enough when the Chamberlain government resigned because of the Norwegian fiasco—which Churchill, more than anyone else, had helped to bring about.[80] As he had fought against a negotiated peace after the fall of Poland, so he continued to resist any suggestion of negotiations with Hitler. Many of the relevant documents are still sealed—after all these years[81]—but it is clear that a strong peace party existed in the country and the government. It included Lloyd George in the House of Commons, and Halifax, the Foreign Secretary, in the Cabinet. Even after the fall of France, Churchill refused even to consider Hitler's renewed peace overtures, whether sincere or not. This, more than anything else, is supposed to be the foundation of his greatness. The British historian John Charmley raised a storm

---

[78] James Leutze, "The Secret of the Churchill–Roosevelt Correspondence: September 1939–May 1940," *Journal of Contemporary History* 10, no. 3 (July 1975), pp. 465–91; Leutze concludes that this was the real reason the two governments colluded to silence Tyler Kent.

[79] John W. Wheeler-Bennett, *King George VI: His Life and Reign* (New York: St. Martin's, 1958), pp. 390–92. Wheeler-Bennett added: "On his return to London the King communicated the essence of his talks with the President to the proper quarters, and so greatly did he esteem their importance that he carried the original manuscript of his notes about him in his dispatch case throughout the war."

[80] Hart, "The Military Strategist," p. 208.

[81] John Charmley, *Churchill: The End of Glory* (London: Hodder and Stoughton, 1993), p 423.

of outraged protest when he suggested that a negotiated peace in 1940 might have been to the advantage of Britain and Europe.[82] A Yale historian, writing in the *New York Times Book Review*, referred to Charmley's thesis as "morally sickening."[83] Yet Charmley's scholarly and detailed work makes the crucial point that Churchill's obdurate refusal even to listen to peace terms in 1940 doomed what he claimed was dearest to him—the Empire and a Britain that was non-socialist and independent in world affairs. One may add that it may also have doomed European Jewry.[84] It is amazing that half a century after the fact, there are critical theses concerning World War II that are off-limits to historical debate.

Lloyd George, Halifax, and the others were open to a compromise peace because they understood that Britain and the Dominions alone could not defeat Germany.[85] After the fall of France, Churchill's aim of total victory could be realized only under one condition: that the United States become embroiled in another world war. No wonder that Churchill put his heart and soul into ensuring precisely that.

After a talk with Churchill, Joseph Kennedy, American ambassador to Britain, noted: "Every hour will be spent by the British in trying to figure out how we can be gotten in." When he left from Lisbon on a ship to New York, Kennedy pleaded with the State Department to announce that if the ship should happen to blow up mysteriously in the mid-Atlantic, the United States would not consider it a cause for war with Germany. In his unpublished memoirs, Kennedy wrote: "I thought that would give me some protection against Churchill's placing a bomb on the ship."[86]

---

[82] See also Charmley's review of Clive Ponting's work, in the *Times Literary Supplement*, May 13, 1994, p. 8.

[83] Gaddis Smith, "Whose Finest Hour?" *New York Times Book Review*, August 29, 1993, p. 3.

[84] On March 27, 1942, Goebbels commented in his diary on the destruction of the European Jews, which was then underway: "Here, too, the Führer is the undismayed champion of a radical solution necessitated by conditions and therefore inexorable. Fortunately, a whole series of possibilities presents itself for us in wartime that would be denied us in peacetime. We shall have to profit by this." *The Goebbels Diaries, 1942–1943*, Louis P. Lochner, ed. and trans. (Garden City, N.Y.: Doubleday, 1948), p. 148.

[85] Paul Addison, "Lloyd George and Compromise Peace in the Second World War," in *Lloyd George: Twelve Essays*, A. J. P. Taylor, ed. (New York: Atheneum, 1971), pp. 359–84.

[86] Irving, *Churchill's War*, pp. 193, 207.

Kennedy's fears were perhaps not exaggerated. For, while it had been important for British policy in World War I, involving America was the *sine qua non* of Churchill's policy in World War II. In Franklin Roosevelt, he found a ready accomplice.

That Roosevelt, through his actions and private words, evinced a clear design for war before December 7, 1941, has never really been in dispute. Arguments have raged over such questions as his possible foreknowledge of the Pearl Harbor attack. In 1948, Thomas A. Bailey, diplomatic historian at Stanford, already put the real pro-Roosevelt case:

> Franklin Roosevelt repeatedly deceived the American people during the period before Pearl Harbor.... He was like a physician who must tell the patient lies for the patient's own good.... The country was overwhelmingly noninterventionist to the very day of Pearl Harbor, and an overt attempt to lead the people into war would have resulted in certain failure and an almost certain ousting of Roosevelt in 1940, with a complete defeat of his ultimate aims.[87]

Churchill himself never bothered to conceal Roosevelt's role as co-conspirator. In January, 1941, Harry Hopkins visited London. Churchill described him as "the most faithful and perfect channel of communication between the President and me ... the main prop and animator of Roosevelt himself":

> I soon comprehended [Hopkins's] personal dynamism and the outstanding importance of his mission ... here was an envoy from the President of supreme importance to our life.

---

[87] Thomas A. Bailey, *The Man in the Street: The Impact of American Public Opinion on Foreign Policy* (New York: Macmillan, 1948), p. 13. A recent writer has commented on Bailey's position: "In reality, when Roosevelt and other presidents lied, they did it for their own good, or what they believed to be their own good. But they were often mistaken because they have tended to be at least as shortsighted as the masses.... Roosevelt's destroyer deal marked a watershed in the use and abuse of presidential power, foreshadowing a series of dangerous and often disastrous adventures abroad." Robert Shogan, *Hard Bargain* (New York: Scribner's, 1995), pp. 271, 278. The classical revisionist case on Roosevelt's war policy was presented in Charles A. Beard, *President Roosevelt and the Coming of War 1941* (New Haven, Conn.: Yale University Press, 1948); and *Perpetual War for Perpetual Peace*, Harry Elmer Barnes, ed. (Caldwell, Idaho: Caxton, 1953), among other works.

With gleaming eye and quiet, constrained passion he said: "The President is determined that we shall win the war together. Make no mistake about it. He has sent me here to tell you that at all costs and by all means he will carry you through, no matter what happens to him—there is nothing that he will not do so far as he has human power." There he sat, slim, frail, ill, but absolutely glowing with refined comprehension of the Cause. It was to be the defeat, ruin, and slaughter of Hitler, to the exclusion of all other purposes, loyalties and aims.[88]

In 1976, the public finally learned the story of William Stephenson, the British agent code named "Intrepid," sent by Churchill to the United States in 1940.[89] Stephenson set up headquarters in Rockefeller Center, with orders to use any means necessary to bring the United States into the war. With the full knowledge and cooperation of Roosevelt and the collaboration of federal agencies, Stephenson and his 300 or so agents "intercepted mail, tapped wires, cracked safes, kidnapped, … rumor mongered" and incessantly smeared their favorite targets, the "isolationists." Through Stephenson, Churchill was virtually in control of William Donovan's organization, the embryonic U.S. intelligence service.[90]

Churchill even had a hand in the barrage of pro-British, anti-German propaganda that issued from Hollywood in the years before the United States entered the war. Gore Vidal, in *Screening History*, perceptively notes that starting around 1937, Americans were subjected to one film after another glorifying England and the warrior heroes who built the Empire. As spectators of these productions, Vidal says: "We served neither Lincoln nor Jefferson Davis; we served the Crown."[91] A key Hollywood figure in generating the movies that "were making us all weirdly English" was the Hungarian émigré and friend of Churchill, Alexander Korda.[92] Vidal very aptly writes:

---

[88]Winston S. Churchill, *The Grand Alliance*, vol. 3, *The Second World War* (Boston: Houghton Mifflin, 1950), pp. 23–24.

[89]William Stevenson, *A Man Called Intrepid* (New York: Harcourt Brace Jovanovich, 1976).

[90]Irving, *Churchill's War*, pp. 524–27.

[91]Gore Vidal, *Screening History* (Cambridge, Mass.: Harvard University Press, 1992), p. 40.

[92]Ibid., p. 47.

> For those who find disagreeable today's Zionist propaganda, I can only say that gallant little Israel of today must have learned a great deal from the gallant little Englanders of the 1930s. The English kept up a propaganda barrage that was to permeate our entire culture.... Hollywood was subtly and not so subtly infiltrated by British propagandists.[93]

While the Americans were being worked on, the two confederates consulted on how to arrange for direct hostilities between the United States and Germany. In August, 1941, Roosevelt and Churchill met at the Atlantic conference. Here they produced the Atlantic Charter, with its "Four Freedoms," including "the freedom from want"—a blank check to spread Anglo-American *Sozialpolitik* around the globe. When Churchill returned to London, he informed the Cabinet of what had been agreed to. Thirty years later, the British documents were released. Here is how the *New York Times* reported the revelations:

> Formerly top secret British Government papers made public today said that President Franklin D. Roosevelt told Prime Minister Winston Churchill in August, 1941, that he was looking for an incident to justify opening hostilities against Nazi Germany.... On August 19 Churchill reported to the War Cabinet in London on other aspects of the Newfoundland [Atlantic Charter] meeting that were not made public...." He [Roosevelt] obviously was determined that they should come in. If he were to put the issue of peace and war to Congress, they would debate it for months," the Cabinet minutes added. "The President had said he would wage war but not declare it and that he would become more and more provocative. If the Germans did not like it, they could attack American forces.... Everything was to be done to force an incident."[94]

On July 15, 1941, Admiral Little, of the British naval delegation in Washington, wrote to Admiral Pound, the First Sea Lord: "the brightest hope for getting America into the war lies in the escorting arrangements to Iceland, and let us hope the Germans will not be slow in attacking them." Little added, perhaps jokingly: "Otherwise

---

[93] Ibid., p. 33.
[94] "War-Entry Plans Laid to Roosevelt," *New York Times*, January 2, 1972.

I think it would be best for us to organise an attack by our own submarines and preferably on the escort!" A few weeks earlier, Churchill, looking for a chance to bring America into the war, wrote to Pound regarding the German warship, *Prinz Eugen*: "It would be better for instance that she should be located by a US ship as this might tempt her to fire on that ship, thus providing the incident for which the US government would be so grateful."[95] Incidents in the North Atlantic did occur, increasingly, as the United States approached war with Germany.[96]

But Churchill did not neglect "the back door to war" — embroiling the United States with Japan — as a way of bringing America into the conflict with Hitler. Sir Robert Craigie, the British ambassador to Tokyo, like the American ambassador Joseph Grew, was working feverishly to avoid war. Churchill directed his foreign secretary, Anthony Eden, to whip Craigie into line:

> He should surely be told forthwith that the entry of the United States into war either with Germany and Italy or with Japan, is fully conformable with British interests. Nothing in the munitions sphere can compare with the importance of the British Empire and the United States being co-belligerent.[97]

Churchill threw his influence into the balance to harden American policy towards Japan, especially in the last days before the Pearl Harbor attack.[98] A sympathetic critic of Churchill, Richard Lamb, has written:

> Was [Churchill] justified in trying to provoke Japan to attack the United States? ... in 1941 Britain had no prospect of defeating Germany without the aid of the USA as an active ally. Churchill believed Congress would never authorize Roosevelt to declare war on Germany.... In war, decisions by national leaders must be made according to their effect on the war effort. There is truth in the old adage: "All's fair in love and war."[99]

---

[95] Beesly, *Room 40*, p. 121 n. 1.

[96] See, for instance, William Henry Chamberlin, *America's Second Crusade* (Chicago: Henry Regnery, 1950), pp. 124–47.

[97] Richard Lamb, *Churchill as War Leader* (New York: Carroll and Graf, 1991), p. 149.

[98] Ibid., pp. 147–62.

[99] Ibid., p. 162.

No wonder that, in the House of Commons, on February 15, 1942, Churchill declared, of America's entry into the war: "This is what I have dreamed of, aimed at, worked for, and now it has come to pass."[100]

Churchill's devotees by no means hold his role in bringing America into World War II against him. On the contrary, they count it in his favor. Professor Harry Jaffa, in his uninformed and frantic apology, seems to be the last person alive who refuses to believe that the Man of Many Centuries was responsible to any degree for America's entry into the war: after all, wasn't it the Japanese who bombed Pearl Harbor?[101]

But what of the American Republic? What does it mean for us that a President collaborated with a foreign head of government to entangle us in a world war? The question would have mattered little to Churchill. He had no concern with the United States as a sovereign, independent nation, with its own character and place in the scheme of things. For him, Americans were one of "the English-speaking peoples." He looked forward to a common citizenship for Britons and Americans, a "mixing together," on the road to Anglo-American world hegemony.[102]

But the Churchill–Roosevelt intrigue should, one might think, matter to Americans. Here, however, criticism is halted before it

---

[100]Chamberlin, *America's Second Crusade*, p. 177. On Churchill's use of the "backdoor to war" for the United States, see John Costello, *Days of Infamy. MacArthur, Roosevelt, Churchill — The Shocking Truth Revealed* (New York: Pocket Books, 1994). On the question of Pearl Harbor, it is interesting to note that even as "mainstream" a historian as Warren F. Kimball, editor of the Churchill–Roosevelt correspondence, writes: "Doubts have not yet been laid to rest concerning still-closed British intelligence files about the Japanese attack on Pearl Harbor: information that Churchill may have chosen not to pass on to the Americans in the hope that such an attack would draw the United States into war." See also Warren F. Kimball, "Wheel Within a Wheel: Churchill, Roosevelt, and the Special Relationship," in *Churchill*, Blake and Louis, eds., p. 298, where Kimball cites James Rusbridger and Eric Nave, *Betrayal at Pearl Harbor: How Churchill Lured Roosevelt into World War II* (New York: Summit, 1991). Kimball complains that, despite written requests from him and other historians, British government files on relations with Japan in late 1941 remain closed. *Churchill*, p. 546 n. 29. Robert Smith Thompson, in *A Time for War: Franklin Delano Roosevelt and the Path to Pearl Harbor* (New York: Prentice Hall, 1991), presents a useful recent account of the coming of the war with Japan.

[101]Jaffa, "In Defense of Churchill," p. 277.

[102]Charmley, *Churchill: The End of Glory*, p. 538.

starts. A moral postulate of our time is that in pursuit of the destruction of Hitler, all things were permissible. Yet why is it self-evident that morality required a crusade against Hitler in 1939 and 1940, and not against Stalin? At that point, Hitler had slain his thousands, but Stalin had already slain his millions. In fact, up to June, 1941, the Soviets behaved far more murderously toward the Poles in their zone of occupation than the Nazis did in theirs. Around 1,500,000 Poles were deported to the Gulag, with about half of them dying within the first two years. As Norman Davies writes: "Stalin was outpacing Hitler in his desire to reduce the Poles to the condition of a slave nation."[103] Of course, there were balance-of-power considerations that created distinctions between the two dictators. But it has yet to be explained why there should exist a double standard ordaining that compromise with one murderous dictator would have been "morally sickening," while collaboration with the other was morally irreproachable.[104]

"First Catch Your Hare"

Early in the war, Churchill, declared: "I have only one aim in life, the defeat of Hitler, and this makes things very simple for me."[105] "Victory—victory at all costs," understood literally, was his policy practically to the end. This points to Churchill's fundamental and fatal mistake in World War II: his separation of operational from political strategy. To the first—the planning and direction of military campaigns—he devoted all of his time and energy; after all, he did *so* enjoy it. To the second, the fitting of military operations to the larger and much more significant political aims they were supposed to serve, he devoted no effort at all.

Stalin, on the other hand, understood perfectly that the entire purpose of war is to enforce certain political claims. This is the meaning of Clausewitz's famous dictum that war is the continuation of policy by other means. On the visit to Moscow of British Foreign Secetary Anthony Eden in December, 1941, with the Wehrmacht in the Moscow suburbs, Stalin was ready with his demands: British

---

[103] Norman Davies, *God's Playground: A History of Poland*, vol. 2, *1795 to the Present* (New York: Columbia University Press, 1982), pp. 447–53.

[104] For a critique of the view that Hitler's aim was to "conquer the world," see Geoffrey Stoakes, *Hitler and the Quest for World Domination* (Leamington Spa, England: Berg, 1986).

[105] Taylor, "The Statesman," p. 43.

recognition of Soviet rule over the Baltic states and the territories he had just seized from Finland, Poland, and Romania. (They were eventually granted.) Throughout the war he never lost sight of these and other crucial political goals. But Churchill, despite frequent prodding from Eden, never gave a thought to his, whatever they might be.[106] His approach, he explained, was that of Mrs. Glass's recipe for Jugged Hare: "First catch your hare."[107] First beat Hitler, then start thinking of the future of Britain and Europe. Churchill put in so many words: "the defeat, ruin, and slaughter of Hitler, to the exclusion of all other purposes, loyalties and aims."

Tuvia Ben-Moshe has shrewdly pinpointed one of the sources of this grotesque indifference:

> Thirty years earlier, Churchill had told Asquith that ... his life's ambition was "to command great victorious armies in battle." During World War II he was determined to take nothing less than full advantage of the opportunity given him — the almost unhampered military management of the great conflict. He was prone to ignore or postpone the treatment of matters likely to detract from that pleasure.... In so doing, he deferred, or even shelved altogether, treatment of the issues that he should have dealt with in his capacity as Prime Minister.[108]

Churchill's policy of all-out support of Stalin foreclosed other, potentially more favorable approaches. The military expert Hanson Baldwin, for instance, stated:

> There is no doubt whatsoever that it would have been in the interest of Britain, the United States, and the world to have allowed — and indeed, to have encouraged — the world's two great dictatorships to fight each other to a frazzle. Such a struggle, with its resultant weakening of both Communism and Nazism, could not but have aided in the establishment of a more stable peace.[109]

---

[106] For instance, in May, 1944, Eden protested to Churchill, regarding the prospect of the "Communization of the Balkans": "We must think of the after-effect of these developments, instead of confining ourselves as hitherto to the short-term view of what will give the best dividends during the war and for the war." Charmley, *Churchill: The End of Glory*, p. 538.

[107] Ben-Moshe, *Churchill: Strategy and History*, pp. 236–37.

[108] Ibid., 241.

[109] Hanson W. Baldwin, *Great Mistakes of the War* (New York: Harper, 1949), p. 10.

Instead of adopting this approach, or, for example, promoting the overthrow of Hitler by anti-Nazi Germans—instead of even considering such alternatives—Churchill from the start threw all of his support to Soviet Russia.

Franklin Roosevelt's fatuousness towards Josef Stalin is well-known. He looked on Stalin as a fellow "progressive" and an invaluable collaborator in creating the future New World Order.[110] But the neo-conservatives and others who counterpose to Roosevelt's inanity in this matter Churchill's Old World cunning and sagacity are sadly in error. Roosevelt's nauseating flattery of Stalin is easily matched by Churchill's. Just like Roosevelt, Churchill heaped fulsome praise on the Communist mass-murderer and was anxious for Stalin's personal friendship. Moreover, his adulation of Stalin and his version of Communism—so different from the repellent "Trotskyite" kind—was no different in private than in public. In January, 1944, he was still speaking to Eden of the "deep-seated changes which have taken place in the character of the Russian state and government, the new confidence which has grown in our hearts towards Stalin."[111] In a letter to his wife, Clementine, Churchill wrote, following the October, 1944 conference in Moscow: "I have had very nice talks with the old Bear. I like him the more I see him. Now they respect us & I am sure they wish to work with us."[112] Writers like Isaiah Berlin, who try to give the impression that Churchill hated or despised all dictators, including Stalin, are either ignorant or dishonest.[113]

---

[110] Roosevelt's attitude is epitomized in his statement: "If I give him [Stalin] everything I possibly can, and ask nothing of him in return, [then] *noblesse oblige*, he won't try to annex anything and will work with me for a world of peace and democracy." Robert Nisbet, *Roosevelt and Stalin: The Failed Courtship* (Washington, D.C.: Regnery, 1988), p. 6. Joseph Sobran's remarks in his brief essay, "Pal Joey," *Sobran's* 2, no. 8 (August 1995): pp. 5–6, are characteristically insightful.

[111] Ben-Moshe, *Churchill: Strategy and History*, pp. 287–88, 305–06.

[112] Ponting, *Churchill*, p. 665.

[113] Isaiah Berlin, "Winston Churchill in 1940," in idem, *Personal Impressions*, Henry Hardy, ed. (New York: Viking, 1980), p. 16., where Churchill is quoted as saying of Stalin that he is "at once a callous, a crafty, and an ill-informed giant." Note, however, that even this quotation shows that Churchill placed Stalin in an entirely different category from the unspeakably evil Hitler. In fact, as the works by Charmley, Ponting, and Ben-Moshe amply demonstrate, until the end of the war Churchill's typical attitude toward Stalin was friendly and admiring. Berlin's essay, with its mawkish infatuation with "the largest human being of

Churchill's supporters often claim that, unlike the Americans, the seasoned and crafty British statesman foresaw the danger from the Soviet Union and worked doggedly to thwart it. Churchill's famous "Mediterranean" strategy—to attack Europe through its "soft underbelly," rather than concentrating on an invasion of northern France—is supposed to be the proof of this.[114] But this was an *ex post facto* defense, invented by Churchill once the Cold War had started: there is little, if any, contemporary evidence that the desire to beat the Russians to Vienna and Budapest formed any part of Churchill's motivation in advocating the "soft underbelly" strategy. At the time, Churchill gave purely military reasons for it.[115] As Ben-Moshe states: "The official British historians have ascertained that not until the second half of 1944 and after the Channel crossing did Churchill first begin to consider preempting the Russians in southeastern Europe by military means."[116] By then, such a move would have been impossible for several reasons. It was another of Churchill's wild military notions, like invading Fortress Europe through Norway,[117] or putting off the invasion of northern France

---

our time," has to be read to be believed. An indication of one source of Berlin's passion is his reference to Churchill's sympathy for "the struggle of the Jews for self-determination [sic] in Palestine."

[114] Cf. Charmley, *Churchill: The End of Glory*, pp. 572–73, on "Operation Armpit," the extension of the Italian campaign and a thrust towards Vienna; Charmley concludes that, contrary to Churchill's Cold War defenders: "there is little evidence to show that Churchill's support for 'Armpit' was based upon political motives.... [He supported it] for the reason which any student of his career will be familiar with—it fired his imagination."

[115] Cf. Taylor, "The Statesman," pp. 56–57: "According to one version, Churchill was alarmed at the growth of Soviet power and tried to take precautions against it, if not in 1942 at least well before the end of the war.... It is hard to sustain this view from contemporary records. Churchill never wavered from his determination that Nazi Germany must be utterly defeated.... Churchill had no European policy in any wider sense. His outlook was purely negative: the defeat of Germany.... With Churchill it was always one thing at a time." See also Ben-Moshe, *Churchill: Strategy and History*, pp. 292–99, on the southern strategy not being aimed at forestalling Soviet gains.

[116] Ibid., p. 287.

[117] After the British had been forced to evacuate Norway, Churchill insisted on recapturing Narvik. General Ironside remarked privately, "He wanted to divert troops from all over the place. He is so like a child in many ways. He tires of a thing, and then wants to hear no more of it.... It is most extraordinary how mercurial he is." Nicholson Baker, *Human Smoke*, p. 173.

until 1945—by which time the Russians would have reached the Rhine.[118]

Moreover, the American opposition to Churchill's southern strategy did not stem from blindness to the Communist danger. General Albert C. Wedemeyer, one of the firmest anti-Communists in the American military, wrote:

> if we had invaded the Balkans through the Ljubljana Gap, we might theoretically have beaten the Russians to Vienna and Budapest. But logistics would have been against us there: it would have been next to impossible to supply more than two divisions through the Adriatic ports.... The proposal to save the Balkans from communism could never have been made good by a "soft underbelly" invasion, for Churchill himself had already cleared the way for the success of Tito ... [who] had been firmly ensconced in Yugoslavia with British aid long before Italy itself was conquered.[119]

Wedemeyer's remarks about Yugoslavia were on the mark. On this issue, Churchill rejected the advice of his own Foreign Office, depending instead on information provided especially by the head of the Cairo office of the SOE—the Special Operations branch—headed by a Communist agent named James Klugman. Churchill withdrew British support from the Loyalist guerrilla army of General Mihailovic and threw it to the Communist Partisan leader Tito.[120] What a victory for Tito would mean was no secret to Churchill.[121]

---

[118] An instance of the lengths to which Churchill's apologists will go is provided by John Keegan, in "Churchill's Strategy," in *Churchill*, Blake and Louis, eds., p. 328, where he states of Churchill: "Yet he never espoused any truly unwise strategic course, nor did he contemplate one. His commitment to a campaign in the Balkans was unsound, but such a campaign would not have risked losing the war." Risking losing the war would appear to be an excessively stringent criterion for a truly unwise strategic course.

[119] Albert C. Wedemeyer, *Wedemeyer Reports!* (New York: Holt, 1958), p. 230. Everyone else was against Churchill's plan, including his own military advisors. Brooke pointed out to his chief that, if they followed through with his idea, "we should embark on a campaign through the Alps in winter." Ponting, *Churchill*, p. 625.

[120] Lamb, *Churchill as War Leader*, pp. 250–75.

[121] Churchill's own Foreign Office informed him that: "we would land ourselves with a Communist state closely linked to the USSR after the war who would employ

When Fitzroy Maclean was interviewed by Churchill before being sent as liaison to Tito, Maclean observed that, under Communist leadership, the Partisans'

> ultimate aim would undoubtedly be to establish in Jugoslavia a Communist regime closely linked to Moscow. How did His Majesty's Government view such an eventuality?... Mr. Churchill's reply left me in no doubt as to the answer to my problem. So long, he said, as the whole of Western civilization was threatened by the Nazi menace, we could not afford to let our attention be diverted from the immediate issue by considerations of long-term policy.... Politics must be a secondary consideration.[122]

It would be difficult to think of a more frivolous attitude to waging war than considering "politics" to be a "secondary consideration." As for the "human costs" of Churchill's policy, when an aide pointed out that Tito intended to transform Yugoslavia into a Communist dictatorship on the Soviet model, Churchill retorted: "Do you intend to live there?"[123]

Churchill's benign view of Stalin and Russia contrasts sharply with his view of Germany. Behind Hitler, Churchill discerned the old specter of Prussianism, which had caused, allegedly, not only the two world wars, but the Franco-Prussian War as well. What he was battling now was "Nazi tyranny and Prussian militarism," the "two main elements in German life which must be absolutely destroyed."[124] In October, 1944, Churchill was still explaining to Stalin

---

the usual terrorist methods to overcome opposition." Ibid., p. 256. Anthony Eden told the Cabinet in June, 1944: "If anyone is to blame for the present situation in which Communist-led movements are the most powerful elements in Yugoslavia and Greece, it is we ourselves." British agents, according to Eden, had done the work of the Russians for them. Charmley, *Churchill: The End of Glory*, p. 580.

[122] Fitzroy Maclean *Eastern Approaches* (London: Jonathan Cape, 1949), p. 281.

[123] Lamb, *Churchill as War Leader*, p. 259. Churchill believed Tito's promises of a free election and a plebiscite on the monarchy; above all, he concentrated on a single issue: killing Germans. See also Charmley, *Churchill: The End of Glory*, p. 558.

[124] On September 21, 1943, for instance, Churchill stated: "The twin roots of all our evils, Nazi tyranny and Prussian militarism, must be extirpated. Until this is achieved, there are no sacrifices we will not make and no lengths in violence to which we will not go." Russell Grenfell, *Unconditional Hatred* (New York: Devin-Adair, 1953), p. 92.

that: "The problem was how to prevent Germany getting on her feet in the lifetime of our grandchildren."[125] Churchill harbored a "confusion of mind on the subject of the Prussian aristocracy, Nazism, and the sources of German militarist expansionism ... [his view] was remarkably similar to that entertained by Sir Robert Vansittart and Sir Warren Fisher; that is to say, it arose from a combination of almost racialist antipathy and balance of power calculations."[126] Churchill's aim was not simply to save world civilization from the Nazis, but, in his words, the "indefinite prevention of their [the Germans] rising again as an Armed Power."[127]

Little wonder, then, that Churchill refused even to listen to the pleas of the anti-Hitler German opposition, which tried repeatedly to establish liaison with the British government. Instead of making every effort to encourage and assist an anti-Nazi coup in Germany, Churchill responded to the feelers sent out by the German resistance with cold silence.[128] Reiterated warnings from Adam von Trott and other resistance leaders of the impending "bolshevization" of Europe made no impression at all on Churchill.[129] A recent historian has written, "by his intransigence and refusal to countenance talks with dissident Germans, Churchill threw away an opportunity to end the war in July 1944."[130] To add infamy to

---

[125] Ponting, *Churchill*, p. 675.

[126] Watt, "Churchill and Appeasement," p. 210.

[127] In a memorandum to Alexander Cadogan, of the Foreign Office; Richard Lamb, *The Ghosts of Peace, 1935–1945* (Salisbury, England: Michael Russell, 1987), p. 133.

[128] Peter Hoffmann, *German Resistance to Hitler* (Cambridge, Mass.: Harvard University Press, 1988), pp. 95–105; idem, *The History of the German Resistance*, Richard Barry, trans. (Cambridge, Mass.: MIT Press, 1977), pp. 205–48; and idem, "The Question of Western Allied Co-Operation with the German Anti-Nazi Conspiracy, 1938–1944," *The Historical Journal* 34, no. 2 (1991), pp. 437–64.

[129] Giles MacDonogh, *A Good German: Adam von Trott zu Solz* (Woodstock, N.Y.: Overlook Press, 1992), pp. 236–37.

[130] Lamb, *Churchill as War Leader*, p. 292. Lamb argues this thesis at length and persuasively in his *The Ghosts of Peace*, pp. 248–320. A less conclusive judgment is reached by Klemens von Klemperer, *German Resistance Against Hitler: The Search for Allies Abroad 1938–1945* (Oxford: Clarendon, 1992), especially pp. 432–41, who emphasizes the difficulties in the way of any agreement between the British government and the German resistance. These included, in particular, the loyalty of the former to its Soviet ally and the insistence of the latter on post-war Germany's keeping ethnically German areas, such as Danzig and the Sudetenland.

stupidity, Churchill and his crowd had only words of derision for the valiant German officers even as they were being slaughtered by the Gestapo.[131]

In place of help, all Churchill offered Germans looking for a way to end the war before the Red Army flooded into Central Europe was the slogan of *unconditional surrender*. Afterwards, Churchill lied in the House of Commons about his role at the Casablanca conference regarding Roosevelt's announcement of the policy of unconditional surrender and was forced to retract his statements.[132] Eisenhower, among others, strenuously and persistently objected to the formula as hampering the war effort by raising the morale of the Wehrmacht.[133] In fact, the slogan was seized on by Goebbels, and contributed to the Germans holding out to the bitter end.

The pernicious effect of the policy was immeasurably bolstered by the Morgenthau Plan, which gave the Germans a terrifying picture of what "unconditional surrender" would mean.[134] This plan, initialed by Roosevelt and Churchill at Quebec, called for turning Germany into an agricultural and pastoral country; even the coal mines of the Ruhr were to be wrecked. The fact that it would have led to the deaths of tens of millions of Germans made it a perfect analog to Hitler's schemes for dealing with Russia and the Ukraine.

Churchill was initially averse to the plan. However, he was won over by Professor Lindemann, as maniacal a German-hater as

---

[131] Marie Vassiltchikov, who was close to the conspirators, in her *Berlin Diaries, 1940–1945* (New York: Knopf, 1987), p. 218, expressed her bafflement at the line taken by the British: "The Allied radio makes no sense to us: they keep naming people who, they claim, took part in the plot. And yet some of these have not yet been officially implicated. I remember warning Adam Trott that this would happen. He kept hoping for Allied support of a 'decent' Germany and I kept saying that at this point they were out to destroy Germany, any Germany, and would not stop at eliminating the 'good' Germans with the 'bad.'"

[132] Ben-Moshe, *Churchill: Strategy and History*, pp. 307–16. See also Anne Armstrong, *Unconditional Surrender* (Westport, Conn.: Greenwood, [1961] 1974); and Lamb, *The Ghosts of Peace*, pp. 215–35. Among the strongest wartime critics of the unconditional surrender policy, as well as of the bombing of civilians, was the military expert, Liddell Hart; see Brian Bond, *Liddell Hart: A Study of his Military Thought* (New Brunswick, N.J.: Rutgers University Press, 1977), pp. 119–63.

[133] Lamb, *The Ghosts of Peace*, p. 232.

[134] Ibid., pp. 236–45.

Morgenthau himself. Lindemann stated to Lord Moran, Churchill's personal physician: "I explained to Winston that the plan would save Britain from bankruptcy by eliminating a dangerous competitor.... Winston had not thought of it in that way, and he said no more about a cruel threat to the German people."[135] According to Morgenthau, the wording of the scheme was drafted entirely by Churchill. When Roosevelt returned to Washington, Hull and Stimson expressed their horror and quickly disabused the President. Churchill, on the other hand, was unrepentant. When it came time to mention the Morgenthau Plan in his history of the war, he distorted its provisions and, by implication, lied about his role in supporting it.[136]

Beyond the issue of the plan itself, Lord Moran wondered how it had been possible for Churchill to appear at the Quebec conference "without any thought out views on the future of Germany, although she seemed to be on the point of surrender." The answer was that "he had become so engrossed in the conduct of the war that little time was left to plan for the future":

> Military detail had long fascinated him, while he was frankly bored by the kind of problem which might take up the time of the Peace Conference.... The P. M. was frittering away his waning strength on matters which rightly belonged to soldiers. My diary in the autumn of 1942 tells how I talked to Sir Stafford Cripps and found that he shared my cares. He wanted the P. M. to concentrate on the broad strategy of the war and on high policy.... No one could make [Churchill] see his errors.[137]

---

[135] Lord Moran, *Churchill: The Struggle for Survival, 1940–1965* (Boston: Houghton Mifflin, 1966), pp. 190–91. Churchill's ready acceptance of this specious argument casts considerable doubt on the claim of Paul Addison, *Churchill on the Home Front*, p. 437, that Churchill was "schooled" in free-trade doctrines, which were "ingrained" in him. More consistent with the evidence, including his outright rejection of free trade beginning in 1930, is that Churchill used or cast aside the economic theory of the market economy as it suited his political purposes.

[136] Moran, *Churchill: The Struggle for Survival, 1940–1965*, pp. 195–96.

[137] Ibid., p. 193. That the spirit at least of the Morgenthau Plan continued to guide Allied policy in post-war Germany is shown in Freda Utley's *The High Cost of Vengeance* (Chicago: Henry Regnery, 1949).

War Crimes Discreetly Veiled

There are a number of episodes during the war revealing of Churchill's character that deserve to be mentioned. A relatively minor incident was the British attack on the French fleet, at Mers-el-Kébir (Oran), off the coast of Algeria. After the fall of France, Churchill demanded that the French surrender their fleet to Britain. The French declined, promising that they would scuttle the ships before allowing them to fall into German hands. Against the advice of his naval officers, Churchill ordered British ships off the Algerian coast to open fire. About 1500 French sailors were killed. The French moved what remained of their fleet in the western Mediterranean to Nice. When the Germans attempted to seize it, the French were true to their word, and scuttled their ships.

Churchill's attack at Mers-el-Kébir was obviously a war crime, by any conceivable definition: an unprovoked assault on the forces of an ally without a declaration of war. At Nuremberg, German officers were sentenced to prison for less. Realizing this, Churchill lied about Mers-el-Kébir in his history and suppressed evidence concerning it in the official British histories of the war.[138] With the attack on the French fleet, Churchill confirmed his position as the prime subverter through two world wars of the system of rules of warfare that had evolved in the West over centuries.

But the great war crime which will be forever linked to Churchill's name is the terror-bombing of the cities of Germany that in the end cost the lives of around 600,000 civilians and left some 800,000 seriously injured.[139] (Compare this to the roughly 70,000 British

---

[138] Lamb, *Churchill as War Leader*, pp. 63–73. See also Ponting, *Churchill*, pp. 450–54; and Hart, "The Military Strategist," pp. 210–21.

[139] The "British obsession with heavy bombers" had consequences for the war effort as well; it led, for instance, to the lack of fighter planes at Singapore. Taylor, "The Statesman," p. 54. On the whole issue, see Stephen A. Garrett, *Ethics and Airpower in World War II: The British Bombing of German Cities* (New York: St. Martin's Press, 1993). See also Max Hastings, *Bomber Command* (New York: Dial Press, 1979); David Irving, *The Destruction of Dresden* (New York: Ballantine, 1963); and Benjamin Colby, *'Twas a Famous Victory* (New Rochelle, N.Y.: Arlington House, 1974), pp. 173–202. On the British use of airpower to "pacify" colonial populations, see Charles Townshend, "Civilization and 'Frightfulness': Air Control in the Middle East Between the Wars," in *Warfare, Diplomacy, and Politics: Essays in Honor of A. J. P. Taylor*, Chris Wrigley, ed. (London: Hamish Hamilton, 1986), pp. 142–62.

lives lost to German air attacks. In fact, there were nearly as many French killed by Allied air attacks as there were English killed by German.[140]) The plan was conceived mainly by Churchill's friend and scientific advisor, Professor Lindemann and carried out by the head of Bomber Command, Arthur Harris ("Bomber Harris"). Harris stated: "In Bomber Command we have always worked on the assumption that bombing anything in Germany is better than bombing nothing."[141] Harris and other British air force leaders boasted that Britain had been the pioneer in the massive use of strategic bombing. J. M. Spaight, former Principal Assistant Secretary of the Air Ministry, noted that while the Germans (and the French) looked on air power as largely an extension of artillery, a support to the armies in the field, the British understood its capacity to destroy the enemy's home-base. They built their bombers and established Bomber Command accordingly.[142]

Brazenly lying to the House of Commons and the public, Churchill claimed that only military and industrial installations were targeted. In fact, the aim was to kill as many civilians as possible — thus, "area" bombing, or "carpet" bombing — and in this way to break the morale of the Germans and terrorize them into surrendering.[143]

---

[140]Ponting, *Churchill*, p. 620.

[141]Hastings, *Bomber Command*, p. 339. In 1945, Harris wrote: "I would not regard the whole of the remaining cities of Germany as worth the bones of one British grenadier." Ibid., p. 344. Harris later wrote "The Germans had allowed their soldiers to dictate the whole policy of the Luftwaffe, which was designed expressly to assist the army in rapid advances.... Much too late in the day they saw the advantage of a strategic bombing force." Hughes, *Winston Churchill: British Bulldog*, p. 189. Harris, "the terrorizer and destroyers of cities" (Robert Bevan, *The Destruction of Memory: Architecture at War*, London: Reaktion Books, 2006) was honored in 1992 with a statue of him erected in front of the Church of St. Clement Danes in London ("the RAF church"). The statue was unveiled by the Queen Mother herself, who was surprised by heckling from protesters in the crowd.

[142]J. M. Spaight, *Bombing Vindicated* (London: Geoffrey Bles, 1944), p. 70–71. Spaight declared that Britons should be proud of the fact that "we began to bomb objectives on the German mainland before the Germans began to bomb objectives on the British mainland." Hitler, while ready enough to use strategic bombing pitilessly on occasion, "did not want [it] to become the practice. He had done his best to have it banned by international agreement." Ibid., pp. 68, 60. Writing during the war, Spaight, of course, lied to his readers in asserting that German civilians were being killed only incidentally by the British bombing.

[143]On February 14, 1942, Directive no. 22 was issued to Bomber Command, stip-

Harris at least had the courage of his convictions. He urged that the government openly announce that:

> the aim of the Combined Bomber Offensive ... should be unambiguously stated [as] the destruction of German cities, the killing of German workers, and the disruption of civilized life throughout Germany.[144]

The campaign of murder from the air leveled Germany. A thousand-year-old urban culture was annihilated, as great cities, famed in the annals of science and art, were reduced to heaps of smoldering ruins. There were high points: the bombing of Lübeck, when that ancient Hanseatic town "burned like kindling"; the 1000-bomber raid over Cologne, and the following raids that somehow, miraculously, mostly spared the great Cathedral but destroyed the rest of the city, including thirteen Romanesque churches; the firestorm that consumed Hamburg and killed some 42,000 people. No wonder that, learning of this, a civilized European like Joseph Schumpeter, at Harvard, was driven to telling "anyone who would listen" that Churchill and Roosevelt were destroying more than Genghis Khan.[145]

The most infamous act was the destruction of Dresden, in February, 1945. According to the official history of the Royal Air Force: "The destruction of Germany was by then on a scale which might have appalled Attila or Genghis Khan."[146] Dresden, the capital of the old Kingdom of Saxony, was an indispensable stop on the Grand Tour, the baroque gem of Europe. The war was practically over, the city filled with masses of helpless refugees escaping the advancing Red Army. Still, for three days and nights, from February 13

---

ulating that efforts were now to be "focused on the morale of the enemy civil population and in particular of the industrial workers." The next day, the chief of the Air Staff added: "Ref the new bombing directive: I suppose it is clear that the aiming points are to be the built-up areas, not, for instance, the dockyards or aircraft factories." Garrett, *Ethics and Air Power in World War II*, p. 11. By lying about the goal of the bombing and attempting a cover-up after the war, Churchill implicitly conceded that Britain had committed breaches of the rules of warfare. Ibid., pp. 36–37.

[144]Ibid., pp. 32–33.

[145]Richard Swedberg, *Schumpeter: A Biography* (Princeton, N.J.: Princeton University Press, 1991), p. 141.

[146]Garrett, *Ethics and Air Power in World War II*, p. 202.

to 15, Dresden was pounded with bombs. At least 30,000 people were killed, perhaps tens of thousands more. The Zwinger Palace; Our Lady's Church (die Frauenkirche); the Brühl Terrace, overlooking the Elbe where, in Turgenev's *Fathers and Sons*, Uncle Pavel went to spend his last years; the Semper Opera House, where Richard Wagner conducted the premieres of *The Flying Dutchman* and *Tannhäuser* and Richard Strauss the premiere of *Rosenkavalier*; and practically everything else was incinerated. Churchill had fomented it. But he was shaken by the outcry that followed. While in Georgetown and Hollywood few had ever heard of Dresden, the city meant something in Stockholm, Zurich, and the Vatican, and even in London. What did our hero do? He sent a memorandum to the Chiefs of Staff:

> It seems to me that the moment has come when the question of bombing of German cities simply for the sake of increasing the terror, though under other pretexts, should be reviewed. Otherwise, we shall come into control of an utterly ruined land.... The destruction of Dresden remains a serious query against the conduct of Allied bombing.... I feel the need for more precise concentration upon military objectives ... rather than on mere acts of terror and wanton destruction, however impressive.[147]

The military chiefs saw through Churchill's cowardly ploy: realizing that they were being set up, they refused to accept the memorandum. After the war, Churchill casually disclaimed any knowledge of the Dresden bombing, saying: "I thought the Americans did it."[148]

And still the bombing continued. On March 16, in a period of twenty minutes, Würzburg was razed to the ground. As late as the middle of April, Berlin and Potsdam were bombed yet again, killing another 5,000 civilians. Finally, it stopped; as Bomber Harris noted, there were essentially no more targets to be bombed in Germany.[149]

---

[147] Hastings, *Bomber Command*, pp. 343–44. In November, 1942, Churchill had proposed that in the Italian campaign: "All the industrial centers should be attacked in an intense fashion, every effort being made to render them uninhabitable and to terrorise and paralyse the population." Ponting, *Churchill*, p. 614.

[148] To a historian who wished to verify some details, Churchill replied: "I cannot recall anything about it. I thought the Americans did it. Air Chief Marshal Harris would be the person to contact." Rose, *Churchill: The Unruly Giant*, p. 338.

[149] Garrett, *Ethics and Air Power in World War II*, p. 21.

It need hardly be recorded that Churchill supported the atom bombing of Hiroshima and Nagasaki, which resulted in the deaths of more tens of thousands of civilians. When Truman fabricated the myth of the "500,000 U.S. lives saved" by avoiding an invasion of the Home Islands—the highest military estimate had been 46,000—Churchill topped his lie: the atom-bombings had saved 1,200,000 lives, including 1,000,000 Americans, he fantasized.[150]

The eagerness with which Churchill directed or applauded the destruction of cities from the air should raise questions for those who still consider him the great "conservative" of his—or perhaps of all—time. They would do well to consider the judgment of an authentic conservative like Erik von Kuehnelt-Leddihn, who wrote: "Non-Britishers did not matter to Mr. Churchill, who sacrificed human beings their lives, their welfare, their liberty—with the same elegant disdain as his colleague in the White House."[151]

1945: The Dark Side

And so we come to 1945 and the ever-radiant triumph of Absolute Good over Absolute Evil. So potent is the mystique of that year that the insipid welfare states of today's Europe clutch at it at every opportunity, in search of a few much-needed shreds of glory.

The dark side of that triumph, however, has been all but suppressed. It is the story of the crimes and atrocities of the victors and their protégés. Since Winston Churchill played a central role

---

[150]See Barton J. Bernstein, "A postwar myth: 500,000 U.S. lives saved," *Bulletin of the Atomic Scientists* 42, no. 6 (June/July 1986), pp. 38–40; and, idem, "Wrong Numbers," *The Independent Monthly* (July 1995), pp. 41–44. See also, idem, "Seizing the Contested Terrain of Early Nuclear History: Stimson, Conant, and Their Allies Explain the Decision to Use the Atomic Bomb," *Diplomatic History* 17, no. 1 (Winter 1993), pp. 35–72, where the point is made that a major motive in the political elite's early propaganda campaign justifying the use of the atomic bombs was to forestall a feared retreat into "isolationism" by the American people. It is interesting to note that Richard Nixon, sometimes known as the "Mad Bomber" of Indo-China, justified "deliberate attacks on civilians" by citing the atomic bombings of the Japanese cities, as well as the attacks on Hamburg and Dresden. Richard M. Nixon, "Letters to the Editor," *New York Times*, May 15, 1983.

[151]Erik von Kuehnelt-Leddihn, *Leftism Revisited: From de Sade and Marx to Hitler and Pol Pot* (Washington, D.C.: Regnery, 1990), p. 281. This work contains numerous perceptive passages on Churchill, e.g., pp. 261–65, 273, and 280–81, as well as on Roosevelt.

in the Allied victory, it is the story also of the crimes and atrocities in which Churchill was implicated. These include the forced repatriation of some two million Soviet subjects to the Soviet Union. Among these were tens of thousands who had fought with the Germans against Stalin, under the sponsorship of General Vlasov and his "Russian Army of Liberation." This is what Alexander Solzhenitsyn wrote, in *The Gulag Archipelago*:

> In their own country, Roosevelt and Churchill are honored as embodiments of statesmanlike wisdom. To us, in our Russian prison conversations, their consistent shortsightedness and stupidity stood out as astonishingly obvious... what was the military or political sense in their surrendering to destruction at Stalin's hands hundreds of thousands of armed Soviet citizens determined not to surrender.[152]

Most shameful of all was the handing over of the Cossacks. They had never been Soviet subjects, since they had fought against the Red Army in the Civil War and then emigrated. Stalin, understandably, was particularly keen to get hold of them, and the British obliged. Solzhenitsyn wrote, of Winston Churchill:

> He turned over to the Soviet command the Cossack corps of 90,000 men. Along with them he also handed over many wagonloads of old people, women, and children.... This great hero, monuments to whom will in time cover all England, ordered that they, too, be surrendered to their deaths.[153]

The "purge" of alleged collaborators in France was a blood bath that claimed more victims than the Reign of Terror in the Great Revolution—and not just among those who in one way or other had aided the Germans: included were any right-wingers the Communist resistance groups wished to liquidate.[154]

The massacres carried out by Churchill's protégé, Tito, must be added to this list: tens of thousands of Croats, not simply the Ustasha, but any "class-enemies," in classical Communist style. There

---

[152] Aleksandr I. Solzhenitsyn, *The Gulag Archipelago, 1918–1956: An Experiment in Literary Investigation*, Thomas P. Whitney, trans. (New York: Harper and Row, 1973), vols. 1–2, p. 259 n.

[153] Ibid., pp. 259–60.

[154] Sisley Huddleston, *France: The Tragic Years, 1939–1947* (New York: Devin-

was also the murder of some 20,000 Slovene anti-Communist fighters by Tito and his killing squads. When Tito's Partisans rampaged in Trieste, which he was attempting to grab in 1945, additional thousands of Italian anti-Communists were massacred.[155]

As the troops of Churchill's Soviet ally swept through Central Europe and the Balkans, the mass deportations began. Some in the British government had qualms, feeling a certain responsibility. Churchill would have none of it. In January, 1945, he noted to the Foreign Office: "Why are we making a fuss about the Russian deportations in Rumania of Saxons [Germans] and others?... I cannot see the Russians are wrong in making 100 or 150 thousand of these people work their passage.... I cannot myself consider that it is wrong of the Russians to take Rumanians of any origin they like to work in the Russian coal-fields."[156] About 500,000 German civilians were deported to work in Soviet Russia, in accordance with Churchill and Roosevelt's agreement at Yalta that such slave labor constituted a proper form of "reparations."[157]

Worst of all was the expulsion of some 12 million Germans from their ancestral homelands in East and West Prussia, Silesia, Pomerania, and the Sudetenland, as well as the Balkans. This was done pursuant to the agreements at Tehran, where Churchill proposed that Poland be "moved west," and to Churchill's acquiescence in the plan of the Czech leader Eduard Beneš for the "ethnic cleansing" of Bohemia and Moravia. Around one-and-a-half to two million German civilians died in this process.[158]

Adair, 1955), pp. 285–324.

[155] See, for instance, Richard West, *Tito and the Rise and Fall of Yugoslavia* (New York: Carroll and Graf, 1995), pp. 192–93.

[156] Ponting, *Churchill*, p. 665.

[157] Herbert Mitzka, *Zur Geschichte der Massendeportationen von Ostdeutschen in die Sowjetunion im Jahre 1945* (Einhausen: Atelier Hübner, 1986). On other crimes against German civilians in the aftermath of the war, see, among other works, Heinz Nawratil, *Die deutschen Nachkriegsverluste unter Vertriebenen, Gefangenen, und Verschleppten* (Munich/Berlin: Herbig, 1986); John Sack, *An Eye for an Eye* (New York: Basic Books, 1993); and James Bacque, *Verschwiegene Schuld: Die alliierte Besatzungspolitik in Deutschland nach 1945*, Hans-Ulrich Seebohm, trans. (Berlin/Frankfurt a. M.: Ullstein, 1995).

[158] Alfred de Zayas, *Nemesis at Potsdam: The Anglo-Americans and the Expulsion of the Germans. Background, Execution, Consequences* (London: Routledge and Kegan Paul, 1977).

Beneš Announces the Expulsion of the Germans

The riot of rape by the Soviet troops was probably the worst in history. Females—Hungarian, even Polish, as well as German, little girls to old women—were multiply violated, sometimes raped to death. (In the west the Americans raped on a very much smaller scale.) Boys who tried to defend their mothers were simply shot by the soldiers, others were forced to look on. But the most brutal sufferings of German civilians (from the ground) were at the hands of the Czechs themselves.

The Nazis were perpetrating horrendous atrocities in most of the rest of their occupied territories, inciting courageous, death-defying resistance movements. In the Czechs' lands, however, the Germans encountered nary a peep. There was no Czech resistance and the population was pretty well content, especially given the welfare state measures introduced by the Nazi "Protector" of Bohemia and Moravia, Reinhard Heydrich. In London it was decided to have Heydrich killed, a plot that succeeded. But assassins had to be flown in from England: none could be found among the natives.

As the Wehrmacht retreated, the Czechs found their virility. Beneš announced, "Woe, woe, woe, thrice woe, we will liquidate you!" In May, he declared, "We have decided ... to liquidate the German problem in our republic once and for all."[159] All over Bohemia and Moravia and in the capital thousands of German civilians were tortured and massacred. In a school in Prague, on the night of May 5, 1945, "groups of ten Germans were led down to the courtyard and shot: men, women, and children—even babies." Professors and physicians at the Charles University of Prague—founded in 1347 and administered for centuries by the Germans (of course), the oldest university in all of Central Europe—were lynched. Germans individually or in groups were beaten to death, to the cheers of onlookers. The American troops "did not meddle in the activities of Czech partisans." More details, for those who can stomach them, can be found in MacDonough's book.[160]

---

[159] Giles MacDonough, *After the Reich: The Brutal History of the Allied Occupation* (New York: Basic Books, 2007), p. 128. The following account is from *After the Reich*.

[160] It is interesting to note that Václav Klaus, the center-right sometime president

As the Hungarian liberal Gaspar Tamas wrote, in driving out the Germans of east-central Europe, "whose ancestors built our cathedrals, monasteries, universities, and railroad stations," a whole ancient culture was effaced.[161] But why should that mean anything to the Winnie worshippers who call themselves "conservatives" in America today?

Churchill Has Second Thoughts

To top it all, came the Nuremberg Trials, a travesty of justice condemned by the great Senator Robert Taft, where British and other Allied jurists joined with Stalin's judges and prosecutors — seasoned veterans of the purges of the '30s — in another great show trial.[162]

By 1946, Churchill was complaining in a voice of outrage of the happenings in Eastern Europe: "From Stettin on the Baltic to Trieste on the Adriatic, an iron curtain has descended over Europe." Goebbels had popularized the phrase "iron curtain," but it was accurate enough.

The European continent now contained a single, hegemonic power. "As the blinkers of war were removed," John Charmley writes, "Churchill began to perceive the magnitude of the mistake which had been made."[163] In fact, Churchill's own expressions of profound self-doubt consort oddly with his admirers' retrospective triumphalism. After the war, he told Robert Boothby: "Historians are apt to judge war ministers less by the victories achieved under their direction than by the political results which flowed from them. Judged by that standard, I am not sure that I shall be held to have done very well."[164] In the preface to the first volume of his history of World War II, Churchill explained why he was so troubled:

---

of the post-World War II Czech Republic, esteemed member the Mont Pèlerin Society and universally acclaimed free-market superstar, has ostentatiously refused to apologize for the explusion of the Germans, not even bothering to mention the torture and murder of thousands of them by his fellow countrymen.

[161] Gaspar M. Tamas, "The Vanishing Germans," *The Spectator*, May 6, 1989, p. 15.

[162] Critiques of the Nuremberg Trials are included in Lord Hankey, *Politics, Trials, and Errors* (Chicago: Henry Regnery, 1950), and F. J. P. Veale, *Advance to Barbarism: The Development of Total Warfare from Serajevo to Hiroshima* (New York: Devin-Adair, 1968), among other works.

[163] Charmley, *Churchill: The End of Glory*, p. 622.

[164] Robert Boothy, *Recollections of a Rebel* (London: Hutchison, 1978), pp. 183–84.

> The human tragedy reaches its climax in the fact that after all the exertions and sacrifices of hundreds of millions of people and of the victories of the Righteous Cause, we have still not found Peace or Security, and that we lie in the grip of even worse perils than those we have surmounted.[165]

On V-E Day, he had announced the victory of "the cause of freedom in every land." But to his private secretary, he mused: "What will lie between the white snows of Russia and the white cliffs of Dover?"[166] It was a bit late to raise the question. Really, what are we to make of a statesman who for years ignored the fact that the extinction of Germany as a power in Europe entailed ... certain consequences? Is this another Bismarck or Metternich we are dealing with here? Or is it a case of a Woodrow Wilson redivivus—of another Prince of Fools?

With the balance of power in Europe wrecked by his own policy, there was only one recourse open to Churchill: to bring America into Europe permanently. Thus, his anxious expostulations to the Americans, including his Fulton, Missouri "Iron Curtain" speech. Having destroyed Germany as the natural balance to Russia on the continent, he was now forced to try to embroil the United States in yet another war—this time a Cold War, that would last 45 years, and change America fundamentally, and irrevocably.[167]

The Triumph of the Welfare State

In 1945, general elections were held in Britain, and the Labour Party won a landslide victory. Clement Attlee and his colleagues took power and created the socialist welfare state. But the socializing of Britain was probably inevitable, given the war. It was a natural outgrowth of the wartime sense of solidarity and collectivist emotion, of the feeling that the experience of war had somehow rendered class structure and hierarchy—normal features of any advanced society—obsolete and indecent. And there was a second factor: British society had already been to a large extent socialized in the war years, under Churchill himself. As Ludwig von Mises wrote:

---

[165] Churchill, *The Gathering Storm*, pp. iv-v.

[166] Nisbet, *Roosevelt and Stalin: The Failed Courtship*, p. 106.

[167] Cf. Robert Higgs, "The Cold War Economy: Opportunity Costs, Ideology, and the Politics of Crisis," *Explorations in Economic History* 31 (1994), pp. 283-312.

> Marching ever further on the way of interventionism, first Germany, then Great Britain and many other European countries have adopted central planning, the Hindenburg pattern of socialism. It is noteworthy that in Germany the deciding measures were not resorted to by the Nazis, but some time before Hitler seized power by Brüning ... and in Great Britain not by the Labour Party but by the Tory Prime Minister, Mr. Churchill.[168]

While Churchill waged war, he allowed Attlee to head various Cabinet committees on domestic policy and devise proposals on health, unemployment, education, etc.[169] Churchill himself had already accepted the master-blueprint for the welfare state, the Beveridge Report. As he put it in a radio speech:

> You must rank me and my colleagues as strong partisans of national compulsory insurance for all classes for all purposes from the cradle to the grave.[170]

That Mises was correct in his judgment on Churchill's role is indicated by the conclusion of W. H. Greenleaf, in his monumental study of individualism and collectivism in modern Britain. Greenleaf states that it was Churchill who

---

[168] Ludwig von Mises, *Human Action* (New Haven, Conn.: Yale University Press, 1949), p. 855.

[169] Charmley, *Churchill: The End of Glory*, p. 610, 618. Cf. Peter Clarke, *Liberals and Social Democrats* (Cambridge: Cambridge University Press, 1978), p. 281: "When the Churchill Coalition was formed in May 1940 it gave progressivism a central political role which it had lacked since 1914.... The people's war brought a people's government in which ordinary Labour and good Liberals were the ascendant elements.... Anti-appeasement was the dominant myth; it helped displace the Guilty Men of Munich; and it prepared the ground for the overthrow of the Chamberlain consensus in domestic policy too. Keynes suddenly moved to a pivotal position inside the Treasury. Labour's patriotic response to the common cause was symbolised by the massive presence of Ernest Bevan as Minister of Labour."

[170] Addison, "Churchill and Social Reform," p. 73. Addison states: "By the spring of 1945 the Coalition government had prepared draft bills for comprehensive social insurance, family allowances, and a national health service." As Leader of the Opposition for the next six years, "in social policy [Churchill] invariably contested the Labour Party's claim to a monopoly of social concern, and insisted that the credit for devising the post-war welfare state should be given to the wartime Coalition, and not to the Attlee government."

during the war years, instructed R. A. Butler to improve the education of the people and who accepted and sponsored the idea of a four-year plan for national development and the commitment to sustain full employment in the post-war period. As well he approved proposals to establish a national insurance scheme, services for housing and health, and was prepared to accept a broadening field of state enterprises. It was because of this coalition policy that Enoch Powell referred to the veritable social revolution which occurred in the years 1942–44. Aims of this kind were embodied in the Conservative declaration of policy issued by the Premier before the 1945 election.[171]

When the Tories returned to power in 1951, "Churchill chose a Government which was the least recognizably Conservative in history."[172] There was no attempt to roll back the welfare state, and the only industry that was reprivatized was road haulage.[173] Churchill "left the core of its [the Labour government's] work inviolate."[174] The "Conservative" victory functioned like Republican victories in the United States, from Eisenhower on — to consolidate the socialist advances that had gone before. Churchill even undertook to make up for "deficiencies" in the welfare programs of the previous Labour government, in housing and public works.[175] Most insidiously of all, he directed his leftist Labour Minister, Walter Monckton, to appease the unions at all costs. Churchill's surrender to the unions, "dictated by sheer political expediency," set the stage for the quagmire in labor relations that prevailed in Britain for the next two decades.[176]

Yet, in truth, Churchill never cared a great deal about domestic affairs, even welfarism, except as a means of attaining and keeping office. What he loved was power, and the opportunities power provided to live a life of drama and struggle and endless war.

---

[171] Greenleaf, *The British Political Tradition*, pp. 254–55.

[172] Roberts, *Eminent Churchillians*, p. 258.

[173] Ibid., p. 254. Roberts points out that "when the iron and steel industries were denationalized in 1953, they effectively continued to be run via the Iron and Steel Board."

[174] Roy Jenkins, "Churchill: The Government of 1951–1955," in *Churchill*, Blake and Louis, eds., p. 499.

[175] Addison, "Churchill and Social Reform," p. 76.

[176] Roberts, *Eminent Churchillians*, pp. 243–85.

There is a way of looking at Winston Churchill that is very tempting: that he was a deeply flawed creature, who was summoned at a critical moment to do battle with a uniquely appalling evil, and whose very flaws contributed to a glorious victory—in a way, like Merlin, in C. S. Lewis's great Christian novel, *That Hideous Strength*.[177]

Such a judgment would, I believe, be superficial. A candid examination of his career, I suggest, yields a different conclusion: that, when all is said and done, Winston Churchill was a Man of Blood and a politico without principle, whose apotheosis serves to corrupt every standard of honesty and morality in politics and history

---

[177] C. S. Lewis, *That Hideous Strength: A Modern Fairy-Tale for Grown-Ups* (New York: Collier, [1946] 1965).

CHAPTER 3

Harry S. Truman: Advancing the Revolution

A "Near-Great"?

When Harry Truman left office in January 1953, he was intensely unpopular, even widely despised. Many of his most cherished schemes, from national health insurance (socialized medicine) to universal military training (UMT) had been soundly rejected by Congress and the public. Worst of all, the war in Korea, which he persisted in calling a "police action," was dragging on with no end in sight.

Yet today, Republican no less than Democratic politicians vie in glorifying Truman. When historians are asked to rank American presidents, he is listed as a "Near-Great." Naturally, historians, like everyone else, have their own personal views and values. Like other academics in the humanities they tend to be overwhelmingly left of center. As Robert Higgs writes: "Left-liberal historians worship

---

This is an expanded version of an essay that first appeared in *Reassessing the Presidency*, edited by John V. Denson in 2001 and published by the Ludwig von Mises Institute.

political power, and idolize those who wield it most lavishly in the service of left-liberal causes."[1] So it is scarcely surprising that they should venerate men like Woodrow Wilson, Franklin Roosevelt, and Harry Truman, and connive to get a gullible public to go along.

But for anyone friendlier to limited government than the ordinary run of history professors, the presidency of Harry Truman will appear in a very different light. Truman's predecessor had massively expanded federal power, especially the power of the president, in what amounted to a revolution in American government. Under Truman, that revolution was consolidated and advanced beyond what even Franklin Roosevelt had ever dared hope for.

The Onset of the Cold War—
Scaring Hell Out of the American People

Most pernicious of all, Truman's presidency saw the genesis of a world-spanning American political and military empire.[2] This was not simply the unintended consequence of some supposed Soviet threat, however. Even before the end of World War II, high officials in Washington were drawing up plans to project American military might across the globe. To start with, the United States would dominate the Atlantic and Pacific Oceans and the Western Hemisphere, including through a network of air and naval bases. Complementing this would be a system of air transit rights and landing facilities from North Africa to Saigon and Manila. This planning continued through the early years of the Truman administration.[3]

---

[1] Robert Higgs, "No More 'Great Presidents,'" *The Free Market* (February 1997), p. 2.

[2] Even such a defender of U.S. policy as John Lewis Gaddis, in "The Emerging Post-Revisionist Synthesis on the Origins of the Cold War," *Diplomatic History* 7, no. 3 (Summer 1983), pp. 171–93, states that part of the "post-revisionist" consensus among diplomatic historians is that an American empire did indeed come into being. But this American empire, according to Gaddis, is a "defensive" one. Why this should be a particularly telling point is unclear, considering that for American leaders "defense" has entailed attempting to control the world.

[3] Melvyn P. Leffler, "The American Conception of National Security and the Beginnings of the Cold War, 1945–1948," *American Historical Review* 89, no. 2 (April 1984), pp. 346–81. See also the comments by John Lewis Gaddis and Bruce Kuniholm, and Leffler's reply, pp. 382–400.

HARRY S. TRUMAN: ADVANCING THE REVOLUTION   105

But the planners had no guarantee that such a radical reversal of our traditional policy could be sold to Congress and the people. It was the confrontation with the Soviet Union and "international Communism," begun and defined by Truman and then prolonged for four decades, that furnished the opportunity and the rationale for realizing the globalist dreams.

That after World War II the Soviet Union would be predominant in Europe was inevitable, given the goals pursued by Roosevelt and Churchill: Germany's unconditional surrender and its annihilation as a factor in the balance of power.[4] At Yalta, the two Western leaders acquiesced in the control over Eastern Europe that had been won by Stalin's armies, while affecting to believe that the Red dictator would cheerfully assent to the establishment of democratic governments in that area. The trouble was that genuinely free elections east of the Elbe (except in Czechoslovakia) would inescapably produce bitterly anti-Communist regimes. Such a result was unacceptable to Stalin, whose position was well-known and much more realistic than the illusions of his erstwhile allies. As he stated in the spring of 1945: "Whoever occupies a territory also imposes on it his own social system [as far] as his army can reach."[5]

When Truman became president in April 1945, he was at first prepared to continue the "Grand Alliance," and in fact harbored sympathetic feelings toward Stalin.[6] But differences soon arose. The raping and murdering rampage of Red Army troops as they rolled over Eastern Europe came as a disagreeable surprise to Americans who had swallowed the wartime propaganda, from Hollywood and elsewhere, on the Soviet "purity of arms." Stalin's apparent intention to communize Poland and include the other conquered territories within his sphere of influence was deeply resented by

---

[4] See Ralph Raico, "Rethinking Churchill," in the present volume.

[5] Walter LaFeber, *America, Russia, and the Cold War, 1945–1990*, 6th rev. ed. (New York: McGraw-Hill, 1991), p. 13. Cf. Stalin's comment at Yalta: "A freely elected government in any of these countries would be anti-Soviet, and that we cannot allow." Hans J. Morgenthau, "The Origins of the Cold War," in Lloyd C. Gardner, Arthur Schlesinger, Jr., and Hans J. Morgenthau, *The Origins of the Cold War* (Waltham, Mass.: Ginn, 1970), pp. 87–88.

[6] Melvyn R. Leffler, "Inside Enemy Archives: The Cold War Reopened," *Foreign Affairs* (July/August 1996), pp. 134–35.

leaders in Washington, who at the same time had no qualms about maintaining their own sphere of influence throughout all of Latin America.[7]

Stalin's predictable moves to extend his sway around the periphery of the USSR further alarmed Washington. Exploiting the presence of Soviet forces in northern Iran (a result of the wartime agreement of the Big Three to divide up control of that country), he pressed for oil concessions similar to those gained by the United States and Britain. After the Soviets withdrew in return for a promise of concessions by the Iranian parliament, Iran, supported by the United States, reneged on the deal. Turning to Turkey, Stalin revived traditional Russian claims dating from Tsarist days, pressuring Ankara to permit unimpeded transit for Soviet warships through the Straits.

Most ominous, in Washington's view, was the civil war in Greece, where Royalist forces faced Red insurgents. Britain, bankrupted by the war, was compelled to abandon its support of the Royalist cause. Would the United States take up the torch from the faltering hand of the great imperial power? Here, Truman told his cabinet, he "faced a decision more serious than ever confronted any president."[8] The hyperbole is ludicrous, but one can appreciate Truman's problem. The United States had never had the slightest interest in the eastern Mediterranean, nor was it possible to discern any threat to American security in whatever outcome the Greek civil war might produce. Moreover, Stalin had conceded Greece to Britain, in his famous deal with Churchill in October 1944, whereby Russia was given control of most of the rest of the Balkans, a deal approved by Roosevelt. Accordingly, the Greek Communists did not enjoy Soviet backing: they were not permitted to join the Cominform, and their provisional government was not recognized by the Soviet Union or any other Communist state.[9]

---

[7] At the State Department, Henry Stimson and John J. McCloy agreed in May 1945 that (in McCloy's words) "we ought to have our cake and eat it too," that is, control South America and "at the same time intervene promptly in Europe; we oughtn't to give away either asset [sic]." Stephen E. Ambrose, *Rise to Globalism: American Foreign Policy Since 1938*, 3rd rev. ed. (New York: Penguin, 1983), p. 103.

[8] Alonzo L. Hamby, *Man of the People: A Life of Harry S. Truman* (New York: Oxford University Press, 1995), p. 391.

[9] Frank Kofsky, *Harry S. Truman and the War Scare of 1948: A Successful*

Given all this, how would Truman be able to justify U.S. involvement? Urged on by hardliners like Navy Secretary James Forrestal, who were emboldened by the (temporary) American monopoly of the atom bomb, he decided to frame the Communist uprising in Greece, as well as Soviet moves in Iran and Turkey, in apocalyptic terms. In countering them, he mused: "We might as well find out whether the Russians are as bent on world conquest now as in five or ten years."[10] World conquest. Now, it seems, it was a Red Hitler who was on the march.[11]

Still, after the landslide Republican victory in the congressional elections of 1946, Truman had to deal with a potentially recalcitrant opposition. The Republicans had promised to return the country to some degree of normalcy after the statist binge of the war years. Sharp cuts in taxes, abolition of wartime controls, and a balanced budget were high priorities.

But Truman could count on allies in the internationalist wing of the Republican Party, most prominently Arthur Vandenberg, a former "isolationist" turned rabid globalist, now chairman of the Senate Foreign Relations Committee. When Truman revealed his new "doctrine" to Vandenberg, the Republican leader advised him that, in order to get such a program through, the President would have to "scare hell out of the American people."[12] That Truman proceeded to do.

On March 12, 1947, in a speech before a joint session of Congress, Truman proclaimed a revolution in American foreign policy. More important than the proposed $300 million in aid for Greece and $100 million for Turkey was the vision he presented. Declaring that henceforth "it must be the policy of the United States to support free peoples who are resisting attempted subjugation by armed

---

Campaign to Deceive the Nation (New York: St. Martin's Press, 1993), pp. 244–45.

[10] Ambrose, *Rise to Globalism*, p. 117.

[11] In their attacks on Patrick Buchanan's *A Republic, Not an Empire: Reclaiming America's Destiny* (Washington, D.C.: Regnery, 1999) for his insistence that Nazi Germany posed no threat to the United States after 1940, Buchanan's critics have generally resorted to fatuous smears. This is understandable, since they are wedded to a fantasy of Hitlerian power that, ironically, is itself a reflection of Hitlerian propaganda. The fact is that Nazi Germany never conquered any militarily important nation but France. The danger of 80 million Germans "conquering the world" is a scarecrow that has, obviously, served the globalists well.

[12] Ambrose, *Rise to Globalism*, pp. 132–33.

minorities or by outside pressure," Truman situated aid to Greece and Turkey within a world-encompassing, life-or-death struggle "between alternative ways of life."[13] As one historian has written, he

> escalated the long, historic struggle between the Left and Right in Greece for political power, and the equally historic Russian urge for control of the Dardanelles [sic], into a universal conflict between freedom and slavery. It was a very broad jump indeed.[14]

At first, Truman's radical initiative provoked uneasiness, even within his administration. George Kennan, often credited with fathering the Cold War "containment" idea, strongly opposed military aid to Turkey, a nation which was under no military threat and which bordered the Soviet Union. Kennan also scoffed at the "grandiose" and "sweeping" character of the Truman Doctrine.[15] In Congress, the response of Senator Robert Taft was to accuse the President of dividing the world into Communist and anti-Communist zones. He asked for evidence that our national security was involved in Greece, adding that he did not "want war with Russia."[16] But Taft turned out to be the last, sometimes vacillating, leader of the Old Right, whose ranks were visibly weakening.[17] Although he was called "Mr. Republican," it was the internationalists who were now in charge of that party. In the Senate, Taft's doubts were answered with calm, well-reasoned rebuttals. Vandenberg intoned:

---

[13]Ronald E. Powaski, *The Cold War: The United States and the Soviet Union, 1917–1991* (New York: Oxford University Press, 1998), p. 72.

[14]Ambrose, *Rise to Globalism*, p. 133. That self-interest played a role in the exaggeration of the "crisis" is the conclusion of Ronald Steel, "The End of the Beginning," *Diplomatic History* 16, no. 2 (Spring 1992), p. 297, who writes that universalizing the struggle would "enable the United States greatly to expand its military and political reach," which "enhanced its appeal to American foreign policy elites eager to embrace the nation's new opportunities."

[15]LaFeber, *America, Russia, and the Cold War*, pp. 53–54.

[16]Ronald Radosh, *Prophets on the Right: Profiles of Conservative Critics of American Globalism* (New York: Simon and Schuster, 1975), pp. 155–56.

[17]See Ted Galen Carpenter's scholarly and highly informative *The Dissenters: American Isolationists and Foreign Policy, 1945–1954* (Ph.D. dissertation, University of Texas, 1980). On the same topic, but concentrating on the intellectual leaders of the Old Right, see Joseph R. Stromberg's perceptive analysis, *The Cold War and the Transformation of the American Right: The Decline of Right-Wing Liberalism* (M.A. thesis, Florida Atlantic University, 1971).

"If we desert the President of the United States at [this] moment we cease to have any influence in the world forever." Massachusetts Senator Henry Cabot Lodge, Jr., averred that repudiating Truman would be like throwing the American flag on the ground and stomping on it.[18] In May, Congress appropriated the funds the president requested.

Meanwhile, the organs of the national security state were being put into place.[19] The War and Navy Departments and the Army Air Corps were combined into what was named, in Orwellian fashion, the Defense Department. Other legislation established the National Security Council and upgraded intelligence operations into the Central Intelligence Agency.

In the following decades, the CIA was to play a sinister, extremely expensive, and often comically inept role—especially in its continually absurd overestimations of Soviet strength.[20] In establishing the CIA, Congress had no intention of authorizing it to conduct secret military operations, but under Truman this is what it quickly began to do, including waging a secret war on the Chinese mainland even before the outbreak of the Korean War (with no appreciable results).[21] In 1999, after it targeted the Chinese embassy in Belgrade for bombing—supposedly a mistake, even though

---

[18] Melvyn P. Leffler, *A Preponderance of Power: National Security, the Truman Administration, and the Cold War* (Stanford, Calif.: Stanford University Press, 1992), p. 146.

[19] See Michael J. Hogan, *A Cross of Iron: Harry S. Truman and the Origins of the National Security State, 1945–1954* (Cambridge: Cambridge University Press, 1998).

[20] Cf. Daniel Patrick Moynihan, *Secrecy: The American Experience* (New Haven, Conn.: Yale University Press, 1997), pp. 195–99 and *passim*. In 1997, former President Gerald Ford recalled his days as a member of the House Defense Appropriations Committee, when spokesmen for the CIA would warn over and over again of the imminent danger of the Soviet Union's surpassing the United States "in military capability, in economic growth, in the strength of our economies. It was a scary presentation."

[21] Truman later maintained that he never intended the CIA to involve itself in "peacetime cloak-and-dagger operations." This, however, was a lie. See John Prados, *Presidents' Secret Wars: CIA and Pentagon Covert Operations from World War II through the Persian Gulf War*, rev. ed. (Chicago: Ivan R. Dee, 1996), pp. 20–21, 28–29, 65–67; also Peter Grose, *Operation Rollback: America's Secret War Behind the Iron Curtain* (Boston: Houghton Mifflin, 2000), which discusses George Kennan's 1948 plan, approved by the Truman administration, to carry out paramilitary actions behind the Iron Curtain, including guerrilla attacks and sabotage.

American diplomats had dined at the embassy and its location was known to everyone in the city—CIA has come to stand, in the words of one British writer, for "Can't Identify Anything."[22]

In June 1947, Secretary of State George Marshall announced a wide-ranging scheme for economic aid to Europe. In December, the Marshall Plan was presented as an appropriations bill calling for grants of $17 billion over four years. The plan, it was claimed, would reconstruct Europe to the point where the Europeans could defend themselves. Congress at first was cold to the idea. Taft grumbled that American taxpayers should not have to support an "international WPA," arguing that the funds would subsidize the socialization programs under way in many of the recipient countries.[23] The Marshall Plan led to intensified tensions with the Russians, who saw it as further proof that Washington aimed to undermine their rule over Eastern Europe. Stalin instructed his satellite states to refuse to take part.[24]

---

[22]Geoffrey Wheatcroft, in the *Times Literary Supplement* (July 16, 1999), p. 9. For an excellent analysis of the United States' and NATO's successive lies on the bombing of the Chinese embassy, and the American media's characteristic endorsement and propagation of the lies, see Jared Israel, "The Arrogance of Rome," www.emperors-clothes.com, April 18, 2000.

[23]Radosh, *Prophets on the Right*, pp. 159–61. The Marshall Plan and its supposed successes are now enveloped by what Walter A. McDougall, in *Promised Land, Crusader State: The American Encounter with the World Since 1776* (Boston: Houghton Mifflin, 1997), p. 180, rightly calls a "mythology." The basic cause of Europe's recovery was the relatively free-market principles put into practice (in West Germany, for instance), and, more than anything else, the character of the European peoples, sometimes called "human capital." What the Marshall Plan and the billions in U.S. military aid largely accomplished was to allow the European regimes to construct their welfare states, and, in the case of France, for one, to continue trying to suppress colonial uprisings, as in Vietnam. Cf. George C. Herring, *America's Longest War: the United States and Vietnam, 1950–1976* (New York: Knopf, 1979), p. 8: "substantial American funds under the Marshall Plan enabled France to use its own resources to prosecute the war in Indochina." See also Tyler Cowen, "The Marshall Plan: Myths and Realities," in *U.S. Aid to the Developing World: A Free Market Agenda*, Doug Bandow, ed. (Washington, D.C.: Heritage, 1985), pp. 61–74; and Alan S. Milward, "Was the Marshall Plan Necessary?" *Diplomatic History* 13 (Spring 1989), pp. 231–53, who emphasizes the pressures placed on European governments by the Plan's administrators to adopt Keynesian policies.

[24]Vladislav Zubok, "Stalin's Plans and Russian Archives," *Diplomatic History* 21, no. 2 (Spring 1997), p. 299. The Soviet documents show that Stalin and Molotov were "convinced that the U.S. aid was designed to lure the Kremlin's East Euro-

"World-Conquest" Red Alert

Nineteen forty-eight was a decisive year in the Cold War. There was great reluctance in the conservative Eightieth Congress to comply with Truman's program, which included funding for the European Recovery Act (Marshall Plan), resumption of the draft, and Universal Military Training (UMT). To deal with this resistance, the administration concocted the war scare of 1948.

The first pretext came in February, with the so-called Communist coup in Czechoslovakia. But Czechoslovakia, was, for all intents and purposes, already a Soviet satellite. Having led the Czechs in the "ethnic cleansing" of 3.5 million Sudeten Germans, the Communists enjoyed great popularity. In the general elections, they won 38 per cent of the vote, constituting by far the largest single party. The American ambassador reported to Washington that Communist consolidation of power in early 1948 was the logical outgrowth of the Czech–Soviet military alliance dating back to 1943. George Marshall himself, Secretary of State at the time, stated in private that "as far as international affairs are concerned," the formal Communist assumption of power made no difference: it would merely "crystallize and confirm for the future previous Czech policy."[25] Still, the Communist "coup" was painted as a great leap forward in Stalin's plan for "world conquest."

Then, on March 5, came the shocking letter from General Lucius Clay, U.S. military governor in Germany, to General Stephen J. Chamberlin, head of Army Intelligence, in which Clay revealed his foreboding that war "may come with dramatic suddenness." Years later, when Clay's biographer asked him why, if he sensed an impending war, this was the only reference he ever made to it, he replied:

> General Chamberlin ... told me that the Army was having trouble getting the draft reinstituted and they needed a strong message from me that they could use in congressional testimony. So I wrote this cable.[26]

On March 11, Marshall solemnly warned in a public address that: "The world is in the midst of a great crisis." Averell Harriman asserted:

---

pean neighbors out of its orbit and to rebuild German strength." See also Leffler, "Inside Enemy Archives," p. 133.

[25] Kofsky, *Truman*, p. 99.
[26] Ibid., p. 106.

> There are aggressive forces in the world coming from the Soviet Union which are just as destructive as Hitler was, and I think are a greater menace than Hitler was.[27]

And so Harriman laid down the Hitler card, which was to become the master trump in the globalists' propaganda hand for the next half-century and most likely for many decades to come.

Taft, campaigning for the Republican presidential nomination, was angered by the war hysteria drummed up by the administration:

> I know of no indication of Russian intention to undertake military aggression beyond the sphere of influence that was originally assigned to them [at Yalta]. The situation in Czechoslovakia was indeed a tragic one, but Russian influence has predominated there since the end of the war.

Taft tried to introduce a note of sanity: "If President Truman and General Marshall have any private intelligence" regarding imminent war, "they ought to tell the American people about it." Otherwise, we should proceed on "the basis of peace."[28]

In reality, the administration had no such "private intelligence," hence the need to stage-manage Clay's letter. On the contrary, Colonel Robert B. Landry, Truman's air aide, reported that in their zone in eastern Germany the Russians had dismantled hundreds of miles of railroad track and shipped them home—in other words, they had torn up the very railroad lines required for any Soviet attack on western Europe.[29] Field Marshal Montgomery, after a trip to Russia in 1947, wrote to General Eisenhower: "The Soviet Union is very, very tired. Devastation in Russia is appalling, and the country is in no fit state to go to war."[30] Today it would be very difficult to find any scholar anywhere willing to subscribe to Truman's frenzied vision of a Soviet Union about to set off to conquer the world. As John Lewis Gaddis wrote:

---

[27] Ronald E. Powaski, *Toward an Entangling Alliance: American Isolationism, Internationalism, and Europe, 1901–1950* (Westport, Conn.: Greenwood, 1991), pp. 201–02.

[28] Harry W. Berger, "Senator Robert A. Taft Dissents from Military Escalation," in *Cold War Critics: Alternatives to American Foreign Policy in the Truman Years*, Thomas G. Paterson, ed. (Chicago: Quadrangle Books, 1971), pp. 181–82; and Kofsky, *Truman*, p. 130.

[29] Ibid., pp. 294–95.

[30] Michael Parenti, *The Sword and the Dollar: Imperialism, Revolution, and the*

> Stalin is now seen as a cagey but insecure opportunist, taking advantage of such tactical opportunities as arose to expand Soviet influence, but without any long-term strategy for or even very much interest in promoting the spread of communism beyond the Soviet sphere.[31]

The non-existence of Soviet plans to launch an attack on Europe holds for the entire Cold War period. One scholar in the field concludes that

> despite the fact that the Russian archives have yielded ample evidence of Soviet perfidy and egregious behavior in many other spheres, nothing has turned up to support the idea that the Soviet leadership at any time actually planned to start World War III and send the "Russian hordes" westward.[32]

Arms Race (New York: St. Martin's, 1989), p. 147.

[31] Gaddis, "The Emerging Post-Revisionist Synthesis," p. 181. Hans Morgenthau, "The Origins of the Cold War," p. 95, anticipated this conclusion: "The limits of Stalin's territorial ambition were the traditional limits of Russian expansionism." Even Vladislav Zubok, who believes that the now available Soviet documents show the U.S. leaders in a much better light than many had thought, nonetheless concedes, "Stalin's Plans," p. 305: "there was an element of overreaction, arrogance, and selfish pragmatism in the American response to Stalin's plans.... The Soviet military machine was not a military juggernaut, western Europe was not under threat of a direct Soviet military assault, and the Sino-Soviet bloc lacked true cohesion.... American containment of Stalin's Soviet Union may indeed have helped the dictatorship to mobilize people to the task of building a superpower from the ashes and ruins of the impoverished and devastated country. It may even have helped Stalin to trample on the seeds of liberalism and freedom in Soviet society." Cf. Leffler, "Inside Enemy Archives," pp. 132, 134: "The new research clearly shows that American initiatives intensified Soviet distrust and reinforced Soviet insecurities ... [recent research indicates] that American policies made it difficult for potential reformers inside the Kremlin to gain the high ground."

[32] Matthew Evangelista, "The 'Soviet Threat': Intentions, Capabilities, and Context," *Diplomatic History* 22, no. 3 (Summer 1998), pp. 445–46. On how information from recently opened Soviet archives has undermined the old Cold War account, see Leffler, "Inside Enemy Archives," pp. 120–35. Leffler, hardly a "New Left" (or libertarian) historian, concludes: "Americans should reexamine their complacent belief in the wisdom of their country's cold war policies."

The fact that Stalin was the worst tyrant and greatest mass-murderer in twentieth-century European history has by now been established beyond a doubt. However, here one should heed Murray Rothbard's admonition against doing "*a priori* history," that is, assuming that in a given international conflict it is always

So why the war scare in 1948? In a 1976 interview, looking back on this period, Air Force Brigadier General Robert C. Richardson, who served at NATO headquarters in the early 1950s, candidly admitted:

> there was no question about it, that [Soviet] threat that we were planning against was way overrated and intentionally overrated, because there was the problem of reorienting the [U.S.] demobilization ... [Washington] made this nine-foot-tall threat out there. And for years and years it stuck. I mean, it was almost immovable.[33]

Yet, anyone who doubted the wisdom of the administration's militaristic policy was targeted for venomous smears. According to Truman, Republicans who opposed his universal crusade were "Kremlin assets," the sort of traitors who would shoot "our soldiers in the back in a hot war,"[34] a good example of Truman's acclaimed

---

the relatively liberal state that is in the right as against the relatively illiberal state, which must always be the aggressor. Murray N. Rothbard, *For a New Liberty: The Libertarian Manifesto*, rev. ed. (New York: Collier–Macmillan, 1978), pp. 289–91.

[33] Evangelista, "The Soviet Threat," p. 447. See also Steel, "The End of the Beginning," "Unquestionably, the Soviet Union was far weaker ideologically, politically, structurally, and, of course, economically, than was generally assumed." An astonishing admission that the whole Cold War was fueled, on the American side, by wild overestimations of Soviet strength was made in 1990 by Strobe Talbott, Deputy Secretary of State: "for more than four decades, Western policy has been based on a grotesque exaggeration of what the USSR could do if it wanted, therefore what it might do, therefore what the West must be prepared to do in response.... Worst-case assumptions about Soviet intentions have fed, and fed upon, worst-case assumptions about Soviet capabilities." John A. Thompson, "The Exaggeration of American Vulnerability: The Anatomy of a Tradition," *Diplomatic History* 16, no. 1 (Winter 1992), p. 23. Thompson's article is highly instructive on how hysteria regarding impending attacks on the United States during the twentieth century—a time when America grew ever stronger—has contributed to entanglement in foreign conflicts.

[34] Justus D. Doenecke, *Not to the Swift: The Old Isolationists in the Cold War Era* (Lewisburg, Penn.: Bucknell University Press, 1979), p. 216. Truman's slanders were particularly vile, since his own motivation in generating the war-scare was at least in part self-aggrandizement. As his trusted political adviser Clark Clifford noted in a memo to the President: "There is considerable political advantage to the administration in its battle with the Kremlin. The worse matters get up to a fairly certain point—real danger of imminent war—the more is there a sense of crisis. In times of crisis, the American citizen tends to back up his president." (Kofsky, *Truman*, p. 92)

"plain speaking."[35] Averell Harriman charged that Taft was simply helping Stalin carry out his aims. As always, the establishment press, led by the *New York Times*, echoed the government's slanders. Amusingly, Republican critics of the war hysteria were labeled pro-Soviet even by journals like *The New Republic* and *The Nation*, which had functioned as apologists for Stalin's terror regime for years.[36]

Truman's campaign could not have succeeded without the enthusiastic cooperation of the American media. Led by the *Times*, the *Herald Tribune*, and Henry Luce's magazines, the press acted as volunteer propagandists for the interventionist agenda, with all its calculated deceptions. (The principal exceptions were the *Chicago Tribune* and the *Washington Times–Herald*, in the days of Colonel McCormick and Cissy Paterson.)[37] In time, such subservience in foreign affairs became routine for the "fourth estate," culminating during and after the 1999 war against Yugoslavia in reporting by the press corps that surpassed the mendacity of the Serbian Ministry of Information.

Overwhelmed by the propaganda blitz from the administration and the press, a Republican majority in Congress heeded the Secretary of State's high-minded call to keep foreign policy "above politics" and voted full funding for the Marshall Plan.[38]

---

[35] Cf. George Will's judgment, in *The Leveling Wind: Politics, the Culture, and Other News, 1990–1994* (New York: Viking, 1994), p. 380: "Truman's greatness was a product of his goodness, his straight-ahead respect for the public, respect expressed in decisions briskly made and plainly explained." In truth, despite Will's ignorant blather, Truman was all of his life a demagogue, a political garbage-mouth, whose first instinct was to besmirch his opponents. In his tribute to Truman, Will employs his usual ploy whenever he is moved to extol some villainous politico or other: his subject's greatness could only be denied by pitiful postmodernist creatures who reject all human excellence, nobility of soul, etc. This maneuver is nowhere sillier than in the case of Harry Truman.

[36] Doenecke, *Not to the Swift*, pp. 200, 216.

[37] Ted Galen Carpenter, *The Captive Press: Foreign Policy Crises and the First Amendment* (Washington, D.C.: Cato Institute, 1995), pp. 45–52. Carpenter's excellent study covers the whole period of the Cold War.

[38] The commotion over Soviet plans to "conquer the world" intensified in June 1948 with the blockade of West Berlin. The United States and its allies had unilaterally decided to jettison four-power control of Germany and instead to integrate their occupation zones and proceed to create a West German state. Stalin's clumsy response was to exploit the absence of any formal agreement permitting the Western powers access to Berlin, and to institute the blockade.

The next major step was the creation of the North Atlantic Treaty Organization. The true significance of the NATO treaty was hidden, as the new Secretary of State Dean Acheson assured Congress that it would not be followed by other regional pacts, that no "substantial" numbers of American troops would be stationed in Europe, and that the Germans would under no circumstances be rearmed—all untrue. Congress was likewise promised that the United States was under no obligation to extend military aid to its new allies, nor would an arms race with the Soviet Union ensue.[39] Events came to the aid of the globalists. In September 1949, the Soviets exploded an atomic bomb. Congress approved the military appropriation for NATO that Truman had requested, which, in the nature of things, was followed by a further Soviet buildup. This escalating back and forth became the pattern for the Cold War arms race for the next fifty years, much to the delight of U.S. armaments contractors and the generals and admirals on both sides.

The Korean War

In June 1950, the National Security Council adopted a major strategic document, NSC-68, which declared, implausibly enough, that "a defeat of free institutions anywhere is a defeat everywhere." The United States should no longer attempt to "distinguish between national and global security." Instead, it must stand at the "political and material center with other free nations in variable orbits around it." NSC-68, not declassified until 1975, called for an immediate three- or four-fold increase in military spending, which would serve also to prime the pump of economic prosperity—thus formalizing military Keynesianism as a permanent fixture of American life. Moreover, public opinion was to be conditioned to accept the "large measure of sacrifice and discipline" needed to meet the protean Communist challenge for the indefinite future.[40]

---

[39]LaFeber, *America, Russia, and the Cold War*, pp. 83–84. Some minor award for Orwellian Newspeak is due the Democratic foreign affairs leader in the Senate, Tom Connally, who stated that NATO "is but the logical extension of the principle of the Monroe Doctrine."

[40]See especially Jerry W. Sanders, *Peddlers of Crisis: The Committee on the Present Danger and the Politics of Containment* (Boston: South End Press, 1983); also Gabriel Kolko, *Century of War: Politics, Conflict, and Society Since 1914* (New York: New Press, 1994), pp. 397–98; and Powaski, *Cold War*, pp. 85–86.

HARRY S. TRUMAN: ADVANCING THE REVOLUTION

Even Truman was dubious on the prospects for such a quantum leap in globalism in a time of peace. But again, events—and Truman's shrewd exploitation of them—came to the aid of the internationalist planners. As one of Truman's advisers later expressed it: in June 1950, "we were sweating over it," and then, "thank God Korea came along."[41]

For years, skirmishes and even major engagements had occurred across the 38th parallel, which divided North from South Korea. On January 12, 1950, Secretary of State Acheson described the American defensive perimeter as extending from the Aleutians to Japan to the Philippines. South Korea (as well as Taiwan) was conspicuously placed outside this perimeter. One reason was that it was not considered to be of any military value. Another was that Washington did not trust South Korean strongman Syngman Rhee, who repeatedly threatened to reunite the country by force. Rhee was advocating a march north to American officials as late as mid-June 1950.[42]

On June 25, it was North Korea that attacked.[43] The next day, Truman instructed U.S. air and naval forces to destroy Communist supply lines. When bombing failed to prevent the headlong retreat of the South Korean army, Truman sent American troops stationed in Japan to join the battle. General Douglas MacArthur was able to hold the redoubt around Pusan, then, in an amphibious invasion at Inchon, to begin the destruction of the North Korean position.

After the North Koreans retreated behind the 38th parallel, Truman decided against ending the war on the basis of the *status quo ante.* Instead, he ordered MacArthur to move north. Pyongyang was to be the first Communist capital liberated, and the whole peninsula was to be unified under the rule of Syngman Rhee. As U.N. forces (mainly American and South Korean) swept north, the

---

[41] Michael Schaller, *The United States and China in the Twentieth Century* (New York: Oxford University Press, 1979), pp. 131–32.

[42] Bruce Cumings, *Korea's Place in the Sun: A Modern History* (New York: Norton, 1997), pp. 257–58. Japan was unable to act as a counterweight to Communist regimes in East Asia because, like Germany, it had been annulled as a military power. In addition, the constitution imposed on Japan by the American occupiers forced it to renounce warmaking as a sovereign right.

[43] The attack was authorized by Stalin, "in expectation that the United States might eventually turn [South Korea] into a beachhead for a return to the Asian mainland in alliance with a resurgent Japan" (Zubok, "Stalin's Plans," p. 301).

Chinese issued warnings against approaching their border at the Yalu River. These were ignored by an administration somehow unable to comprehend why China might fear massive U.S. forces stationed on its frontier. Chinese troops entered the war, prolonging it by another three years, during which most of the American casualties were sustained.[44] MacArthur, who proposed bombing China itself, was dismissed by Truman, who at least spared the nation an even wider war, possibly involving Russia as well.

Korea afforded unprecedented opportunities for advancing the globalist program. Truman assigned the U.S. Seventh Fleet to patrol the strait between Taiwan and the Chinese mainland. Four more U.S. divisions were sent to Europe, to add to the two already there, and another $4 billion was allocated for the rearmament of our European allies. Some months before the start of the Korean War, Truman had already initiated America's fateful involvement in Indochina, supporting the French imperialists and their puppet ruler Bảo Đại against the nationalist and Communist revolutionary Hồ Chí Minh. Korea furnished welcome cover for stepping up aid to the French, which soon amounted to a half-billion dollars a year. The United States was thus providing the great bulk of the material resources for France's colonialist war. The State Department defended this commitment, rather ridiculously, by citing Indochina's production of "much-needed rice, rubber, and tin." More to the point was the fear expressed that the "loss" of Indochina, including Vietnam, would represent a defeat in the struggle against what was portrayed as a unified and coordinated Communist push to take over the world.[45]

At the same time, the degradation of political language went into high gear, where it remained for the rest of the Cold War and probably permanently. To the authoritarian regimes in Greece and Turkey were now added, as components of "the Free World" which Americans were obligated to defend, Rhee's autocratic Republic of

---

[44]Eric A. Nordlinger, *Isolationism Reconfigured: American Foreign Policy for a New Century* (Princeton, N.J.: Princeton University Press, 1995), pp. 168–69.

[45]Walter LaFeber, *America, Russia, and the Cold War*, pp. 107–08; see also Herring, *America's Longest War*, pp. 6–23. France's war against the Việt Minh began in 1946 with a typical colonialist atrocity, when a French cruiser bombarded Hải Phòng, killing 6,000 civilians; ibid., p. 5. Acts of brutality such as this were on the minds of the "isolationist" Republicans like Taft, George Bender, and Howard Buffet when they inveighed against American support of Western imperialism in terms which would be considered "leftist" today.

Korea, Chiang's dictatorship on Taiwan, and even colonialist French Indochina.

With the outbreak of the Korean War, the Republicans' capitulation to globalism was practically complete.[46] As is standard procedure in American politics, foreign policy was a non-issue in the 1948 presidential campaign. Thomas E. Dewey, a creature of the Eastern establishment centered in Wall Street, was as much of an overseas meddler as Truman. Now, in the struggle against "international Communism," even erstwhile "isolationists" showed themselves to be arch-interventionists when it came to Asia, going so far as to make a hero of MacArthur for demanding an expansion of the war and the "unleashing" of Chiang's army on the mainland. Taft supported sending troops to fight in Korea, while entering one major objection. Characteristically, it was on the constitutional question.

The President as War-Maker At Will

When North Korea invaded the South, Truman and Acheson claimed unlimited presidential authority to engage the United States in the war, which they kept referring to as a "police action." Truman stated: "The president, as Commander-in-Chief of the Armed Forces of the United States, has full control over the use thereof."[47] This flies in the face of Article 1, section 8 of the U.S. Constitution, where the power to declare war is vested in Congress. The deliberations at the Constitutional Convention and other statements of the Founding Fathers are unequivocal in this respect. While the president, as commander-in-chief, is given authority to deploy American forces in wartime, it is Congress that decides on war or peace. Wouldn't it be surpassing strange if the Founders, so concerned to limit, divide, and balance power, had left the decision to engage the country in war to the will of a single individual?[48]

---

[46]On the shift of conservatives from "isolationism" to internationalism, see Murray N. Rothbard, "The Transformation of the American Right," *Continuum* (Summer 1964), pp. 220–31.

[47]John Hart Ely, *War and Responsibility: Constitutional Lessons of Vietnam and Its Aftermath* (Princeton, N.J.: Princeton University Press, 1993), pp. 10–11.

[48]See, for example, James Wilson's statement: "This system will not hurry us into war; it is calculated to guard against it. It will not be in the power of a single man, or a single body of men, to involve us in such distress; for the important power of declaring war is vested in the legislature at large." Ibid., p. 3. Illustrative

So well-established was this principle that even Woodrow Wilson and Franklin Roosevelt, no minimizers of executive prerogatives, bowed to it and went to Congress for their declarations of war. It was Truman who dared what even his predecessor had not. As two constitutional scholars, Francis D. Wormuth and Edwin B. Firmage, have written:

> The Constitution is not ambiguous.... The early presidents, and indeed everyone in the country until the year 1950, denied that the president possessed [the power to initiate war]. There is no sustained body of usage to support such a claim.[49]

At the time, college history professors rushed to blazon the allegedly countless occasions when presidents sent U.S. forces into war or warlike situations without congressional approval. Lists of such occasions were afterward compiled by other apologists for executive power in foreign affairs—in 1971, for instance, by the revered conservative Barry Goldwater. These incidents have been carefully examined by Wormuth and Firmage, who conclude:

> One cannot be sure, but the number of cases in which presidents have personally made the decision [in contrast, for instance, to overzealous military and naval officers] unconstitutionally to engage in war or in acts of war probably lies between one and two dozen. And in all those cases the presidents have made false claims of authorization, either by statute or by treaty or by international law. They have not relied on their powers as commander in chief or as chief executive.[50]

At all events, as Chief Justice Earl Warren held in 1969, articulating a well-known constitutional principle on behalf of seven other Justices: "That an unconstitutional action has been taken before surely does not render that action any less unconstitutional at a later date."[51]

---

of the present-day decay of constitutional thinking is the statement of the noted conservative advocate of the doctrine of "original intent" Robert Bork (ibid., p. 5): "The need for presidents to have that power [to use military force abroad without Congressional approval], particularly in the modern age, should be obvious to almost anyone."

[49] Francis D. Wormuth and Edwin B. Firmage, *To Chain the Dog of War: The War Power of Congress in History and Law*, 2nd ed. (Urbana: University of Illinois Press, 1989), p. 151.

[50] Ibid.

[51] Ibid., p. 135.

The administration sometimes alluded to the vote of the U.N. Security Council approving military action in Korea as furnishing the necessary authority. This was nothing but a smokescreen. First, because according to the U.N. Charter, any Security Council commitment of members' troops must be consistent with the members' "respective constitutional processes." The United Nations Participation Act of 1945 also required congressional ratification for the use of American forces. In any case, Truman stated that he would send troops to Korea whether or not authorized by the Security Council. His position really was that any president may plunge the country into war simply on his own say-so.[52]

Today presidents assert the right to bomb at will countries which, like North Korea in 1950, never attacked us and with which we are not at war—Sudan, Afghanistan, Iraq, and, repeatedly, Yugoslavia. They are eagerly seconded in this by "conservative" politicians and publicists, nor does the American public demur. Back in 1948, Charles Beard already noted the dismal ignorance among our people of the principles of our republican government:

> American education from the universities down to the grade schools is permeated with, if not dominated by, the theory of presidential supremacy in foreign affairs. Coupled with the flagrant neglect of instruction in constitutional government, this propaganda ... has deeply implanted in the minds of rising generations the doctrine that the power of the president over international relations is, for all practical purposes, illimitable.[53]

---

[52]Ely, *War and Responsibility*, pp. 151–52 n. 60. A year earlier the North Atlantic Treaty had been submitted to the Senate for approval. Article 5 specifically ensured that "U.S. response to aggression in the area covered by the alliance would be governed by 'constitutional processes' thereby requiring congressional approval." Ponawski, *Toward Entangling Alliance*, pp. 208–09. On the origins of unlimited presidential warmaking powers, see Robert Shogan, *Hard Bargain: How FDR Twisted Churchill's Arm, Evaded the Law, and Changed the Role of the American Presidency*, paperback edition (Boulder, Colo.: Westview, 1999), preface to the paperback edition, "Paving the Way to Kosovo."

[53]Charles A. Beard, *President Roosevelt and the Coming of the War, 1941: A Study in Appearances and Realities* (New Haven, Conn.: Yale University Press, 1948), p. 590. Beard listed as among the major purveyors of this doctrine "powerful private agencies engaged nominally in propaganda for 'peace,'" which look to the president to advance their ideas for "ordering and reordering the world."

Needless to say, the situation has in no way improved, as the public schools grind out tens of millions of future voters to whom the notion, say, that James Madison had something to do with the Constitution of the United States would come as an uninteresting revelation.

The Korean War lasted three years and cost 36,916 American deaths and more than 100,000 other casualties. Additionally, there were millions of Korean dead and the devastation of the peninsula, especially in the north, where the U.S. Air Force pulverized the civilian infrastructure—with much "collateral damage"—in what has since become its emblematic method of waging war.[54] Today, nearly a half-century after the end of the conflict, the United States continues to station troops as a "tripwire" in yet another of its imperial outposts.[55]

The indirect consequences of Truman's "police action" have been equally grim. Hans Morgenthau wrote:

---

[54] Kolko, *Century of War*, pp. 403–08. General Curtis LeMay boasted of the devastation wreaked by the Air Force: "We burned down just about every city in North and South Korea both ... we killed off over a million civilian Koreans and drove several million more from their homes." Callum A. MacDonald, *Korea: The War Before Vietnam* (New York: Free Press, 1986), p. 235. I am grateful to Joseph R. Stromberg for drawing my attention to this quotation. It gives one pause to realize that the savagery of the U.S. air war was such as to lead even Winston Churchill to condemn it. Ibid., pp. 234–35. In Fall 1999, it was finally disclosed that "early in the Korean War, American soldiers machine-gunned hundreds of helpless civilians under a railroad bridge in the South Korean countryside," allegedly in order to thwart the infiltration of North Korean troops. Former U.S. soldiers "described other refugee killings as well in the war's first weeks, when U.S. commanders ordered their troops to shoot civilians of an allied nation, as a defense against disguised enemy soldiers, according to once-classified documents found in U.S. military archives" (*Washington Post*, September 30, 1999). A few months later, other declassified U.S. military documents revealed that the South Korean government executed without trial more than 2,000 leftists as its forces retreated in the first stages of the war; the occurrence of such executions was known to the American military authorities at the time (*New York Times*, April 21, 2000). In addition, there is evidence that the United States may, in fact, have experimented with bacteriological warfare in Korea, as charged by China and North Korea. See Stephen Endicott and Edward Hagerman, *The United States and Biological Warfare: Secrets from the Early Cold War and Korea* (Bloomington: Indiana University Press, 1998).

[55] Doug Bandow, *Tripwire: Korea and U.S. Foreign Policy in a Changed World* (Washington, D.C.: Cato Institute, 1996).

The misinterpretation of the North Korean aggression as part of a grand design at world conquest originating in and controlled by Moscow resulted in a drastic militarization of the cold war in the form of a conventional and nuclear armaments race, the frantic search for alliances, and the establishment of military bases.[56]

Truman is glorified for his conduct of foreign affairs more than anything else. Whether one concurs in this judgment depends mainly on the kind of country one wishes America to be. Stephen Ambrose has summed up the results of the foreign policy of Harry Truman:

> When Truman became president he led a nation anxious to return to traditional civil-military relations and the historic American foreign policy of noninvolvement. When he left the White House his legacy was an American presence on every continent of the world and an enormously expanded armament industry. Yet so successfully had he scared hell out of the American people, the only critics to receive any attention in the mass media were those who thought Truman had not gone far enough in standing up to the communists. For all his troubles, Truman had triumphed.[57]

The *Führerprinzip* in the Economic Arena

Harry Truman's conception of presidential power as in principle unlimited was as manifest in his domestic as in his foreign policy. Some key episodes illustrate this.

In May 1946, Truman decided that the proper response to the strike of railroad workers was to draft the strikers into the Army. Even his Attorney General, Tom Clark, doubted that the Draft Act permitted "the induction of occupational groups" or that the move was at all constitutional. But, as Truman's Pulitzer Prize-winning biographer David McCullough wrote, in his typical stupefied adoration: "Truman was not interested in philosophy. The strike must

---

[56] Morgenthau, "Origins of the Cold War," p. 98.

[57] Ambrose, *Rise to Globalism*, p. 185. On the ultimate price paid by the nation for Truman's "triumph," see the important article by Robert Higgs, "The Cold War Economy: Opportunity Costs, Ideology, and the Politics of Crisis," *Explorations in Economic History* 31 (1994), pp. 283–312.

stop. 'We'll draft them and think about the law later,' he reportedly remarked."[58] McCullough neglected to note that bold "action" in defiance of law is considered a characteristic of fascist regimes.

On May 25, Truman addressed Congress, requesting the authority "to draft into the Armed Forces of the United States all workers who are on strike against their government." His proposal was greeted with tumultuous applause, and the House quickly approved the bill by 306 to 13. In the Senate, though, the bill was stopped in its tracks by Senator Taft. He was joined by left-liberals like Claude Pepper of Florida. Eventually, the Senate rejected the bill by 70 to 13.

Later that year, another "crisis" led Truman to contemplate further exercise of dictatorial power. While most of the wartime price controls had been lifted by this time, controls remained on a number of items, most prominently meat. Strangely enough, it was precisely in that commodity that a shortage and a black market developed. The meat shortage was eroding support for the Democrats, who began to look with trepidation on the upcoming congressional elections. Party workers were told by usually loyal voters, "No meat, no votes." Truman was forced to act. He would address the nation again, announcing and explaining the decision he had made.

In his draft for the speech, Truman was bitter. He indicted the American people for their greed and selfishness, so different from the selfless patriotism of the heroes who had won the Medal of Honor. The draft continued:

> You've deserted your president for a mess of pottage, a piece of beef—a side of bacon.... If you the people insist on following Mammon instead of Almighty God, your president can't stop you all by himself. I can no longer enforce a law you won't support.... You've gone over to the powers of selfishness and greed.[59]

This crazy tirade was omitted from the speech Truman made on October 14.[60] But ever the cheap demagogue, he pilloried the meat

---

[58] David McCullough, *Truman* (New York: Simon and Schuster, 1992), pp. 501–06.
[59] Hamby, *Man of the People*, pp. 382–83.
[60] *Public Papers of the Presidents of the United States: Harry S. Truman, 1946* (Washington, D.C.: U.S. Government Printing Office, 1962), pp. 451–55.

HARRY S. TRUMAN: ADVANCING THE REVOLUTION 125

industry as responsible for the shortage, "those who, in order further to fatten their profits, are endangering the health of our people by holding back vital foods which are now ready for market and for which the American people are clamoring." The failed haberdasher, it appears, had little understanding of the role that *prices* might play in a market economy In his speech, Truman confided that he had carefully weighed and discussed with his cabinet and economic experts a number of possible solutions. One was "to have the Government seize the packing houses." But this would not have helped, since the packing houses were empty. Then came a notion that "would indeed be a drastic remedy": "that the government go out onto the farms and ranges and seize the cattle for slaughter." Truman gave the idea "long and serious consideration." Here is why, in the end, he declined to go the route of the Bolsheviks in the Ukraine:

> We decided against the use of this extreme wartime emergency power of Government. It would be wholly impracticable because the cattle are spread throughout all parts of the country.[61]

This statement from the feisty, "Near-Great" Man of the People deserves to be read more than once.[62]

So, sadly and reluctantly Truman announced the end of price controls on meat, although he advised the country that "some items, like rent, will have to be controlled for a long time to come."

On April 8, 1952, as a nationwide strike loomed in the steel industry, Truman issued Executive Order 10340, directing his Secretary of Commerce Charles Sawyer to seize the steel mills.

He acted, he claimed, "by virtue of the authority vested in me by the Constitution and the laws of the United States, and as President of the United States and Commander-in-Chief of the armed forces of the United States."[63] He could not, however, point to any such law, despite his reference to "the laws of the United States." Nor did any provision of the Constitution give the president the right to

---

[61] Ibid., p. 453.

[62] Murray N. Rothbard dealt with this grab for power in a brilliant piece of economic journalism, "Price Controls Are Back!" in his *Making Economic Sense* (Auburn, Ala.: Ludwig von Mises Institute, 1995), pp. 123–27.

[63] Wormuth and Firmage, *To Chain the Dog of War*, p. 174.

seize private property by proclamation. But, as McCullough tells us, Truman was convinced "from his reading of history" that "his action fell within his powers as President and Commander-in-Chief." After all, hadn't Lincoln suspended the writ of *habeas corpus* during a national emergency?[64] On April 9, the Star-Spangled Banner was raised over the nation's steel mills, and the steel companies immediately took the case to court.

At a news conference on April 17, Truman was asked: "Mr. President, if you can seize the steel mills under your inherent powers, can you, in your opinion, also seize the newspapers and/or the radio stations?" Truman replied: "Under similar circumstances the President of the United States has to act for whatever is for the best of the country. That's the answer to your question."[65]

The next day, the New York Times reported:

> The president refused to elaborate. But White House sources said the president's point was that he had power in an emergency, to take over "any portion of the business community acting to jeopardize all the people."

The case of *Youngstown Sheet & Tube Co. v. Sawyer* quickly reached the Supreme Court, where Truman's argument was rejected by a vote of 6 to 3. Speaking for the three was Truman's old crony, Chief Justice Fred Vinson, who argued that the president had the authority to enact all laws necessary for carrying out laws previously passed by Congress. Any man worthy of the office of president, Vinson wrote, should be "free to take at least interim action necessary to execute legislative programs essential to the survival of the nation." The majority, including Hugo Black, William O. Douglas, Felix Frankfurter, and even Truman's former Attorney General, Tom Clark, decided otherwise.[66]

At that April 17 news conference, no reporter thought to ask a follow-up question to Truman's stunning reply. His claim of the

---

[64] McCullough, *Truman*, pp. 896–97. McCullough's implied apology for Truman here is a good indication of the tenor and caliber of his gargantuan puff-piece. For a debunking of McCullough by two scholars, see the review by Gar Alperovitz and Kai Bird, "Giving Harry Hell," *The Nation* (May 10, 1993), pp. 640–41.

[65] *The Public Papers of Harry S. Truman, 1952–53* (Washington, D.C.: U.S. Government Printing Office, 1966), pp. 272–73.

[66] McCullough, *Truman*, pp. 900–01.

unlimited right to dispose at his discretion of the property of any and all citizens—a viewpoint for which a king of England was beheaded—made as little impression on the press then as it has on his admirers ever since. One wonders what it would take to spark their outrage or even their interest.[67]

In economic policy, the years of Truman's "Fair Deal" were a time of consolidation and expansion of government power. In February 1946, the Employment Act was passed. Inspired by the newly dominant Keynesian economics, it declared that henceforth the economic health of the nation was primarily the responsibility of the Federal government. With the coming of the Korean War, economic controls were again the order of the day (Bernard Baruch was once more, for the third time since 1917, a prime agitator for their introduction.) Truman declared a "national emergency." New boards and agencies oversaw prices and wages, established priorities in materials allocation, and instituted controls over credit and other sectors of the economy.[68] As in the world wars, the aftermath of Truman's Korean War exhibited the ratchet-effect, whereby Federal government spending, though diminished, never returned to the previous peacetime level.[69]

A Heritage of Sinkholes

Truman's legacy includes programs and policies that continue to inflict damage to this day. Three cases are especially noteworthy.

---

[67] One Congressman was led by Truman's remarks and his seizure of the steel mills to demand his impeachment (*New York Times*, April 19, 1952). George Bender, Republican of Ohio, stated: "I do not believe that our people can tolerate the formation of a presidential precedent which would permit any occupant of the White House to exercise his untrammeled discretion to take over the industry, communications system or other forms of private enterprise in the name of 'emergency.'" But Bender was one of the last, and best, of the Old Right leaders and thus out of tune with the times. Of course the American people could and did tolerate such a precedent. What is still uncertain is whether there is any limit whatever to their tolerance of acts of oppression by the government.

[68] Robert Higgs, *Crisis and Leviathan: Critical Episodes in the Growth of American Government* (New York: Oxford University Press, 1987), pp. 227, 244–45.

[69] Jonathan R. T. Hughes, *The Governmental Habit: Economic Controls from Colonial Times to the Present* (New York: Basic Books, 1977), pp. 208–09. Federal expenditures in the early Eisenhower years were, on average, twice as high as in the period 1947–1950.

In his message to Congress on January 20, 1949, Truman launched the concept of aid from Western governments to the poorer nations that were soon to be called, collectively, the Third World. Point Four of his speech sketched a new program to provide technical assistance to the "more than half the people of the world [who] are living in conditions approaching misery," and whose "economic life is primitive and stagnant." This was to be "a cooperative enterprise in which all nations work together through the United Nations and its specialized agencies"—in other words, a state-funded and state-directed effort to end world poverty.[70]

According to Peter Bauer, Point Four "inaugurated a far-reaching policy and a supporting terminology."[71] In the decades that followed, foreign aid was promoted by a proliferating international bureaucracy, as well as by religious and secular zealots ignorantly confident of the purity of their anti-social cause. Western guilt feelings, fostered by the leftist intelligentsia and self-seeking Third World politicians, have facilitated the channeling of hundreds of billions of dollars to governments in Asia, Africa, and Latin America. Today, even "conservative" politicians and publicists are devotees. "Development aid" has become institutionalized and is intended to continue indefinitely, with all its attendant harm: reinforced statism, inferior economic performance, and corruption on the greatest scale the world has ever known.[72]

Truman began the "special relationship" between the United States and Zionism. Franklin Roosevelt, while not blind to Zionist interests, favored an evenhanded approach in the Middle East as between Arabs and Jews. Truman, on the other hand, was an all-out champion of the Zionist cause.[73]

There were two major reasons for Truman's support. One was a sentimental attachment that was strongly reinforced by many who

---

[70] *The Public Papers of Harry S. Truman, 1949* (Washington, D.C.: U.S. Government Printing Office, 1964), pp. 114–15.

[71] Peter Bauer, *Equality, the Third World, and Economic Delusion* (Cambridge, Mass.: Harvard University Press, 1981), pp. 139, 275 n. 1. See also Peter Bauer and Cranley Onslow, "Fifty Years of Failure," *The Spectator* (September 5, 1998), pp. 13–14.

[72] Graham Hancock, *Lords of Poverty: The Power, Prestige, and Corruption of the International Aid Business* (New York: Atlantic Monthly Press, 1989).

[73] Alfred M. Lilienthal, *The Zionist Connection: What Price Peace?* (New York: Dodd, Mead, 1978), pp. 45–100.

had influence with him, including his old business partner, Eddie Jacobson as well as David K. Niles and Eleanor Roosevelt.[74] Visiting the president, the Chief Rabbi of Israel told him: "God put you in your mother's womb so that you could be the instrument to bring about the rebirth of Israel after two thousand years." Instead of taking offense at such chutzpah, the president was deeply moved. One of his biographers reports: "At that, great tears started rolling down Harry Truman's cheeks."[75]

The second reason for Truman's support was political opportunism. With congressional elections coming up in 1946 and then a very difficult presidential campaign in 1948, the votes of Zionist sympathizers in New York, Illinois, California, and other states could be critical. White House Counsel Clark Clifford was particularly persistent in arguing this angle, to the point that Secretary of State Marshall, who was skeptical of the pro-Zionist bias, angrily objected. Clifford, said Marshall, was trying to have the President base a crucial foreign policy position on "domestic political considerations."[76]

American backing was indispensable in the birth of the State of Israel. In November 1947, the United Nations, led by the United States, voted to partition Palestine. The mandate had to be gerrymandered in order to create a bare majority in the territory allotted the Jews, who, while comprising one-third of the population, were given 56 per cent of the land. On America's role, veteran State Department official Sumner Welles wrote:

> By direct order of the White House every form of pressure, direct and indirect, was brought to bear upon countries outside the Moslem world that were known to be either uncertain or opposed to partition.[77]

---

[74]The depth of Eleanor's understanding of the Middle East situation is illustrated by her statement: "I'm confident that when a Jewish state is set up, the Arabs will see the light: they will quiet down; and Palestine will no longer be a problem." Evan M. Wilson, *Decision on Palestine: How the U.S. Came to Recognize Israel* (Stanford, Cal.: Hoover Institution Press, 1979), p. 116.

[75]Merle Miller, *Plain Speaking: An Oral Biography of Harry S. Truman* (New York: G.P Putnam, 1973), p. 218.

[76]Wilson, *Decision on Palestine*, pp. 134, 142; Lilienthal, *The Zionist Connection*, pp. 82–83.

[77]Wilson, *Decision on Palestine*, p. 126.

In her biography of her father, Margaret Truman spoke, in terms that today would be viewed as verging on anti-Semitism, of "the intense pressure which numerous Jews put on Dad from the moment he entered the White House and his increasing resentment of this pressure." She quotes from a letter Truman sent to Eleanor Roosevelt:

> I fear very much that the Jews are like all underdogs. When they get on top, they are just as intolerant and as cruel as the people were to them when they were underneath. I regret this situation very much, because my sympathy has always been on their side.[78]

But Truman's sporadic resentment did not prevent him from promoting Zionist plans for Palestine at the important points. He stubbornly ignored the advice not only of his own State Department, but also of his British ally who kept reminding him of the commitment made by Roosevelt, and by Truman himself, that the Arab states would be consulted on any settlement of the Palestine question.[79] When Israel declared its independence, on May 15, 1948, the United States extended *de facto* recognition ten minutes later. Since then, with the exception of the Eisenhower years, the bonds linking the United States to Israel have grown ever tighter, with American leaders seemingly indifferent to the costs to their own country.[80]

---

[78]Margaret Truman, *Harry S. Truman* (New York: William Morrow, 1973), pp. 381, 384–85.

[79]Clement Attlee, British prime minister during the decisive years, was a strong critic of Truman's policy: "The president went completely against the advice of his own State Department and his own military people.... The State Department's view was very close to ours, they had to think internationally, but most of the politicians were influenced by voting considerations. There were crucial elections coming up at the time, and several big Jewish firms had contributed to Democratic Party funds." Attlee reminded Truman of the American promises to Arab leaders that they, as well as the Zionists, would be fully consulted on Palestine: "It would be very unwise to break these solemn pledges and so set aflame the whole Middle East." Clement Attlee, *Twilight of Empire: Memoirs of Prime Minister Clement Attlee*, Francis Williams, ed. (New York: A. S. Barnes, 1963), pp. 181, 190.

[80]See Lilienthal, *The Zionist Connection*, and Sheldon L. Richman, "Ancient History": *U.S. Conduct in the Middle East Since World War II and the Folly of Intervention* (Washington, D.C.: Cato Institute, 1991).

HARRY S. TRUMAN: ADVANCING THE REVOLUTION   131

In the end, the part of Truman's legacy with the greatest potential for harm is NATO. Allegedly created in response to a (nonexistent) Soviet threat to overrun Europe, it has already outlived the Soviet Union and European Communism by a decade. At the beginning of the new century, there is no possibility that this entrenched military and civilian bureaucratic apparatus will simply fade away. When did such a huge collection of functionaries ever surrender their lucrative, tax-funded positions without a revolution?

In the course of NATO's aggression against Yugoslavia—illegal, according to the U.S. Constitution, the Charter of the United Nations, and NATO's own charter—its mission has been "redefined." No longer merely a defensive alliance (against whom?), it will now roam the world, a law unto itself, perpetually "in search of monsters to destroy." In 1951, General Eisenhower, then supreme Allied commander in Europe, stated: "If, in ten years time, all American troops stationed in Europe for national defense purposes have not been returned to the United States, then this whole project [NATO] will have failed."[81] A growing threat to the independence, the well-being, and the very lives of the peoples of the world, NATO may turn out in the end to have been Truman's greatest failure.

There are also episodes in Truman's presidency that have been forgotten in the rush to certify him as a "Near-Great" but that should not go unmentioned. Among the more notable ones:

Truman endorsed the Nuremberg trials of the top German leaders, appointing Robert H. Jackson, a Justice of the U.S. Supreme Court, as chief American prosecutor.[82] The trials were exposed as a vindictive violation of the canons of Anglo-American law by Senator Taft, who was labeled a pro-Nazi by Democratic and labor union leaders for his pains.[83] At Nuremberg, when the question came up of responsibility for the murder of thousands of Polish POWs at Katyn, Truman followed the craven policy laid down by FDR: the proof already in the possession of the U.S. government—that it was the Soviets who had murdered the Poles—was suppressed.[84]

---

[81]Eugene J. Carroll, Jr., "NATO Enlargement: To What End?" in *NATO Enlargement: Illusions and Reality*, Ted Galen Carpenter and Barbara Conry, eds. (Washington, D.C.: Cato Institute, 1998), p. 199.

[82]See, for example, *The Public Papers of Harry S. Truman, 1946*, pp. 455, 480–81.

[83]James A. Patterson, *Mr. Republican: A Biography of Robert A. Taft* (Boston: Houghton Mifflin, 1972), pp. 327–29.

[84]Werner Maser, *Nuremberg: A Nation on Trial*, Richard Barry, trans. (New York: Scribener's, 1979), pp. 112–13.

In the early months of Truman's presidency the United States and Britain directed the forced repatriation of many tens of thousands of Soviet subjects—and many who had never been Soviet subjects—to the Soviet Union, where they were executed by the NKVD or cast into the Gulag. Their crime had been to fight against Stalinist domination on the side of the Germans. Terrible scenes occurred in the course of this repatriation (sometimes called "Operation Keelhaul"), as the condemned men, and in some cases women with their children, were forced or duped into returning to Stalin's Russia. American soldiers had orders to "shoot to kill" those refusing to go. Some of the victims committed suicide rather than fall into the hands of the Soviet secret police.[85]

At home, the Truman administration brought the corrupt practices of the President's mentor to the White House. Truman had entered politics as the protégé of Tom Pendergast, the boss of the Kansas City Democratic machine. One of Truman's first acts as president was to fire the U.S. Attorney General for western Missouri, who had won 259 convictions for vote fraud against the machine and had sent Boss Pendergast to federal prison, where he died. Over the years, the Truman administration was notorious for influence-peddling, cover-ups, and outright theft.[86] It ranks with the administration of Bill Clinton for the dishonest practices of its personnel, although Truman and his wife Bess were never themselves guilty of malfeasance.

On the Road to the Atom Bombings[87]

U.S. planes had been systematically bombing the civilians of over sixty Japanese cities for months before Hiroshima, under the direction of Bomber Commander (later General) Curtis LeMay. The high

---

[85] Julius Epstein, *Operation Keelhaul: The Story of Forced Repatriation from 1944 to the Present* (Old Greenwich, Conn.: Devin-Adair, 1973), especially pp. 99–104. See especially Nicholas Bethell, *The Last Secret: Forcible Repatriation to Russia, 1944–47* (London: Andre Deutsch, 1974); and also Jason Kendall Moore, "Between Expediency and Principle: U.S. Repatriation Policy Toward Russian Nationals, 1944–1949," *Diplomatic History* 24, no. 3 (Summer 2000).

[86] Jules Abels, *The Truman Scandals* (Chicago: Regnery, 1956); Henry Regnery, *Memoirs of a Dissident Publisher* (New York: Harcourt, Brace, Jovanovich, 1979), pp. 132–38.

[87] All important arguments in favor of the destruction of enemy cities through Allied aircraft in the Second World War are presented in their best possible light, and thoroughly refuted, by the philosopher A. C. Grayling in *Among the Dead*

point of LeMay's campaign was the fire- and napalm-bombing of Tokyo by 334 B-29s on the night of March 9–10. At least 100,000 persons were killed, in one way or another, probably considerably more. The U.S. Strategic Bombing Survey concluded that "the largest number of victims were the most vulnerable: women, children, and the elderly." After the attack LeMay asserted that he wanted Tokyo "burned down—wiped right off the map," of course in order to "shorten the war." Through all this he had the full support of Roosevelt as he did later of Truman. The Japanese could do nothing against the American aerial onslaught except evacuate some 400,000 children to the countryside.[88]

Puzzlingly, high decision-makers continued to justify the mass-murder of Japanese civilians by reference to atrocities committed by Japan's military. In May, for instance, Marshall met with General Leslie Groves, head of the Manhattan Project and Henry ("Hap") Arnold, commander of the Army Air Force. Marshall cautioned that "we should guard against too much gratification" over the success of the air campaign because of the number of innocent casualities. Groves replied that he wasn't thinking of those victims but rather of the victims of the Bataan death march. When Groves and Arnold left, Arnold slapped his companion on the back, saying, "I'm glad you said that—it's just the way I feel."[89] Arguments along these lines were used by many leaders, up to and including Truman.

It is difficult to come to grips with what these men were saying. How *could* cruelty on the part of the Japanese army—at Bataan, in China, or anywhere else—*possibly* validate the deliberate killing of Japanese innocents, let alone hundreds of thousands of them? Those who employed, or continue to employ, such a calculus live in a strangely amoral mental world.

Genocidal fantasies flitted about in the minds of some. Admiral Halsey, commander in the South Pacific, compared the Japanese

---

Cities, op. cit.

[88] Mark Selden, "A Forgotten Holocaust," in Yuki Tanaka and Marilyn B. Young, eds., *Bombing Civilians: A Twentieth-Century History* (New York: The New Press, 2009), pp. 82–86, 93. LeMay later held various high military positions, including head of the Stratetic Air Command. He continued doing God's work in Korea and Vietnam, where, he boasted, he planned to bomb North Vietnam "back to the Stone Age." In the Cuban missile crisis he urged an invasion of Cuba even after the Russians agreed to withdraw.

[89] Hasegawa, "Were the Atomic Bombings Justified?", p. 124.

unfavorably to the Germans. While the Germans were at worst misled, "at least they react like men. But the Japanese are like animals.... They take to the jungle as if they had been bred there, and like some beasts you never see them until they are dead." Such beasts had simply to be annihilated. At the first interdepartmental meeting of a committee on how Japan was to be treated after the war, a representative of the Navy recommended "the almost total elimination of the Japanese as a race." Paul V. McNutt, former Democratic governor of Indiana and before and after the war U.S. High Commissioner to the Philippines, was chairman of the War Manpower Commission. His recommendation was "the extermination of the Japanese in toto." Elliott Roosevelt, one of the President's sons, proposed bombing Japan until "half the Japanese civilian population" was killed off.[90]

Such fond dreams of genocide were never realized, of course. Instead, the conventional bombing of Japan continued unabated, until the mid-summer of 1945.

Hiroshima and Nagasaki

The most spectacular episode of Truman's presidency that will never be forgotten, but will be forever linked to his name is the atomic bombings of Hiroshima on August 6, 1945 and of Nagasaki three days later.[91] Probably close to 200,000 persons were killed in the attacks and through radiation poisoning; the vast majority were civilians, including thousands of Korean workers. Twelve U.S. Navy fliers incarcerated in a Hiroshima jail were also among the dead, as well as other Allied prisoners of war.[92]

Great controversy has always surrounded the bombings. One

---

[90] Ibid., p. 119.

[91] On the atomic bombings, see Gar Alperovitz, *The Decision to Use the Atomic Bomb and the Architecture of an American Myth* (New York: Knopf, 1995); and idem, "Was Harry Truman a Revisionist on Hiroshima?" *Society for Historians of American Foreign Relations Newsletter* 29, no. 2 (June 1998); also Martin J. Sherwin, *A World Destroyed: The Atomic Bomb and the Grand Alliance* (New York: Vintage, 1977); and Dennis D. Wainstock, *The Decision to Drop the Atomic Bomb* (Westport, Conn.: Praeger, 1996).

[92] For decades after the war's end the U.S. government kept secret the deaths of the U.S. prisoners of war at Hiroshima (and also Nagasaki). At the military cemetary in Missouri where the remains of eight of the Americans who died in the Hiroshima bombing are buried, the place and cause of their deaths is unmen-

thing Truman insisted on from the start: the decision to use the bombs, and the responsibility it entailed, was his alone. Over the years, he gave different, and contradictory, grounds for his decision. Sometimes he implied that he had acted simply out of revenge. To a clergyman who criticized him, Truman responded, testily:

> Nobody is more disturbed over the use of Atomic bombs than I am but I was greatly disturbed over the unwarranted attack by the Japanese on Pearl Harbor and their murder of our prisoners of war. The only language they seem to understand is the one we have been using to bombard them.[93]

Such reasoning will not impress anyone who fails to see how the brutality of the Japanese military could justify deadly retaliation against innocent old men, women, and children. Truman perhaps was aware of this, so from time to time he advanced other pretexts. On August 9, 1945, he stated: "The world will note that the first atomic bomb was dropped on Hiroshima, a military base. That was because we wished in this first attack to avoid, insofar as possible, the killing of civilians."[94] This, however, is absurd. Pearl Harbor was a military base. Hiroshima was a city, inhabited by some three hundred thousand people, which contained military elements, as San Francisco contains the Presidio. In any case, since the harbor was mined and the U.S. Navy and Army Air Force were in control of the waters around Japan, whatever troops were stationed in Hiroshima had been effectively neutralized.

On other occasions, Truman claimed that Hiroshima was bombed because it was an industrial center. But, as noted in the U.S. Strategic Bombing Survey, "all major factories in Hiroshima were on the periphery of the city — and escaped serious damage."[95] The target was the center of the city. That Truman realized the kind of victims the bombs consumed is evident from his comment to his Cabinet on August 10, explaining his reluctance to drop a third bomb: "The

---

tioned. Hasegawa, "Were the Atomic Bombing Justified," p. 132.

[93] Alperovitz, *Decision*, p. 563. Truman added: "When you deal with a beast you have to treat him as a beast. It is most regrettable but nevertheless true." For similar statements by Truman, see ibid., p. 564. Alperovitz's monumental work is the end-product of four decades of study of the atomic bombings and is indispensable for comprehending the argumentation on the issue.

[94] Ibid., p. 521.

[95] Ibid., p. 523.

thought of wiping out another 100,000 people was too horrible," he said; he didn't like the idea of killing "all those kids."[96] *Wiping out another one hundred thousand people ... all those kids.*

Moreover, the notion that Hiroshima was a major military or industrial center is implausible on the face of it. The city had remained untouched through years of devastating air attacks on the Japanese Home Islands and never figured in Bomber Command's list of the thirty-three primary targets.[97]

Thus, the rationale for the atomic bombings has come to rest on a single colossal fabrication which has gained surprising currency: that they were necessary in order to save a half-million or more American lives. These, supposedly, are the lives that would have been lost in the planned invasion of Kyushu in December, then in the all-out invasion of Honshu the next year, if that was needed. But the worst-case scenario for a full-scale invasion of the Japanese Home Islands was 46,000 American lives lost.[98] The ridiculously inflated figure of a half-million for the potential death toll—more than the total of U.S. dead in all theaters in the Second World War—is now routinely repeated in high school and college textbooks and bandied about by ignorant commentators. Unsurprisingly the prize for sheer fatuousness on this score goes to President George Bush, who claimed in 1991 that dropping the bomb "spared millions of American lives."[99]

Still, Truman's multiple deceptions and self-deceptions are un-

---

[96] Barton J. Bernstein, "Understanding the Atomic Bomb and the Japanese Surrender: Missed Opportunities, Little-Known Near Disasters, and Modern Memory," *Diplomatic History* 19, no. 2 (Spring 1995), pp. 257. General Carl Spaatz, Commander of U.S. strategic bombing operations in the Pacific, was so shaken by the destruction at Hiroshima that he telephoned his superiors in Washington, proposing that the next bomb be dropped on a less populated area, so that it "would not be as devastating to the city and the people." His suggestion was rejected. Ronald Schaffer, *Wings of Judgment: American Bombing in World War II* (New York: Oxford University Press, 1985), pp. 147–48.

[97] This is true also of Nagasaki.

[98] See Barton J. Bernstein, 'A Post-War Myth: 500,000 U.S. Lives Saved," *Bulletin of the Atomic Scientists* 42, no. 6 (June–July 1986), pp. 38–40; and idem, "Wrong Numbers," *The Independent Monthly* (July 1995), pp. 41–44.

[99] J. Samuel Walker, "History, Collective Memory, and the Decision to Use the Bomb," *Diplomatic History* 19, no. 2 (Spring 1995), pp. 320, 323–25. Walker details the frantic evasions of Truman's lapdog biographer, David McCullough when confronted with the unambiguous record.

derstandable, considering the horror he unleashed. It is equally understandable that the U.S. occupation authorities censored reports from the shattered cities and did not permit films and photographs of the thousands of corpses and the frightfully mutilated survivors to reach the public.[100] Otherwise, Americans—and the rest of the world—might have drawn disturbing comparisons to scenes then coming to light from the Nazi concentration camps.

The bombings were condemned as barbaric and unnecessary by high American military officers, including Eisenhower and MacArthur.[101] The view of Admiral William D. Leahy, Truman's own chief of staff, was typical:

> the use of this barbarous weapon at Hiroshima and Nagasaki was of no material assistance in our war against Japan.... My own feeling was that in being the first to use it, we had adopted an ethical standard common to the barbarians of the Dark Ages. I was not taught to make wars in that fashion, and wars cannot be won by destroying women and children.[102]

The political elite implicated in the atomic bombings feared a backlash that would aid and abet the rebirth of horrid prewar "isolationism." Apologias were rushed into print, lest public disgust at the sickening war crime result in erosion of enthusiasm for the globalist project.[103] No need to worry. A sea-change had taken place in the

---

[100] Paul Boyer, "Exotic Resonances: Hiroshima in American Memory," *Diplomatic History* 19, no. 2 (Spring 1995), p. 299. On the fate of the bombings' victims and the public's restricted knowledge of them, see John W. Dower, "The Bombed: Hiroshimas and Nagasakis in Japanese Memory," in ibid., pp. 275–95.

[101] Alperovitz, *Decision*, pp. 320–65. On MacArthur and Eisenhower, see ibid., pp. 352 and 355–56.

[102] William D. Leahy, *I Was There* (New York: McGraw-Hill, 1950), p. 441. Leahy compared the use of the atomic bomb to the treatment of civilians by Genghis Khan, and termed it "not worthy of Christian man." Ibid., p. 442. Curiously, Truman himself supplied the foreword to Leahy's book. In a private letter written just before he left the White House, Truman referred to the use of the atomic bomb as "murder," stating that the bomb "is far worse than gas and biological warfare because it affects the civilian population and murders them wholesale." Barton J. Bernstein, "Origins of the U.S. Biological Warfare Program," *Preventing a Biological Arms Race*, Susan Wright, ed. (Cambridge, Mass.: MIT Press, 1990), p. 9.

[103] Barton J. Bernstein, "Seizing the Contested Terrain of Early Nuclear History:

attitudes of the American people. Then and ever after, all surveys have shown that the great majority supported Truman, believing that the bombs were required to end the war and save hundreds of thousands of American lives, or more likely, not really caring one way or the other.

Those who may still be troubled by such a grisly exercise in cost-benefit analysis — innocent Japanese lives balanced against the lives of Allied servicemen — might reflect on the judgment of the Catholic philosopher G. E. M. Anscombe, who insisted on the supremacy of moral rules.[104] When, in June 1956, Truman was awarded an honorary degree by her university, Oxford, Anscombe protested.[105] Truman was a war criminal, she contended, for what is the difference between the U.S. government massacring civilians from the air, as at Hiroshima and Nagasaki, and the Nazis wiping out the inhabitants of some Czech or Polish village?

Anscombe's point is worth following up. Suppose that, when we invaded Germany in early 1945, our leaders had believed that executing all the inhabitants of Aachen, or Trier, or some other Rhineland city would finally break the will of the Germans and lead them to surrender. In this way, the war might have ended quickly, saving the lives of many Allied soldiers. Would that then have justified shooting tens of thousands of German civilians, including women and children? Yet how is that different from the atomic bombings?

By early summer 1945, the Japanese fully realized that they were beaten. Why did they nonetheless fight on? As Anscombe wrote: "It was the insistence on unconditional surrender that was the root

---

Stimson, Conant, and Their Allies Explain the Decision to Use the Bomb," *Diplomatic History* 17, no. 1 (Winter 1993), pp. 35–72.

[104] One writer in no way troubled by the sacrifice of innocent Japanese to save Allied servicemen — indeed, just to save him — is Paul Fussell; see his *Thank God for the Atom Bomb and Other Essays* (New York: Summit, 1988). The reason for Fussell's little *Te Deum* is, as he states, that he was among those scheduled to take part in the invasion of Japan, and might very well have been killed. It is a mystery why Fussell takes out his easily understandable terror, rather unchivalrously, on Japanese women and children instead of on the men in Washington who conscripted him to fight in the Pacific in the first place.

[105] G. E. M. Anscombe, "Mr. Truman's Degree," in idem, *Collected Philosophical Papers*, vol. 3, *Ethics, Religion and Politics* (Minneapolis: University of Minnesota Press, 1981), pp. 62–71.

of all evil."[106]

That mad formula was coined by Roosevelt at the Casablanca conference, and, with Churchill's enthusiastic concurrence, it became the Allied shibboleth. After prolonging the war in Europe, it did its work in the Pacific. At the Potsdam conference, in July 1945, Truman issued a proclamation to the Japanese, threatening them with the "utter devastation" of their homeland unless they surrendered unconditionally. Among the Allied terms, to which "there are no alternatives," was that there be "eliminated for all time the authority and influence of those who have deceived and misled the people of Japan into embarking on world conquest [sic]." "Stern justice," the proclamation warned, "would be meted out to all war criminals."[107]

Many of Truman's influential advisors, including his own Secretary of War, Henry Stimson, Joseph Grew, James Forrestal, and Admiral Leahy, urged the president to add the promise that Japan could preserve the monarchy and the imperial dynasty. Truman chose instead to follow the advice of his Secretary of State, James F. Byrnes. Byrnes had never gone beyond grade school, but had had a spectacular political career in South Carolina and then nationally. He was one of Truman's cronies and had been appointed Secretary of State only on July 3. Byrnes knew nothing about Japan or world politics but evidently had strong opinions. He vetoed the recommendation of Stimson and the others.[108]

For months before, Truman had been pressed to clarify the U.S. position by many high officials outside the administration, as well. In May 1945, at the President's request, Herbert Hoover prepared a memorandum stressing the urgent need to end the war as soon as possible. The Japanese should be informed that we would in no way interfere with the Emperor or their chosen form of government. He even raised the possibility that, as part of the terms, Japan might be allowed to hold on to Formosa (Taiwan) and Korea. After meeting with Truman, Hoover dined with Taft and other Republican leaders,

---

[106] Anscombe, "Mr. Truman's Degree," p. 62.

[107] Hans Adolf Jacobsen and Arthur S. Smith, Jr., eds., *World War II: Policy and Strategy. Selected Documents with Commentary* (Santa Barbara, Calif.: ABC–Clio, 1979), pp. 345–46.

[108] Hasegawa, "Were the Atomic Bombing Justified?" pp. 107, 113.

and outlined his proposals.[109] Nothing came of the recommendations.

To the Japanese, Truman's declaration at Potsdam meant that the Emperor—regarded by the great bulk of the population as divine, the direct descendent of the Goddess of the Sun—would certainly be dethroned and probably put on trial as a war criminal, possibly hanged, perhaps in front of his palace.[110] It was not, in fact, the U.S. intention to dethrone or punish the Emperor. But this implicit modification of unconditional surrender was never communicated to the Japanese.

In the end, after Nagasaki, Washington acceded to the Japanese desire to keep the dynasty and even to retain Hirohito as Emperor.

Establishment writers on World War II often like to deal in lurid speculations. For instance: if the United States had not entered the war, then Hitler would have "conquered the world" (a sad undervaluation of the Red Army, it would appear; moreover, wasn't it Japan that was trying to "conquer the world"?) and killed untold millions. Now, applying conjectural history in this case: assume that the Pacific war had ended in the way wars customarily do—through negotiation of the terms of surrender. And assume the worst—that the Japanese had adamantly insisted on preserving part of their Empire, say, Korea and Formosa, even Manchuria. In that event, it is quite possible that Japan would have been in a position to prevent the Communists from coming to power in China. And that could have meant that the many millions of deaths now attributed to the Maoist regime would not have occurred.

But even remaining within the limits of feasible diplomacy in 1945, it is clear that Truman in no way exhausted the possibilities of ending the war without recourse to the atomic bomb. The Japanese were not informed that they would be the victims of by far the most lethal weapon ever invented (one with "more than two thousand times the blast power of the British 'Grand Slam,' which is the largest bomb ever yet used in the history of warfare," as Truman boasted in his announcement of the Hiroshima attack). Nor were

---

[109] Alperovitz, *Decision*, pp. 44–45.

[110] For some Japanese leaders, another reason for keeping the Emperor was as a bulwark against a possible post-war Communist takeover. See also Sherwin, *A World Destroyed*, p. 236: "the [Potsdam] proclamation offered the military diehards in the Japanese government more ammunition to continue the war than it offered their opponents to end it."

they told that the Soviet Union was set to declare war on Japan, an event that demoralized important leaders in Tokyo much more than the bombings. Pleas by some of the scientists involved in the project to demonstrate the power of the bomb in some uninhabited or evacuated area were rebuffed. All that mattered was to formally preserve the unconditional surrender formula and save the servicemen's lives that might have been lost in the effort to enforce it. Yet, as Major General J. F. C. Fuller, one of the century's great military historians, wrote in connection with the atomic bombings:

> Though to save life is laudable, it in no way justifies the employment of means which run counter to every precept of humanity and the customs of war. Should it do so, then, on the pretext of shortening a war and of saving lives, every imaginable atrocity can be justified.[111]

Isn't this obviously true? And isn't this the reason that rational and humane men, over generations, developed rules of warfare in the first place?

While the mass media parroted the government line in praising the atomic incinerations, prominent conservatives denounced them as unspeakable war crimes. Felix Morley, constitutional scholar and one of the founders of *Human Events*, drew attention to the horror of Hiroshima, including the "thousands of children trapped in the thirty-three schools that were destroyed." He called on his compatriots to atone for what had been done in their name, and proposed that groups of Americans be sent to Hiroshima, as Germans were sent to witness what had been done in the Nazi camps. The Paulist priest, Father James Gillis, editor of *The Catholic World* and another stalwart of the Old Right, castigated the bombings as "the most powerful blow ever delivered against Christian civilization and the moral law." David Lawrence, conservative owner of *U.S.*

---

[111] J. F. C. Fuller, *The Second World War, 1939–45: A Strategical and Tactical History* (London: Eyre and Spottiswoode, 1948), p. 392. Fuller, who was similarly scathing on the terror bombing of the German cities, characterized the attacks on Hiroshima and Nagasaki as "a type of war that would have disgraced Tamerlane." Cf. Barton J. Bernstein, who concludes, in "Understanding the Atomic Bomb," p. 235: "In 1945, American leaders were not seeking to avoid the use of the A-bomb. Its use did not create ethical or political problems for them. Thus, they easily rejected or never considered most of the so-called alternatives to the bomb."

News and World Report, continued to denounce them for years.[112] The distinguished conservative philosopher Richard Weaver was revolted by

> the spectacle of young boys fresh out of Kansas and Texas turning nonmilitary Dresden into a holocaust ... pulverizing ancient shrines like Monte Cassino and Nuremberg, and bringing atomic annihilation to Hiroshima and Nagasaki.

Weaver considered such atrocities as deeply "inimical to the foundations on which civilization is built."[113]

Today, self-styled conservatives slander as "anti-American" anyone who is in the least troubled by Truman's massacre of so many tens of thousands of Japanese innocents from the air. This shows as well as anything the difference between today's "conservatives," heartless hacks for the American military machine, and those who once deserved the name.

Leo Szilard was the world-renowned physicist who drafted the original letter to Roosevelt that Einstein signed, instigating the Manhattan Project, the program to create the atom bomb. In 1960, shortly before his death, Szilard stated another obvious truth:

> If the Germans had dropped atomic bombs on cities instead of us, we would have defined the dropping of atomic bombs on cities as a war crime, and we would have sentenced the Germans who were guilty of this crime to death at Nuremberg and hanged them.[114]

The destruction of Hiroshima and Nagasaki was a war crime worse than any that Japanese generals were executed for in Tokyo and Manila. If Harry Truman was not a war criminal, then no one ever was.

---

[112] Felix Morley, "The Return to Nothingness," *Human Events* (August 29, 1945) reprinted in *Hiroshima's Shadow*, Kai Bird and Lawrence Lifschultz, eds. (Stony Creek, Conn.: Pamphleteer's Press, 1998), pp. 272–74; James Martin Gillis, "Nothing But Nihilism," *The Catholic World*, September 1945, reprinted in ibid., pp. 278–80; Alperovitz, *Decision*, pp. 438–40.

[113] Richard M. Weaver, "A Dialectic on Total War," in idem, *Visions of Order: The Cultural Crisis of Our Time* (Baton Rouge: Louisiana State University Press, 1964), pp. 98–99.

[114] Wainstock, *Decision*, p. 122.

CHAPTER 4

Marxist Dreams and Soviet Realities

The sharp contrast that Alexis de Tocqueville drew in 1835 between the United States and Tsarist Russia—"the principle of the former is freedom; of the latter, servitude"[1]—became much sharper after 1917, when the Russian Empire was transformed into the Soviet Union.

Like the United States, the Soviet Union is a nation founded on a distinct ideology. In the case of America, the ideology was fundamentally Lockean liberalism; its best expressions are the Declaration of Independence and the Bill of Rights of the U.S. Constitution. The Ninth Amendment, in particular, breathes the spirit of the world-view of late-eighteenth-century America.[2] The Founders believed that there exist natural, individual rights that, taken together,

---

This essay was originally published in 1988, by the Cato Institute, Washington, D.C.

[1] Alexis de Tocqueville, *Democracy in America*, vol. 1 (New York: Vintage, 1945), p. 452.

[2] "The enumeration in the Constitution of certain rights shall not be construed to deny or disparage others retained by the people." Needless to say, the U.S. government has seldom lived up to its proclaimed credo, or anything close to it.

constitute a moral framework for political life. Translated into law, this framework defines the social space within which men voluntarily interact; it allows for the spontaneous coordination and ongoing mutual adjustment of the various plans that the members of society form to guide and fill their lives.

The Soviet Union was founded on a very different ideology, Marxism, as understood and interpreted by V. I. Lenin. Marxism, with its roots in Hegelian philosophy, was a quite conscious revolt against the individual rights doctrine of the previous century. The leaders of the Bolshevik party (which changed its name to Communist in 1918) were virtually all revolutionary intellectuals, in accordance with the strategy set forth by Lenin in his 1902 work *What Is to Be Done?*[3] They were avid students of the works of Marx and Engels published in their lifetimes or shortly thereafter and known to the theoreticians of the Second International. The Bolshevik leaders viewed themselves as the executors of the Marxist program, as those whom History had called upon to realize the apocalyptic transition to Communist society foretold by the founders of their faith.

The aim they inherited from Marx and Engels was nothing less than the final realization of human freedom and the end of the "prehistory" of the human race. Theirs was the Promethean dream of the rehabilitation of Man and his conquest of his rightful place as master of the world and lord of creation.

Building on the work of Michael Polanyi and Ludwig von Mises, Paul Craig Roberts has demonstrated—in books that deserve to be much better known than they are, since they provide an important key to the history of the twentieth century[4]—the meaning of freedom in Marxism. It lies in the abolition of alienation, i.e., of commodity production, production for the market. For Marx and Engels, the market represents not merely the arena of capitalist exploitation but, more fundamentally, a systematic insult to the dignity of Man. Through it, the consequences of Man's action escape from his control and turn on him in malign ways. Thus, the insight

---

[3] V. I. Lenin, *What Is to Be Done? Burning Questions of Our Movement* (New York: International Publishers, 1929).

[4] *Alienation and the Soviet Economy: Towards a General Theory of Marxian Alienation, Organizational Principles, and the Soviet Economy* (Albuquerque: University of New Mexico Press, 1971) and (with Matthew A. Stephenson) *Marx's Theory of Exchange, Alienation, and Crisis* (Standford: Hoover Insitution Press, 1973).

that market processes generate results that were no part of anyone's intention becomes, for Marxism, the very reason to condemn them. As Marx wrote of the stage of Communist society before the total disappearance of scarcity,

> freedom in this field can consist only in socialized man, the associated producers, rationally regulating their interchange with Nature, bringing it under their common control, instead of being ruled by it as by the blind forces of Nature.[5]

The point is made most clearly by Engels:

> With the seizure of the means of production by society, production of commodities is done away with, and with it the dominion of the product over the producers. Anarchy of social production is replaced by conscious organization according to plan. The whole sphere of the conditions of life which surround men, which ruled men up until now comes under the dominion and conscious control of men, who become for the first time the real, conscious lords of nature, because and in that they become master of their own social organization. The laws of their own social activity, which confronted them until this point as alien laws of nature, controlling them, then are applied by men with full understanding, and so mastered by them. Only from then on will men make their history themselves in full consciousness; only from then on will the social causes they set in motion have in the main and in constantly increasing proportion, also the results intended by them. It is the leap of mankind from the realm of necessity to the realm of freedom.[6]

Thus, Man's freedom would be expressed in the total control exercised by the associated producers in planning the economy and, with it, all of social life. No longer would the unintended consequences of Man's actions bring disaster and despair—there *would be no such consequences.* Man would determine his own fate. Left unexplained was how millions upon millions of separate individuals could be expected to act with one mind and one will—could

---

[5] Karl Marx, *Capital: A Critique of Political Economy*, vol. 3, Friedrich Engels, ed. (New York: International Publishers, 1967), p. 820.

[6] Friedrich Engels, "Socialism: Utopian and Scientific," in Karl Marx and

suddenly become "Man"—especially since it was alleged that the state, the indispenable engine of coercion, would wither away.

Already in Marx and Engels's day—decades before the establishment of the Soviet state—there were some with a shrewd idea of just who it was that would assume the title role when the time came to perform the heroic melodrama, Man Creates His Own Destiny. The most celebrated of Marx's early critics was the Russian anarchist Michael Bakunin, for whom Marx was "the Bismarck of socialism" and who warned that Marxism was a doctrine ideally fitted to function as the ideology—in the Marxist sense: the systematic rationalization and obfuscation—of the power urges of revolutionary intellectuals. It would lead, Bakunin warned, to the creation of "a new class," which would establish "the most aristocratic, despotic, arrogant, and contemptuous of all regimes"[7] and entrench its control over the producing classes of society. Bakunin's analysis was extended and elaborated by the Pole Waclaw Machajski.[8]

Despite this analysis—or perhaps as a confirmation of it—the Marxist vision came to inspire generations of intellectuals in Europe and even in America. In the course of the vast, senseless carnage that was the First World War, the Tsarist Empire collapsed and the immense Imperial Russian Army was fragmented into atoms. A small group of Marxist intellectuals seized power. What could be more natural than that, once in power, they should try to bring into being the vision that was their whole purpose and aim? The problem was that the audacity of their dream was matched only by the depth of their economic ignorance.

In August 1917—three months before he took power—this is

Friedrich Engels, *Selected Works* (Moscow: Progress Publishers, 1968), p. 432.

[7]See, for instance, Michael Bakunin, "Marx, the Bismarck of Socialism," in Leonard I. Krimerman and Lewis Perry, eds., *Patterns of Anarchy. A collection of Writings in the Anarchist Tradition* (Garden City, N.Y.: Anchor/Doubleday, 1966), pp. 80–97, especially p. 87. For a discussion of the theoretical problems involved in a "new class" analysis of Soviet society and a critique of James Burnham's attempt to generalize the interpretation to non-Marxist societies, see Leszek Kolakowski, *Main Currents of Marxism*, P. S. Falla, trans. (Oxford: Oxford University Press, 1981) vol. 3, *The Breakdown*, pp. 157–66.

[8]See Max Nomad, *Political Heretics* (Ann Arbor: University of Michigan Press, 1968), pp. 238–41. Also, Jan Waclav Makaïske, *Le socialisme des intellectuels*, Alexandre Skirda, ed. (Paris: Editions du Seuil, 1979).

how Lenin, in *State and Revolution*, characterized the skills needed to run a national economy in the "first phase" of Communism, the one he and his associates were about to embark upon:

> The accounting and control necessary for this have been simplified by capitalism to the utmost, till they have become the extraordinarily simple operations of watching, recording and issuing receipts, within the reach of anybody who can read and write and knows the first four rules of arithmetic.[9]

Nikolai Bukharin, a leading "Old Bolshevik," in 1919 wrote, together with Evgeny Preobrazhensky, one of the most widely read Bolshevik texts. It was *The ABC of Communism*, a work that went through 18 Soviet editions and was translated into 20 languages. Bukharin and Preobrazhensky "were regarded as the Party's two ablest economists."[10] According to them, Communist society is, in the first place, "an organized society," based on a detailed, precisely calculated plan, which includes the "assignment" of labor to the various branches of production. As for distribution, according to these eminent Bolshevik economists, all products will be delivered to communal warehouses, and the members of society will draw them out in accordance with their self-defined needs.[11]

Favorable mentions of Bukharin in the Soviet press are now taken to be exciting signs of the glories of *glasnost*, and in his speech of November 2, 1987, Mikhail Gorbachev partially rehabilitated him.[12] It should be remembered that Bukharin is the man who wrote, "We shall proceed to a standardization of the intellectuals; we shall manufacture them as in a factory"[13] and who stated, in justification of Leninist tyranny:

---

[9] V. I. Lenin, *State and Revolution* (New York: International Publishers, 1943), pp. 83–84.

[10] Sidney Heitman, in the "New Introduction" (unpaginated) to N. Bukharin and E. Preobrazhensky, *The ABC of Communism* (Ann Arbor: University of Michigan Press, 1966).

[11] Ibid., pp. 68–73.

[12] *New York Times*, no. 3, 1987.

[13] David Caute, *The Left in Europe Since 1789* (New York: McGraw–Hill, 1966), p. 179.

> Proletarian coercion, in all its forms, from executions to forced labor, is, paradoxical as it may sound, the method of molding communist humanity out of the human material of the capitalist period.[14]

The shaping of the "human material" at their disposal into something higher—the manufacture of the New Soviet Man, *Homo sovieticus*—was essential to their vision of all the millions of individuals in society acting together, with one mind and one will,[15] and it was shared by all the Communist leaders. It was to this end, for instance, that Lilina, Zinoviev's wife, spoke out for the "nationalization" of children, in order to mold them into good Communists.[16]

The most articulate and brilliant of the Bolsheviks put it most plainly and best. At the end of his *Literature and Revolution*, written in 1924, Leon Trotsky placed the famous, and justly ridiculed, last lines: Under Communism, he wrote, "The average human type will rise to the heights of an Aristotle, a Goethe, or a Marx. And above this ridge new peaks will rise." This dazzling prophecy was justified in his mind, however, by what he had written in the few pages preceding. Under Communism, Man will "reconstruct society and himself in accord with his own plan." "Traditional family life" will be transformed, the "laws of heredity and blind sexual selection" will be obviated, and Man's purpose will be "to create a higher social biological type, or, if your please, a superman."[17] (The full quotation can be found in the article on Trotsky in this volume.)

---

[14] Ibid., p. 112.

[15] "The principal task of the fathers of the October Revolution was the creation of the New Man, *Homo sovieticus*." Michel Heller and Aleksandr Nekrich, *L'utopie au pouvoir: Histoire de l'U.R.S.S. de 1917 á nos jours* (Paris: Calmann-Lévy, 1982), p. 580. As for the result, Kolakowski states: "Stalinism really produced 'the new Soviet man': an ideological schizophrenic, a liar who believed what he was saying, a man capable of incessant, voluntary acts of intellectual self-mutilation." Kolakowski, vol. 3, p. 97.

[16] Heller and Nekrich, p. 50.

[17] Leon Trotsky, *Literature and Revolution* (Ann Arbor: University of Michigan Press, 1971), pp. 246, 249, 254–56. Bukharin entertained similarly absurd collectivist-Promethean notions of socialist achievement. He stated, in 1928 (when Stalin's domination was already apparent): "We are creating and we shall create a civilization compared to which capitalism will have the same aspect as an air played on a kazoo to Beethoven's *Eroica* Symphony." Heller and Nekrich, p. 181.

I suggest that what we have here, in the sheer willfulness of Trotsky and the other Bolsheviks, in their urge to replace God, nature, and spontaneous social order with total, conscious planning by themselves, is something that transcends politics in any ordinary sense of the term. It may well be that to understand what is at issue we must ascend to another level, and that more useful in understanding it than the works of the classical liberal economists and political theorists is the superb novel of the great Christian apologist C. S. Lewis, *That Hideous Strength*.

Now, the fundamental changes in human nature that the Communist leaders undertook to make require, in the nature of the case, absolute political power in a few directing hands. During the French Revolution, Robespierre and the other Jacobin leaders set out to transform human nature in accordance with the theories of Jean-Jacques Rousseau. This was not the only cause but it was surely one of the causes of the Reign of Terror. The Communists soon discovered what the Jacobins had learned: that such an enterprise requires that Terror be erected into a system of government.[18]

The Red Terror began early on. In his celebrated November 1987 speech, Gorbachev confined the Communist Reign of Terror to the Stalin years and stated:

> Many thousands of people inside and outside the party were subjected to wholesale repressive measures. Such, comrades, is the bitter truth.[19]

But by no means is this the whole of the bitter truth. By the end of 1917, the repressive organs of the new Soviet state had been organized into the Cheka, later known by other names, including OGPU, NKVD, and KGB. The various mandates under which the Cheka operated may be illustrated by an order signed by Lenin on February 21, 1918: that men and women of the bourgeoisie be drafted into labor battalions to dig trenches under the supervision of Red Guards, with "those resisting to be shot." Others, including "speculators" and counter-revolutionary agitators, were "to be shot on the scene of their crime." To a Bolshevik who objected to the

---
[18] Cf. J. L. Talmon, *The Origins of Totalitarian Democracy* (London: Mercury Books, 1961).

[19] *New York Times*, Nov. 3, 1987.

phrasing, Lenin replied, "Surely you do not imagine that we shall be victorious without applying the most cruel revolutionary terror?"[20]

The number of Cheka executions that amounted to legalized murder in the period from late 1917 to early 1922—including neither the victims of the Revolutionary Tribunals and the Red Army itself nor the insurgents killed by the Cheka—has been estimated by one authority at 140,000.[21] As a reference point, consider that the number of political executions under the repressive Tsarist regime from 1866 to 1917 was about 44,000, including during and after the Revolution of 1905[22] (except that the persons executed were accorded trials), and the comparable figure for the French Revolutionary Reign of Terror was 18,000 to 20,000.[23] Clearly, with the first Marxist state something new had come into the world.

In the Leninist period—that is, up to 1924—fall also the war against the peasantry that was part of "war communism" and the famine conditions, culminating in the famine of 1921, that resulted from the attempt to realize the Marxist dream. The best estimate of the human cost of those episodes is around 6,000,000 persons.[24]

But the guilt of Lenin and the Old Bolsheviks—and of Marx himself—does not end here. Gorbachev asserted that "the Stalin personality cult was certainly not inevitable."

"Inevitable" is a large word, but if something like Stalinism had not occurred, it would have been close to a miracle. Scorning what Marx and Engels had derided as mere "bourgeois" freedom and "bourgeois" jurisprudence,[25] Lenin destroyed freedom of the press, abolished all protections against the police power, and rejected any hint of division of powers and checks and balances in government. It would have saved the peoples of Russia an immense amount

---

[20] George Leggett, *The Cheka: Lenin's Political Police* (Oxford: Clarendon Press, 1981), pp. 56–57.

[21] Ibid., pp. 466–67

[22] Ibid., p. 468. The great majority of these occurred as a result of the 1905 revolutionary uprising.

[23] Samuel F. Scott and Barry Rothaus, eds., *Historical Dictionary of the French Revolution, 1789–1799*, L–Z (Westport, Conn.: Greenwood Press, 1985), p. 944.

[24] Robert Conquest, *Harvest of Sorrow: Soviet Collectivization and the Terror-Famine* (New York: Oxford University Press, 1986), pp. 53–55.

[25] Karl Marx and Friedrich Engels, *The Communist Manifesto*, in *Selected Works*, p. 49.

MARXIST DREAMS AND SOVIET REALITIES 151

of suffering if Lenin—and Marx and Engels before him—had not quite so brusquely dismissed the work of men like Montesquieu and Jefferson, Benjamin Constant and Alexis de Tocqueville. These writers had been preoccupied with the problem of how to thwart the state's ever-present drive toward absolute power. They laid out, often in painstaking detail, the political arrangements that are required, the social forces that must be nurtured, in order to avert tyranny. But to Marx and his Bolshevik followers, this was nothing more than "bourgeois ideology," obsolete and of no relevance to the future socialist society. Any trace of decentralization or division of power, the slightest suggestion of a countervailing force to the central authority of the "associated producers," ran directly contrary to the vision of the unitary planning of the whole of social life.[26]

The toll among the peasantry was even greater under Stalin's collectivization[27] and the famine of 1933—a deliberate one this time, aimed at terrorizing and crushing the peasants, especially of the Ukraine. We shall never know the full truth of this demonic crime, but it seems likely that perhaps ten or 12,000,000 persons lost their lives as a result of these Communist policies—as many or more than the total of all the dead in all the armies in the First World War.[28]

---

[26] On Marx's responsibility, Kolakowski (vol. 3, pp. 60–61) writes, "He undoubtedly believed that socialist society would be one of perfect unity, in which conflicts of interest would disappear with the elimination of their economic bases in private property. This society, he thought, would have no need of bourgeois institutions such as representative political bodies ... and rules of law safeguarding civil liberties. The Soviet despotism was an attempt to apply this doctrine." See also ibid., p. 41.

[27] The "war against the nation"—Stalin's forced collectivization—was not the product of a power-mad cynic. As Adam Ulam has argued, "Stalin was seldom cynical.... He was sincere and obsessed." His obsession was Marxism-Leninism, the science of society that unerringly points the way to total human freedom. If reality proved refractory, then the cause had to be the "wreckers"—whole categories and classes of people engaged in deliberate sabotage. Surely, the Marxist dream could not be at fault. Adam Ulam, *Stalin. The Man and His Era* (Boston: Beacon Press, 1973), pp. 300–01.

[28] Conquest, *Harvest of Sorrow*, pp. 299–307. The terrible famine year was 1933; after that, concessions were made to the peasant: a half-acre plot that he could work for himself and the right to sell crops on the market after the state's quota had been met. Stalin, however, begrudged these "concessions" to "individualism." Ulam, pp. 350–52.

One is stunned. Who could have conceived that within a few years what the Communists were to do in the Ukraine would rival the appalling butcheries of World War I—Verdun, the Somme, Passchendaele?

> They died in hell,
> They called it Passchendaele.

But what word to use, then, for what the Communists made of the Ukraine?

Vladimir Grossman, a Russian novelist who experienced the famine of 1933, wrote about it in his novel *Forever Flowing*, published in the West. An eyewitness to the famine in the Ukraine stated,

> Then I came to understand the main thing for the Soviet power is the Plan. Fulfill the Plan.... Fathers and mothers tried to save their children, to save a little bread, and they were told: You hate our socialist country, you want to ruin the Plan, you are parasites, kulaks, fiends, reptiles. When they took the grain, they told the kolkhoz [collective farm] members they would be fed out of the reserve fund. They lied. They would not give grain to the hungry.[29]

The labor camps for "class-enemies" had already been established under Lenin, as early as August 1918.[30] They were vastly enlarged under his successor. Alexander Solzhenitsyn compared them to an archipelago spread across the great sea of the Soviet Union. The camps grew and grew. Who were sent there? Any with lingering Tsarist sentiments and recalcitrant members of the middle classes, liberals, Mensheviks, anarchists, priests and laity of the Orthodox Church, Baptists and other religious dissidents, "wreckers," suspects of every description, then, "kulaks" and peasants by the hundreds of thousands.

During the Great Purge of the middle 1930s, the Communist bureaucrats and intellectuals themselves were victims, and at that point there was a certain sort of thinker in the West who now began to notice the camps, and the executions, for the first time. More

---

[29] Cited in ibid., p. 346.
[30] Héléne Carrére d'Encausse, *Stalin: Order Through Terror*, Valence Ionescu, trans. (London and New York: Longman, 1981), pp. 6–7.

MARXIST DREAMS AND SOVIET REALITIES 153

masses of human beings were shipped in after the annexations of eastern Poland and the Baltic states; then enemy prisoners of war, the internal "enemy nationalities," and the returning Soviet prisoners of war (viewed as traitors for having surrendered), who flooded into the camps after 1945—in Solzhenitsyn's words, "vast dense gray shoals like ocean herring."[31]

The most notorious of the camps was Kolyma, in eastern Siberia —in actuality, a system of camps four times the size of France. There the death rate may have been as high as 50 per cent per year[32] and the number of deaths was probably on the order of 3,000,000. It goes on and on. In 1940 there was Katyn and the murder of the Polish officers; in 1952, the leaders of Yiddish culture in the Soviet Union were liquidated en masse[33]—both drops in the bucket for Stalin. During the Purges there were probably about 7,000,000 arrests, and one out of every ten arrested was executed.[34]

How many died altogether? No one will ever know. What is certain is that the Soviet Union has been the worst reeking charnel house of the whole awful twentieth century, worse even than the one the Nazis created (but then they had less time).[35] The sum total of deaths due to Soviet policy—in the Stalin period alone—deaths from the collectivization and the terror famine, the executions and the Gulag, is probably on the order of 20,000,000.[36]

As *glasnost* proceeds and these landmarks of Soviet history are uncovered and explored to a greater or lesser degree, it is to be hoped that Gorbachev and his followers will not fail to point an

---

[31] Aleksandr I. Solzhenitsyn, *The Gulag Archipelago, 1918–1956. An Experiment in Literary Investigation*, vols. 1–2.

[32] Nikolai Tolstoy, *Stalin's Secret War* (New York: Holt, Rinehart and Winston, 1981), p. 15.

[33] David Caute, *The Fellow-Travellers. A Postscript to the Enlightenment* (New York: Macmillan, 1973), p. 286.

[34] Robert Conquest, *The Great Terror: Stalin's Purge of the Thirties* (New York: Macmillan, 1968), p. 527.

[35] It should be obvious that, in logic and justice, the enumeration of Soviet crimes can in no way exculpate any other state—for instance, any Western democracy—for the crimes it has committed or is committing.

[36] Conquest, *The Great Terror*, pp. 525–35, especially p. 533. Caute, *The Fellow-Travellers*, p. 107, estimates the deaths in the camps between 1936 and 1950 at 12,000,000. He adds, "Stalin's policies may have accounted for twenty million deaths." Ibid., p. 303.

accusing finger at the West for the part it played in masking these crimes. I am referring to the shameful chapter in twentieth-century intellectual history involving the fellow travelers of Soviet Communism and their apologias for Stalinism. Americans, especially American college students, have been made familiar with the wrongs of McCarthyism in our own history. This is as it should be. The harassment and public humiliation of innocent private persons is iniquitous, and the U.S. government must always be held to the standards established by the Bill of Rights. But surely we should also remember and inform young Americans of the accomplices in a far different order of wrongs—those progressive intellectuals who "worshiped at the temple of [Soviet] planning"[37] and lied and evaded the truth to protect the homeland of socialism, while millions were martyred. Not only George Bernard Shaw,[38] Sidney and Beatrice Webb, Harold Laski, and Jean-Paul Sartre, but, for instance, the Moscow correspondent of the *New York Times*, Walter Duranty, who told his readers, in August 1933, at the height of the famine:

> Any report of famine in Russia is today an exaggeration or malignant propaganda. The food shortage which has affected almost the whole population in the last year and particularly in the grain-producing provinces—the Ukraine, North Caucasus, the lower Volga region—has, however, caused heavy loss of life.[39]

For his "objective" reporting from the Soviet Union, Duranty won a Pulitzer Prize.[40]

---

[37] Caute, *The Fellow-Travellers*, p. 259.

[38] George Bernard Shaw, for example, expressed his scorn for those who protested when the Soviet Union "judiciously liquidates a handful of exploiters and speculators to make the world safe for honest men." Ibid., p. 113.

[39] Quoted by Eugene Lyons, "The Press Corps Conceals a Famine," in Julien Steinberg, ed., *Verdict of Three Decades. From the Literature of Individual Revolt Against Soviet Communism, 1917–1950* (New York: Duell, Sloan, and Pearce, 1950), pp. 272–73.

[40] Conquest, *Harvest of Sorrow*, pp. 319–20. As Conquest mentions, as of 1983 the *New York Times* still listed Duranty's Pulitzer Prize among the paper's honors. If the *Times* reporter and other correspondents lied so contemptibly about conditions in Soviet Russia and their causes, however, others were soon telling the truth: Eugene Lyons and William Henry Chamberlin published articles and books detailing, from personal experience, what Chamberlin called the "organized famine" that had been used as a weapon against the Ukrainian peasantry.

MARXIST DREAMS AND SOVIET REALITIES 155

Or—to take another fellow traveler virtually at random—we should keep in mind the valuable work of Owen Lattimore of Johns Hopkins University. Professor Lattimore visited Kolyma in the summer of 1944, as an aide to the Vice President of the United States, Henry Wallace. He wrote a glowing report on the camp and on its chief warden, Commandant Nikishov, for the *National Geographic*.[41] Lattimore compared Kolyma to a combination of the Hudson's Bay Company and the TVA.[42] The number of the influential American fellow travelers was, in fact, legion, and I can think of no moral principle that would justify our forgetting what they did and what they did it in aid of.

In his speech of November 2, Gorbachev declared that Stalin was guilty of "enormous and unforgivable crimes" and announced that a special commission of the Central Committee is to prepare a history of the Communist party of the Soviet Union that will reflect the realities of Stalin's rule. Andrei Sakharov has called for the full disclosure of "the entire, terrible truth of Stalin and his era."[43] But can the Communist leaders really afford to tell the entire truth? At the Twentieth Party Congress in 1956, Nikita Khrushchev revealed the tip of the iceberg of Stalinist crimes, and Poland rose up and there took place the immortal Hungarian Revolution, when they did

> high deeds in Hungary
> To pass all men's believing.

What would it mean to reveal the entire truth? Could the Communist leaders admit, for instance, that during World War II, "the losses inflicted by the Soviet state upon its own people rivaled any the Germans could inflict on the battlefield"? That "the Nazi concentration camps were modified versions of Soviet originals," whose evolution the German leadership had followed with some care. That, in short, "the Soviet Union is not only the original killer state, but the model one"?[44] If they did that, what might the consequences not be this time?

See William Henry Chamberlin, "Death in the Villages," in Steinberg, p. 291.

[41] Caute, *The Fellow-Travellers*, p. 102.

[42] Conquest, *The Great Terror*, p. 354.

[43] *New York Times*, Nov. 7, 1987.

[44] Nick Eberstadt, Introduction to Iosif G. Dyadkin, *Unnatural Deaths in the U.S.S.R., 1928–1954* (New Brunswick, N.J., and London: Transaction Books, 1983), pp. 8, 4.

But the fact that the victims of Soviet Communism can never be fully acknowledged in their homelands is all the more reason that, as a matter of historical justice, we in the West must endeavor to keep their memory alive.

CHAPTER 5

Nazifying the Germans

Not long ago a German friend remarked to me, jokingly, that he imagined the only things American college students were apt to associate with Germany nowadays were beer, Lederhosen, and the Nazis. I replied that, basically, there was only one thing that Americans, whether college students or not, associated with Germany. When the Germans are mentioned, it is Nazism that first springs to mind; whatever else may brought up later will be colored and contaminated by thoughts of the Nazis. When Molly Ivins (described by Justin Raimondo, in his *Colin Powell and the Power Elite*, as a "liberal columnist and known plagiarist") remarked, of Pat Buchanan's speech at the 1992 Republican convention, "it sounded better in the original German," everyone instantly knew what she meant. The casual slander was picked up by William Safire and others, and made the rounds. A constant din from Hollywood and the major media has instructed us on what "German" really stands for.

This is a slightly modified version of an article that first appeared in the January 1997 issue of *Chronicles* magazine, published by the Rockford Institute, of Rockford, Illinois.

And yet, as some Germans plaintively insist, there are a thousand years of history "on the other side" of the Third Reich. In cultural terms, it is not an unimpressive record (in which the Austrians must be counted; at least until 1866, Austria was as much a part of the German lands as Bavaria or Saxony). From printing to the automobile to the jet engine to the creation of whole branches of science, the German contribution to European civilization has been, one might say, rather significant. Albertus Magnus, Luther, Leibniz, Kant, Goethe, Humboldt, Ranke, Nietzsche, Carl Menger, Max Weber—these are not negligible figures in the history of thought.

And then, of course, there's the music.

The German role over centuries in transmitting advanced culture to the peoples to the east and southeast was critical at certain stages of their development. The Hungarian liberal, Gaspar M. Tamas, speaking for his own people, the Czechs, and others, wrote of the Germans who had lived among them for centuries and were driven out in 1945, that their "ancestors built our cathedrals, monasteries, universities, and railway stations." As for our country, the highly laudatory chapter that Thomas Sowell devotes to the German immigrants in *Ethnic America* is one of the best in a fascinating book. More than five million Germans came to the United States in the nineteenth century alone. According to recent census figures, around fifty-seven million Americans claim to be of German heritage. Together with the descendants of the immigrants from the British Isles, Germans form the basic American stock. They were highly valued as neighbors, and their ways were woven into the fabric of American life—the Christmas tree and *Silent Night*, for instance, and the family-centered Sunday, with its "jovial yet orderly activities," as an admiring Anglo contemporary put it. Is there any doubt that when Germans composed the leading population in many American cities and towns, these were happier places to live in than they are today?

Yet the air is filled with incessant harping on an interval of twelve years in the annals of this ancient European race. In the normal course of things, one would expect a countervailing defense to emanate from Germany itself. But it is precisely there, among the left intelligentsia, that some of the prime German-haters are to be found. The reasons for this are fairly clear.

Over the last decades, these intellectuals have grown increasingly frustrated at their own people, who remain firmly bourgeois and order-loving, with little interest in neo-Marxist transformations of their way of life. Increasingly, too, that frustration has been vented in hatred and contempt for everything German. Most of all, the Germans were condemned for their hopelessly misguided past and bourgeois social structure, which supposedly produced Nazism. Anguished complaints like that from the conservative historian Michael Stürmer, that "we cannot live while continually pulverizing ourselves and our own history into nothing, while we make that history into a permanent source of infinite feelings of guilt," were merely further evidence that the Germans stood in dire need of radical re-education. A large segment of the left intelligentsia made no bones of its sympathy for the "German Democratic Republic" [Communist East Germany] which at least did not enslave its subjects to consumerism and the "elbow society" prevalent in the West. Naturally, there were certain excesses, but these could be explained by the pressures issuing from Bonn and Washington. For these intellectuals, the GDR dictatorship—kept in existence by Soviet tanks and forced to resort to building a wall to keep its subjects in— was a "normal state"; they denounced any attempts to "destabilize" it, even by the forthright expression of anti-Communist opinion ("primitive anti-Communism," it was called). They spoke warmly of Communism's "humanistic values" and "positive core," which sharply distinguished it from National Socialism. In this way, they exhibited one of the characteristic failings of intellectuals: preferring to look to their preferred theory rather than to social reality.

The German left's "march through the institutions" after 1968 was spectacularly successful in the media, schools and universities, churches, and more and more in politics. Its control of the cultural infrastructure produced a situation where the public declaration of any pro-German attitude was viewed as evidence of *Rechtsradikalismus*. Some thirty years ago, when Israeli Prime Minister Levi Eshkol, at a dinner in Jerusalem, expressed to Konrad Adenauer his confidence that "under your leadership the German people will return to the community of civilized peoples," the old Chancellor retorted: "Mr. Prime Minister, what you think is of no concern to me ... I represent the German people. You have insulted them, and so tomorrow morning I shall depart." It is impossible to imagine any recent German leader, in particular, the lickspittle former Federal President Richard von Weizsäcker, responding with such unabashed patriotism, especially to an Israeli.

Then came 1989, the fall of the Berlin Wall, and signs that the Germans might still harbor some sense of national pride. The conservative historian and publicist Rainer Zitelmann writes that "the left experienced the reunification [of Germany] and the collapse of socialism as a defeat," a grave setback that had to be made good, lest a "turn" occur and the left lose its power to control political debate. The perfect opportunity presented itself when a few halfwits firebombed the homes and asylums of foreign residents. (These incidents were strategically exploited in the same way as the Oklahoma City bombing has been exploited in the United States.) Now came an all-out campaign against allegedly deep-seated German "racism" and "hostility to foreigners," accompanied, naturally, by hysterical warnings of a "Nazi resurgence" and endless allusions to the affinities between Nazism and bourgeois Germany. Thus, the normal human desire to live in one's own country among one's own kind was equated with the will to annihilate other peoples manifested by Hitler and his butchers.

The latest spasm of German abuse and German self-hatred occurred with the publication of Daniel Jonah Goldhagen's *Hitler's Willing Executioners: Ordinary Germans and the Holocaust.* Launched with a remarkable publicity barrage by Knopf, absurdly acclaimed by the author's Harvard friends, it was touted by Abe Rosenthal in the *New York Times* for packing the emotional equivalent of a first visit to Auschwitz. The thesis of this work, which won an award from the American Political Science Association, is that the Judeocide is easily explained: for centuries the Germans had been "eliminationist" anti-Semites, and under the Nazis, they became openly and enthusiastically "exterminationist." Suffice it to say that in public debates recognized Holocaust scholars demolished the crooked methodology and unevidenced claims of this academic hustler.

The best review appeared in the *Frankfurter Allgemeine* and the excellent German conservative magazine *Criticòn*, by Alfred de Zayas, an American historian and jurist and respected authority on international law.

Whenever anti-Semitic attitudes or acts are mentioned, de Zayas observes, Goldhagen speaks of "the Germans"—not "the Nazis," or even "many Germans"—offering no justification at all; it is simply a polemical trick. He neglects to mention well-known facts, e.g., that everyone connected with the killing of the Jews was bound by Führer Order no. 1, as well as by special orders from Himmler, mandating the strictest silence, under penalty of death. So it should not be surprising that, for example, the former Chancellor Helmut Schmidt, during the war a Luftwaffe officer, testified that he had never heard or known anything of the annihilation of the Jews; or that Countess Dönhoff, publisher of the liberal paper, *Die Zeit*, should state that, despite her connections to many key people during the war, she knew nothing of the mass-killings in the camps, and that "I heard the name 'Auschwitz' for the first time after the war."

Goldhagen simply disregards major standard works that contradict his thesis. He claims, for example, that the German people approved of and joined in the *Kristallnacht* (the widespread 1938 murder of Jews and destruction of synagogues and businesses by Nazi thugs) in a kind of nation-wide *Volksfest*. Yet Sarah Gordon, in her authoritative *Hitler, Germans, and the "Jewish Question"* wrote: "there was a torrent of reports indicating public disapproval of Kristallnacht ... [whatever the motivation] what is not in doubt, however, is the fact that the majority did disapprove ... after Kristallnacht, the Nazis deliberately tried to conceal their measures against the Jews."

None of the scholarly critics made much of an impression on audiences that witnessed the debates in the United States or during Goldhagen's tour of Germany late last summer, and certainly not on sales of the book. In any case, most of them, except for de Zayas, overlooked the function performed by a work such as Goldhagen's.

While he indicts the Germans as pathologically anti-Semitic and while some of his critics retort that, no, all of Christendom, indeed, Christianity itself, is implicated in the Jewish genocide, attention is kept fixed on the supposed single great crime of the recent past, if not of all of human history to the virtual exclusion of all others. In particular, the misdeeds of Communist regimes are unduly neglected.

A decade ago, Ernst Nolte, then of the Free University of Berlin, ignited the *Historikerstreit*, or dispute of historians, and became the target of a campaign of defamation led by the philosopher Jürgen Habermas, by asking: "Didn't the 'Gulag Archipelago' come before Auschwitz? Wasn't the 'class murder' of the Bolsheviks the logical and factual presupposition of the 'race murder' of the National Socialists?" These are still good questions. In fact, Stalinist—and Maoist—offenses, while acknowledged, are generally downplayed and have achieved nothing remotely approaching the publicity of the Nazi massacre of the Jews. In the United States, it is possible for a person who keeps abreast of the news media to encounter references to the Holocaust virtually every day of his life. Yet who has heard of Kolyma, where more people were done to death than the present official count for Auschwitz? The figures for the victims of Maoist rule that are starting to come out of China suggest a total in the range of tens of millions. Do these facts even make a dent in public consciousness?

Moreover, there is an aspect of Stalinist atrocities that is very pertinent to the "Goldhagen Debate." In their history of the Soviet Union, *Utopia in Power*, Mikhail Heller and Aleksandr M. Nekrich touch on the issue of whether the German people had full knowledge of the Nazi crimes. They state no opinion. But regarding the Soviets' murderous war on the peasantry, including the Ukrainian terror famine, they write:

> There is no question that the Soviet city people knew about the massacre in the countryside. In fact, no one tried to conceal it. At the railroad stations, city dwellers could see the thousands of women and children who had fled from the villages and were dying of hunger. Kulaks, "dekulakized persons," and "kulak henchmen" died alike. They were not considered human.

There has been no outcry for the Russian people to seek atonement and no one speaks of their "eternal guilt." It goes without saying that the misdeeds of Communism, in Russia, China, and elsewhere are never debited to internationalism and egalitarianism as those of Nazism are to nationalism and racism.

Pointing to Communist crimes is not meant to "trivialize" the destruction of European Jewry, nor can it do so. The massacre of the Jews was one of the worst things that ever happened. But even supposing that it was the worst thing that ever happened, couldn't some arrangement be worked out whereby Communist mass-murders are mentioned once for every ten times (or hundred times?) the Holocaust is brought up? Perhaps also, if we must have publicly-financed museums commemorating the foreign victims of foreign regimes, some memorial to the victims of Communism might be considered, not on the Mall itself, of course, but maybe in a low-rent area of Washington?

If the crimes of Communism go relatively unmentioned, what are we to say of crimes committed *against* Germans? One of the most pernicious legacies of Hitler, Stalin, and Mao is that any political leader responsible for less than, say, three or four million deaths is let off the hook. This hardly seems right, and it was not always so. In fact—the reader may find this incredible—there was a time when American conservatives took the lead in publicizing Allied, and especially American, atrocities against Germans. Historians and high-level journalists like William Henry Chamberlin, in *America's Second Crusade* and Freda Utley, in *The High Cost of Vengeance* pilloried those who had committed what Utley called "our crimes against humanity"—the men who directed the terror bombing of the German cities, conspired in the expulsion of some twelve million Germans from their ancestral lands in the east (in the course of which about two million died—see de Zayas's *Nemesis at Potsdam*), and plotted the "final solution of the German question" through the Morgenthau Plan. Utley even exposed the sham "Dachau trials" of German soldiers and civilians in the first years of the Allied occupation, detailing the use of methods "worthy of the GPU, the Gestapo, and the SS" to extort confessions. She insisted that the same ethical standards had to be applied to victors and vanquished alike. If not, then we were declaring that "Hitler was justified in his belief that 'might makes right.'" Both books were brought out by the late Henry Regnery, one of the last of the Old Right greats, whose house was the bastion of post-World War II revisionism, publishing works like Charles Callan Tansill's classic, *Back Door to War*.

Keeping the Nazi period constantly before our eyes serves the ideological interests of a number of influential groups. That it benefits the Zionist cause, at least as many Zionists see it, is obvious. It is highly useful also to the advocates of a globalist America. Hitler and the crying need for the great crusade to destroy him are the chief exhibits in their case against any form of American "isolationism," past or present. Any suggestion that our Soviet ally in that crusade was guilty of even greater offenses than Nazi Germany, that the United States government itself was incriminated in barbarous acts during and in the aftermath of that war, must be downplayed or suppressed, lest the historical picture grow too complex.

The obsession with the never-ending guilt of the Germans also advances the ends of those who look forward to the extinction of the nation-state and national identity, at least for the West. As the philosopher Robert Maurer argues, it inculcates in the Germans "a permanent bad conscience, and keeps them from developing any normal national self-awareness." In this way, it functions "as a model for the cosmopolitan supersession of every nationalism," which many today are striving towards. Ernst Nolte has recently suggested another strategy at work, aiming at the same goal.

Nothing is clearer than that we are in the midst of a vast campaign to delegitimize Western civilization. In this campaign, Nolte writes, radical feminism joins with Third World anti-Occidentalism and multiculturalism within the Western nations "to instrumentalize to the highest degree the 'murder of six millions Jews by the Germans,' and to place it in the larger context of the genocides by the predatory and conquering West, so that 'homo hitlerensis' ultimately appears as merely a special case of 'homo occidentalis.'" The purpose is to strike at "the cultural and linguistic homogeneity of the national states, achieved over centuries, and open the gates to a massive immigration," so that in the end the nations of the West should cease to exist.

There seem to be cultural dynamics operating that will intensify rather than abate the present fixation. Michael Wolffsohn, an Israeli-born Jew who teaches modern history in Germany, has warned that Judaism is being emptied of its religious content and linked solely to the tribulations of the Jews through history, above all, the Holocaust. More than one commentator has noted that as the West loses any sense of morality rooted in reason, tradition, or faith, yet still feels the need for some secure moral direction, it increasingly finds it in the one acknowledged "absolute evil," the Holocaust. If these claims are true, then the growing secularization of Judaism and the moral disarray of our culture will continue to make victims of the Germans and all the peoples of the West.

CHAPTER 6

Trotsky:
The Ignorance and the Evil

(*Leon Trotsky* • Irving Howe • Viking Press, 1978)

Leon Trotsky has always had a certain appeal for intellectuals that the other Bolshevik leaders lacked. The reasons for this are clear enough. He was a writer, an occasional literary critic—at least according to Irving Howe, a very good one—and a historian (of the revolutions of 1905 and 1917). He had an interest in psychoanalysis and modern developments in physics, and even when in power suggested that the new Communist thought-controllers shouldn't be too harsh on writers with such ideas—not exactly a Nat Hentoff position on freedom of expression, but about as good as one can expect among Communists.

Above all, Trotsky was himself an intellectual, and one who played a great part in what many of that breed consider to be *the real world*—the world of revolutionary bloodshed and terror. He

---

This review is a slightly modified version of one that originally appeared in *Libertarian Review*, March 1979.

was second only to Lenin in 1917; in the Civil War he was the leader of the Red Army and the Organizer of Victory. As Howe says, "For intellectuals throughout the world there was something fascinating about the spectacle of a man of words transforming himself through sheer will into a man of deeds."

Trotsky lost out to Stalin in the power struggle of the 1920s, and in exile became a severe critic of his great antagonist. Thus, for intellectuals with no access to other critics of Stalinism—classical liberal, anarchist, conservative, or social democratic—Trotsky's writings in the 1930s opened their eyes to some aspects at least of the charnel house that was Stalin's Russia. During the period of the Great Purge and the Moscow show trials, Trotsky was placed at the center of the myth of treason and collaboration with Germany and Japan that Stalin spun as a pretext for eliminating his old comrades. In 1940, an agent of the Soviet secret police, Ramón Mercader, sought Trotsky out at his home in Mexico City and killed him with an ice axe to the head.

Irving Howe, the well-known literary critic and editor of *Dissent*, tells the story of this interesting life with great lucidity, economy, and grace. The emphasis is on Trotsky's thought, with which Howe has concerned himself for almost the past 40 years. As a young man, he states, "I came for a brief time under Trotsky's influence, and since then, even though or perhaps because I have remained a socialist, I have found myself moving farther and farther away from his ideas."

Howe is in fact considerably more critical of Trotsky than I had expected. He identifies many of Trotsky's crucial errors, and uses them to cast light on the flaws in Marxism, Leninism, and the Soviet regime that Trotsky contributed so much to creating. And yet there is a curious ambivalence in the book. Somehow the ignorance and the evil in Trotsky's life are never allowed their full weight in the balance, and, in the end, he turns out to be, in Howe's view, a hero and "titan" of the twentieth century. It's as if Howe had chosen not to think out fully the moral implications of what it means to have said and done the things that Trotsky said and did.

We can take as our first example Howe's discussion of the final outcome of Trotsky's political labors: the Bolshevik revolution and the Soviet regime. Throughout this book Howe makes cogent points regarding the real class character of this regime and other

Communist governments—which, he notes, manifested itself very early on:

> A new social stratum—*it had sprung up the very morning of the revolution*—began to consolidate itself: the party-state bureaucracy which found its support in the technical intelligentsia, the factory managers, the military officials, and, above all, the party functionaries.... To speak of a party-state bureaucracy in a country where industry has been nationalized means to speak of a new ruling elite, perhaps a new ruling class, which parasitically fastened itself upon every institution of Russian life. [emphasis in original]

Howe goes on to say that it was not to be expected that the Bolsheviks themselves would realize what they had done and what class they had actually raised to power: "It was a historical novelty for which little provision had been made in the Marxist scheme of things, except perhaps in some occasional passages to be found in Marx's writings about the distinctive social character of Oriental despotism."

This is seriously mistaken. Howe himself shows how Trotsky, in his book *1905* (a history of the Russian revolution of that year), had had a glimpse of this form of society, one in which the state bureaucracy was itself the ruling class. In analyzing the Tsarist regime, Trotsky had picked up on the strand of Marxist thought that saw the state as an *independent parasitic body*, feeding on *all* the social classes engaged in the process of production. This was a view that Marx expressed, for instance, in his *The Eighteenth Brumaire of Louis Bonaparte*.

More importantly, the class character of Marxism itself—as well as the probable consequences of the coming to power of a Marxist party—had been identified well before Trotsky's time. The famous nineteenth century anarchist Michael Bakunin—whose name does not appear in Howe's book, just as not a single other anarchist is even mentioned anywhere in it—had already subjected Marxism to critical scrutiny in the 1870s. In the course of this, Bakunin had uncovered the dirty little secret of the future Marxist state:

> The State has always been the patrimony of some privileged class or other; a priestly class, an aristocratic class, a bourgeois class, and finally a bureaucratic class.... But in the

People's State of Marx, there will be, we are told, no privileged class at all ... but there will be a government, which will not content itself with governing and administering the masses politically, as all governments do today, but which will also administer them economically, concentrating in its own hands the production and the just division of wealth, the cultivation of land, the establishment and development of factories, the organization and direction of commerce, finally the application of capital to production by the only banker, the State. All that will demand an immense knowledge and many "heads overflowing with brains" in this government. It will be the reign of *scientific intelligence*, the most aristocratic, despotic, arrogant, and contemptuous of all regimes. There will be a *new class*, a new hierarchy of real and pretended scientists and scholars. [emphasis added]

This perspective was taken up somewhat later by the Polish-Russian revolutionist, Waclaw Machajski, who held, in the words of Max Nomad, that "nineteenth century socialism was not the expression of the interests of the manual workers but the ideology of the impecunious, malcontent, lower middle-class intellectual workers ... behind the socialist 'ideal' was a new form of exploitation for the benefit of the officeholders and managers of the socialized state."

Thus, that Marxism in power would mean the rule of state functionaries was not merely intrinsically probable—given the massive increase of state power envisaged by Marxists, what else *could* it be?—but it had also been *predicted* by writers well known to a revolutionary like Trotsky. Trotsky, however, had not permitted himself to take this analysis seriously before committing himself to the Marxist revolutionary enterprise. More than that: "To the end of his days," as Howe writes, he "held that Stalinist Russia should still be designated as a 'degenerated workers' state' because it preserved the nationalized property forms that were a 'conquest' of the Russian Revolution"—as if nationalized property and the planned economy were not the *very instruments of rule* of the new class in Soviet Russia.

It remained for some of Trotsky's more critical disciples, especially Max Shachtman in the United States, to point out to their master what had actually happened in Russia: that the Revolution had not produced a "workers' State," nor was there any danger that "capitalism" would be restored, as Trotsky continued to fret it would. Instead, there had come into an existence in Russia a "bureaucratic collectivism" even more reactionary and oppressive than what had gone before.

Trotsky rejected this interpretation. In fact he had no choice. For, as Howe states, the dissidents "called into question the entire revolutionary perspective upon which [Trotsky] continued to base his politics.... There was the further possibility, if Trotsky's critics were right, that the whole perspective of socialism might have to be revised." Indeed.

To his credit, Howe recognizes that a key period for understanding Bolshevism, including the thought of Trotsky, is the period of "war communism," from 1918 to 1921. As he describes it, "Industry was almost completely nationalized. Private trade was banned. Party squads were sent into the countryside to requisition food from the peasants." The results were tragic on a vast scale. The economic system simply broke down, with all the immense suffering and all the countless deaths from starvation and disease that such a small statement implies. As Trotsky himself later put it, "The collapse of the productive forces surpassed anything of the kind that history had ever seen. The country, and the government with it, were at the very edge of the abyss."

How had this come about? Here Howe follows the orthodox interpretation: war communism was merely the product of emergency conditions, created by the Revolution and the Civil War. It was a system of "extreme measures [which the Bolsheviks] had never dreamt of in their earlier programs."

Now, this last may be, strictly speaking, correct. It may well be, that is, that the Bolsheviks had never had the slightest idea of what their aims would mean *concretely* for the economic life of Russia, how those aims would of necessity have to be implemented, or what the consequences would be.

But war communism was no mere "improvisation," whose horrors are to be chalked up to the chaos in Russia at the time. The system was *willed* and itself helped *produce* that chaos. As Paul Craig Roberts has argued in his brilliant book *Alienation and the Soviet Economy*, war communism was an attempt to translate into "Reality" the Marxist ideal: the abolition of "commodity production," of the price system and the market.

This, as Roberts demonstrates, was what Marxism was all about. This is what the end of "alienation" and the final liberation of mankind *consisted in*. Why should it be surprising that when self-confident and determined Marxists like Lenin and Trotsky seized power in a great nation, they tried to put into effect the very policy that was their whole reason for being?

As evidence for this interpretation, Roberts quotes Trotsky himself (ironically, from a book of Trotsky's writings edited by Irving Howe):

> The period of so-called "war communism" [was a period when] economic life was wholly subjected to the needs of the front ... it is necessary to acknowledge, however, that in its original conception it pursued broader aims. The Soviet government hoped and strove to develop these methods of regimentation directly into a system of planned economy in distribution as well as production. In other words, from "war communism" it hoped gradually, but without destroying the system, to arrive at genuine communism ... reality, however, came into increasing conflict with the program of "war communism." Production continually declined, and not only because of the destructive action of the war.

Roberts goes on to quote Victor Serge (a revolutionary who joined the Bolsheviks, worked for the Comintern—the Communist International—later turning against the Soviets): "The social system of those years was later called 'War Communism.' At the time it was called simply 'Communism' ... Trotsky had just written that this system would last over decades if the transition to a genuine, unfettered Socialism was to be assured. Bukharin ... considered the present mode of production to be final."

One slight obstacle was encountered, however, on the road to the abolition of the price system and the market: "Reality," as Trotsky noted, "came into increasing conflict" with the economic "system" that the Bolshevik rulers had fastened on Russia. After a few years of misery and famine for the Russian masses—there is no record of any Bolshevik leader having died of hunger in this period—the rulers thought again, and a New Economic Policy (NEP)—including elements of private ownership and allowing for some market transactions—was decreed.

TROTSKY: THE IGNORANCE AND THE EVIL   171

The significance of all this cannot be exaggerated. What we have with Trotsky and his comrades in the Great October Revolution is the spectacle of a few literary-philosophical intellectuals seizing power in a great country with the aim of overturning the whole economic system—*but without the slightest idea how an economic system works.* In *State and Revolution*, written just before he took power, Lenin wrote:

> The accounting and control necessary [for the operation of a national economy] have been *simplified* by capitalism to the utmost, till they have become the extraordinarily simple operations of watching, recording and issuing receipts, within the reach of anybody who can read and write and knows the first four rules of arithmetic. [emphasis in original]

With this piece of cretinism Trotsky doubtless agreed. And why wouldn't he? Lenin, Trotsky, and the rest had all their lives been professional revolutionaries, with no connection at all to the process of production and, except for Bukharin, no interest in the real workings of an economic system. Their concerns had been the strategy and tactics of revolution and the perpetual, monkish exegesis of the holy books of Marxism.

The nitty-gritty of how an economic system functions—how, in our world, men and women work, produce, exchange, and survive—was something from which they prudishly averted their eyes, as pertaining to the nether regions. These "materialists" and "scientific socialists" lived in a mental world where understanding Hegel, Feuerbach, and the hideousness of Eugen Dühring's philosophical errors was infinitely more important than understanding what might be the meaning of a price.

Of the actual operations of social production and exchange they had about the same appreciation as a medieval mystic. This is a common enough circumstance among intellectuals; the tragedy here is that the Bolsheviks came to rule over millions of real workers, real peasants, and real businessmen.

Howe puts the matter rather too sweetly: once in power, he says, "Trotsky was trying to think his way through difficulties no Russian Marxist had quite foreseen." And what did the brilliant intellectual propose as a solution to the problems Russia now faced? "In December 1919 Trotsky put forward a series of 'theses' [sic] before the party's Central Committee in which he argued for compulsory work and labor armies ruled through military discipline...."

So, forced labor, and not just for political opponents, but for *the whole Russian working class*. Let Daniel and Gabriel Cohn-Bendit, the left-anarchists from the May days of 1968 in Paris, take up the argument:

> "Was it so true," Trotsky asked, "that compulsory labor was always unproductive?" He denounced this view as "wretched and miserable liberal prejudice," learnedly pointing out that "chattel slavery, too, was productive" and that compulsory serf labor was in its times "a progressive phenomenon." He told the unions [at the Third Congress of Trade Unions] that "coercion, regimentation, and militarization of labor were no mere emergency measures and that the workers' State *normally* had the right to coerce *any* citizen to perform any work at any place of its choosing." [emphasis in original]

And why not? Hadn't Marx and Engels, in their ten-point program for revolutionary government in *The Communist Manifesto*, demanded as point eight, "Equal liability for all to labor. Establishment of industrial armies, especially for agriculture"? Neither Marx nor Engels ever disavowed their claim that those in charge of "the workers' state" had the right to enslave the workers and peasants whenever the need might arise. Now, having annihilated the hated market, the Bolsheviks found that the need for enslavement had, indeed, arisen. And of all the Bolshevik leaders, the most ardent and aggressive advocate of forced labor was Leon Trotsky.

There are other areas in which Howe's critique of Trotsky is not penetrating enough, in which it turns out to be altogether too soft-focused and oblique. For instance, he taxes Trotsky with certain philosophical contradictions stemming from his belief in "historical materialism." All through his life, Howe asserts, Trotsky employed "moral criteria by no means simply derived from or reducible to class interest. He would speak of honor, courage, and truth as if these were known constants, for somewhere in the orthodox Marxist there survived a streak of nineteenth century Russian ethicism, earnest and romantic."

Let us leave aside the silly implication that there is something "romantic" about belief in ethical values as against the "scientific" character of orthodox Marxism. In this passage, Howe seems to be saying that adherence to certain commonly accepted values is, among Marxists, a rare kind of atavism on Trotsky's part. Not at all.

Of course historical materialism dismisses ethical rules as nothing more than the "expression," or "reflection," or whatever, of "underlying class relationships" and, ultimately, of "the material productive forces." But no Marxist has ever taken this seriously, except as pretext for *breaking* ethical rules (as when Lenin and Trotsky argued in justification of their terror). Even Marx and Engels, in their "Inaugural Address of the First International," wrote that the International's foreign policy would be to "vindicate the simple laws of morals and justice [sic] which ought to govern the relations of private individuals, as the laws paramount of the intercourse of nations."

That Trotsky admired honor, courage, and truth is not something that cries out for explanation by reference to some Russian tradition of "ethicism" (whatever that might be). The admiration of those values is a part of the common heritage of us all. To think that there is a problem here that needs explaining is to take "historical materialism" much too seriously to begin with.

Similarly with other contradictions Howe thinks he has discovered between Trotsky's Marxist philosophy and certain statements Trotsky made in commenting on real political events. Of the Bolshevik Revolution itself, Trotsky says that it would have taken place even if he had not been in Petrograd, "on condition that Lenin was present and in command." Howe asks, "What happens to historical materialism?" The point Howe is making, of course, is that in the Marxist view individuals are not allowed to play any critical role in shaping really important historical events, let alone in determining whether or not they occur.

But the answer to Howe's question is that, when Trotsky commits a blunder like this, *nothing* happens. Nothing happens, because "historical materialism" was pretentious nonsense from the beginning, a political strategy rather than a philosophical position.

Occasionally, in trying to daub in some light patches of sky to make up for the dark ones in Trotsky's life, Howe begins to slip into a fantasy world. He says that in the struggle with Stalin, Trotsky was at a disadvantage, because he "fought on the terrain of the enemy, accepting the damaging assumption of a Bolshevik monopoly of power." But why is this assumption located on the enemy's terrain? Trotsky shared that view with Stalin. He no more believed that a supporter of capitalism had a right to propagate his ideas than a Spanish inquisitor believed in a witch's right to her own personal lifestyle. And as for the rights even of other socialists—Trotsky in 1921 had led the attack on the Kronstadt rebels, who merely demanded freedom for socialists other than the Bolsheviks. At the time, Trotsky boasted that the rebels would be shot "like partridges"—as, pursuant to his orders, they were.

Howe even stoops to trying a touch of pathos. In sketching the tactics Stalin used in the struggle with Trotsky, he speaks of "the organized harassment to which Trotskyist leaders, distinguished Old Bolsheviks, were subjected by hooligans in the employ of the party apparatus, the severe threats made against all within the party...." Really, now—is it political violence used against *Leon Trotsky* and his "distinguished" followers that is supposed to make our blood run cold? No: if there was ever a satisfying case of poetic justice, the "harassment" and "persecution" of Trotsky—down to and including the ice axe incident—is surely it.

The best example of Howe's strange gentleness toward Trotsky I have left for last. What, when all is said and done, was Trotsky's picture of the Communist society of the future? Howe does quote from Trotsky's *Literature and Revolution* the famous, and ridiculous, last lines: "The average human type [Trotsky wrote] will rise to the heights of an Aristotle, a Goethe, or a Marx. And above this ridge new peaks will rise." He doesn't, however, tell us what precedes these lines—Trotsky's sketch of the future society, his passionate dream. Under Communism, Trotsky states, Man will

> reconstruct society and himself in accordance with his own plan.... The imperceptible, ant-like piling up of quarters and streets, brick by brick, from generation to generation, will give way to the titanic construction of city-villages, with map and compass in hand.... Communist life will not be formed blindly, like coral islands, but will be built up consciously, will be erected and corrected.... Even purely physiologic life will become subject to collective experiments. The human species, the coagulated *Homo sapiens*, will once more enter into a state of radical transformation, and, in his own hands, will become an object of the most complicated methods of artificial selection and psycho-physical training.... [It

will be] possible to reconstruct fundamentally the traditional family life.... The human race will not have ceased to crawl on all fours before God, kings and capital, in order later to submit humbly before the laws of heredity and sexual selection!... Man will make it his purpose ... to create a higher social biological type, or, if you please, a superman.

"Man ... *his* own plan ... *his* purpose ... *his* own hands." When Trotsky promoted the formation of worker-slave armies in industry, he believed that his own will was the will of Proletarian Man. It is easy to guess whose will would stand in for that of Communist Man when the time came to direct the collective experiments on the physiological life, the complicated methods of artificial selection and psycho-physiological training, the reconstruction of the traditional family, the substitution of "something else" for blind sexual selection in the reproduction of human beings, and the creation of the superman.

This, then, is Trotsky's final goal: a world where mankind is "free" in the sense that Marxism understands the term—where all of human life, starting from the economic, but going on to embrace everything, even the most private and intimate parts of human existence—is consciously *planned* by "society," which is assumed to have a single will. And it is *this*—this disgusting positivist nightmare—that, for him, made all the enslavement and killings acceptable.

Surely, this was another dirty little secret that Howe had an obligation to let us in on.

Howe ends by saying of Trotsky that "the example of his energy and heroism is likely to grip the imagination of generations to come," adding that, "even those of us who cannot heed his word may recognize that Leon Trotsky, in his power and his fall, is one of the titans of our century."

This is the kind of writing that covers the great issues of right and wrong in human affairs with a blanket of historicist snow. The fact is that Trotsky used his talents to take power in order to impose his willful dream—the abolition of the market, private property, and the bourgeoisie. His actions brought untold misery and death to his country

Yet, to the end of his life, he tried in every way he could to bring the Marxist revolution to other peoples—to the French, the

Germans, the Italians, even the Americans—with what probable consequences if successful, he, better than anyone else, had reason to know. He was a champion of thought-control, prison camps, and the firing squad for his opponents, and of forced labor for ordinary, non-brilliant working people. He openly defended chattel slavery—which, even in our century, must surely put him into a quite select company.

He was an intellectual who never asked himself such a simple question as: "What reason do I have to believe that the economic condition of workers under socialism will be better than under capitalism?" To the last, he never permitted himself to glimpse the possibility that the bloody, bureaucratic tyranny over which Stalin presided might never have come into existence but for his own efforts.

A hero? Well, no, thank you—I'll find my own heroes elsewhere. A titan of the the twentieth century? In a sense, yes. Leon Trotsky shares with the other "titans" of our century this characteristic: it would have been better if he had never been born.

CHAPTER 7

The Two "Testaments" of American Foreign Policy

(*Promised Land, Crusader State: The American Encounter with the World since 1776* • Walter A. McDougall • Houghton Mifflin, 1997)

As the title suggests, in this work Walter A. McDougall, professor of international relations at Penn and Pulitzer Prize winner, examines the whole history of U.S. foreign policy, utilizing religious terminology. His examination yields an American "Bible," which happens to be divided into two "Testaments," each containing four "Books."

The "Old Testament," which dominated the rhetoric and "for the most part, the practice," from the founding to the last decade of the nineteenth century, preached the doctrines of Liberty (or Exceptionalism), Unilateralism (often "mislabeled Isolationism"), the American System (or the Monroe Doctrine), and Expansion (or Manifest Destiny). Similarly, in the twentieth century, rhetoric and for the most part practice have been under the sway of a "New Testament"

This somewhat modified discussion of Walter A. McDougall's *Promised Land, Crusader State: The American Encounter with the World since 1776* (Houghton Mifflin, 1997) first appeared in *The Independent Review*, Fall, 1998.

composed of Progressive Imperialism, Wilsonianism (or Liberal Internationalism), Containment, and, today increasingly, Global Meliorism. (The capitalizations are McDougall's.) Each of these doctrines remains a part of "the collection of options" available to the United States in its international dealings. For the record, the author's use of religious terminology and frequent religious imagery is of no evident heuristic value and diverts attention from sources of American foreign policy originating far from religious faith.

McDougall's presentation of the first tradition—liberty, or exceptionalism—is well done. He states that to the Republic's founding generation, America's calling "was not *to do* anything special in foreign affairs, but *to be* a light to lighten the world" (p. 20; emphasis in original). The Founders "agreed to limit the content of American Exceptionalism to Liberty at home, period" (p. 21). He sums it up pithily: "Foreign policy existed to defend, not define, what America was" (p. 37).

His exposition of the second tradition, unilateralism, presents conceptual problems, however. First of all, if Washington's Farewell Address is its inaugurating document, it is not a tradition separate from liberty, but simply the means of defending the first tradition. Moreover, one of McDougall's main purposes throughout is to show that unilateralism was not isolationism, which in fact never existed. "Our vaunted tradition of 'isolationism,'" he states, "is no tradition at all, but a dirty word that interventionists, especially since Pearl Harbor, hurl at anyone who questions their policies" (p. 40). That the term functions as a smear and a proven method of forestalling debate is true enough. But it is hard to see how Washington's doctrine can be equated with McDougall's unilateralism. After all, it is possible to pursue a policy of intense global activism *unilaterally*.

McDougall tries to debunk the customary isolationist interpretation of the Farewell Address. As Washington put it, "taking care always to keep ourselves by suitable establishments on a respectable defensive posture, we may safely trust to temporary alliances for extraordinary emergencies." And, he declared, "The great rule of conduct for us in regard to foreign nations is, in extending our commercial relations to have with them as little *political* connection as possible" (emphasis in original). The latter statement was the motto Richard Cobden, the greatest libertarian thinker on international relations, placed on the title page of his first published pamphlet.

THE TWO "TESTAMENTS" OF AMERICAN FOREIGN POLICY 179

The author comments that "real isolationism" would have required "an unequivocal denunciation of *all* cooperation with foreign powers" (p. 47). Even treaties on fisheries? Again and again, McDougall implies that isolationism has to mean a kind of pre-Meiji Japanese closure to the rest of the world. Why this strange insistence? Because, ultimately, McDougall wants to maintain that, despite surface appearances, Washington's "unilateralism" "meshes rather well" with his own favored policy, containment in the post–World War II and post-Soviet periods. That containment involves numerous entangling alliances is a negligible point, because the United States is always "in control."

Thus the rupture with our founding policy is whisked away. But that move is merely a conjurer's trick. For how does the rationale for NATO in its past or presently expanding forms meet Washington's criterion of "extraordinary emergencies"? How can an alliance already lasting half a century count as "temporary"? Do we presently have "as little *political* connection" with foreign countries as possible? One wonders also whether great armies and navies stationed all around the globe are really what the Founders had in mind for America.

In general, McDougall's treatment of the "mythical beast" of "pure isolationism" is confused and confusing. He refers to it as "an ostrich posture in foreign policy" (who would ever adopt that?), and he claims that the flow of capital and labor to the United States and expanding American overseas trade are evidence of the absence of isolationism in the nineteenth century (the pre-Meiji model). McDougall asks, "When did Americans first act on the belief that they had a mission to transform foreign societies?" It was back "in 1819, when the American Board of Foreign Missions decided to evangelize the Sandwich (Hawaiian) Islands." The donation of tens of millions of dollars to foreign missions "prefigured the governmental aid projects of the mid-twentieth century" (pp. 174–75). To argue in this fashion is to blot out, for whatever reason, the basic distinction between civil society, based on voluntarism, and the state, based on coercion.

In any case, McDougall at one point concedes that the Old Testament traditions, in contrast with what came later, "were coherent, mutually supportive, and reflective of our original image of America as a Promised Land" (p. 5). This view is not far from Charles

Beard's in *A Foreign Policy for America* (New York: Knopf, 1940). What McDougall calls the Old Testament, Beard called Continental Americanism. The purpose of our foreign policy has indeed been to protect the unique civilization growing up on this continent. (Beard was too much a progressive to talk about liberty in any Jeffersonian sense.) Continental expansion served to round out our territory, providing largely empty lands for settlement. These additions required only small land forces, and their defense entailed no "entanglements with the great powers of Europe or Asia" — in the cases of Florida and the Louisiana Purchase, they entailed *ejection* of European powers. Thus, they brought with them no danger of serious conflicts. The Monroe Doctrine served the same purpose, because the presence of European powers in Mexico, Central America, or the Caribbean would embroil us in the aggressive diplomacy of the Old World and pose a clear danger of war.

Avoiding war was always the fundamental rationale for isolationism (of course, "neutrality" or "non-intervention" would be preferable terms, but replacing the old slander may by now be impossible). James Madison wrote of war as perhaps the greatest of all enemies of public liberty, producing armies, debts, and taxes, "the known instruments for bringing the many under the domination of the few." Everything abhorrent about the European monarchies was connected with the fact that they were war machines — "nations of eternal war," in James Monroe's words. If we followed their example, we would fall prey to a host of Old World evils, which would wreck our constitutional balance. Accordingly, we were ready to recognize de facto governments as legitimate, and through much of the nineteenth century our navy — the necessary tool for global meddling — was such that, as McDougall states, it was "incapable of beating up on Chile" (p. 73).

Those whom historians have labeled "isolationists" never adopted an "ostrich posture." They argued general principles — the horrors of war, the burdens on the people, the dangers of increased state power, the likely distortions of our constitutional system — but they also argued from the specific circumstances of their times. Such was the case with Robert La Follette in 1917, the America Firsters of 1940–41, and the foes of NATO in 1949, as well as the first great isolationist movement, the Anti-Imperialist League, at the turn of the century. It should not go unremarked that McDougall indulges in a bit of smearing of his own, when he refers to the Anti-Imperialist League as a group of "strange bedfellows," "mostly mugwumps who bemoaned all the change industrialization had wrought in American life" (p. 113; Andrew Carnegie as an enemy of industrialization?). Instead of dealing with their reasoning, McDougall resorts to the usual ploy of writing off as hankerers after a vanished (or imaginary) Golden Age anyone who stood in the way of the imperialist juggernaut. He touches on Carl Schurz's objections to the Philippines war, which nowadays sound "racist" to many. But he avoids mentioning what is surely the best-known and most enduring contribution of those gallant anti-imperialists, William Graham Sumner's formidable critique, "The Conquest of the United States by Spain."

It is difficult to know how to tackle *Promised Land, Crusader State*. It consists largely of obiter dicta, written in an excessively (to my taste) breezy style, in which the author almost never pauses to debate a point. For example, McDougall calls Eric Nordlinger, the author of the excellent *Isolationism Reconfigured*, "by far the most sophisticated 'neo-isolationist' " (p. 201), but does not even suggest a rebuttal of Nordlinger's arguments.

Some of the book's faults, however, may be gathered by looking at McDougall's treatment of Wilson and U.S. participation in the First World War. The American note to Berlin following the sinking of the *Lusitania* was hardly "stern but innocuous." It embraced the ridiculous principle that the U.S. government had the right and duty to protect U.S. citizens traveling on ships flying the flags of belligerents. By holding the Germans to "strict accountability" for any American lives lost through U-boat action, it set the United States on a collision course with Germany. The Zimmermann telegram, offering Mexico an alliance *in case* war broke out between Germany and the United States, was stupid and futile, but, given that hostilities were imminent, hardly "infamous"—that was Wilson's line. The author endorses U.S. entry into the war because a triumphant Germany would have dominated the Atlantic. But, even assuming that our non-intervention would have led to a total German victory (highly doubtful), more probable results than German control of the Atlantic would have been the downfall of the Bolsheviks in Russia and the prevention of Hitler's coming to power.

The most serious defect, however, is that from time to time McDougall pays lip service to the notion that, when all is said and done, the purpose of our foreign policy is to defend our freedom at home. At the end, he lists some of the evils besetting us today: high taxes, an intrusive central government, a "semi-militarized economy," an immense welfare state fed by "a lust for public entitlement," besides a number of what are called social problems. He concludes that we must "husband the rare liberty and fragile unity our ancestors won" (p. 222).

Pious sentiments. But just how seriously can we take his concern for American liberty when, in discussing Wilson and justifying the entry into Wilson's war, McDougall breathes not a word regarding the war's frightful cost to that liberty? The savage assault on economic freedoms and civil liberties and the precedents created for their subsequent erosion are well known (see the section on Wilsonian authoritarianism in the essay on World War I, in the present volume). Why were these outcomes not worth mentioning, as actual results of the war, to balance the *speculative* danger of New Jersey's quaking under the guns of an Imperial German *Kriegsflotte*? In fact, World War I presents a perfect illustration of why the Founders wished to keep clear of war, and McDougall's silence is itself exemplary of how involvement in foreign wars leads to ignoring the destruction of liberty at home.

Still, in contrast to many other analysts, the author makes some useful points. "Vietnam was a liberal war," he rightly states (p. 195). "The mythology that enveloped the Marshall Plan" (p. 180) set the stage for attempts to fabricate viable and prosperous societies through the infusion of American billions. (He could have strengthened his case had he been familiar with Tyler Cowen's demolition of that mythology, "The Marshall Plan: Myths and Realities," in *U.S. Aid to the Developing World: A Free Market Agenda*.) Lyndon Johnson's statement that "our foreign policy must always be an extension of our domestic policy" promised disaster, because his domestic program was the War on Poverty. Now U.S. aims included ending ignorance and disease in a far-off land in the throes of a revolution. McDougall aptly remarks, "South Vietnam's cities—like much of inner-city America—soon became corrupt and dependent welfare zones" (p. 193).

McDougall confutes the current shibboleth of the urgent need for the United States to spread "democracy" throughout the world. Other peoples may democratically choose anti-liberal regimes. In any case, what business is it of ours? He is soundest on foreign aid, where he has clearly learned from the great Peter Bauer, whom he cites. "Our half-century of experience with foreign aid has been almost a total loss" (p. 209). The method used, government-to-government aid, is intrinsically statist. The blunder continues today, as "we attempt to teach ex-Soviet peoples how to be good capitalists through the medium of government grants administered by government agencies for the benefit of our own and foreign bureaucracies" (p. 209). If other countries want a market economy and American-style democracy, "they know what steps to take to achieve them" (p. 210). We should use aid bribes to advance American security, for instance, in persuading the Russians to dismantle their nuclear warheads (of course, as we dismantle our own). "Otherwise, the best way to promote our institutions and values abroad is to strengthen them at home" (p. 210). Good advice, as the author tries once again to demonstrate his allegiance to the first and most American of the "books" of American foreign policy.

But ultimately that effort won't wash. While McDougall rejects global meliorism, what he advocates is a highly interventionist form of containment, including preventing disturbances from regional powers such as Iraq and Iran; using the government to expand trade (NAFTA, GATT, and "jawboning Beijing"); joining in Margaret Thatcher's "New Atlantic Initiative" (why, incidentally, is this lady, who pressed the first Bush to go to war in the Gulf and was the last-ditch friend of Gorbachev and last-ditch foe of German reunification, supposed to be worth listening to?); and, above all, maintaining "the balance of power" throughout Eurasia. This last task alone gives U.S. leaders license to extend their activities, if not to Rwanda and Colombia, then virtually anywhere else they wish.

In the end, *Promised Land, Crusader State* turns out to be disappointingly superficial, never even broaching key questions. We are told, for instance, that the American public "never raised a ruckus" over this or that interventionist move. Yet there is no hint of the unfathomed ignorance, "rational" or otherwise, of Americans in foreign affairs. Even George Will, a Princeton Ph.D., who constantly pontificates on the Middle East, thought Iranians were Arabs. No hint of the leverage that ignorance gives to political elites and special interests pushing their own agendas. Why suppose that U.S. leaders are immune to such pressures or to the blandishments of institutional and personal power? Why even assume that they are any better—any more expert or far-seeing or public-spirited—in handling international relations than they are in running domestic affairs? If they aren't, why shouldn't they be reined in, sharply?

Most important, how is incessant intervention abroad compatible with the Herculean task of restoring liberty at home? In reality, McDougall doesn't have an inkling of how radical and hard that task will be. It is vanishingly improbable that our leaders and their supporting political class will cheerfully welcome the changes required. Much more likely is that, faced with any real challenge to the status quo, they will exploit the range of pretexts McDougall affords them, resorting, in Richard Cobden's words, to "the true secret of despots"—"to employ one nation in cutting the throats of another, so that neither may have time to reform the abuses in their own domestic government."

CHAPTER 8

The Other War that Never Ends: A Survey of Some Recent Literature on World War I

The Second World War has been called the war that never ends. To a lesser degree, the same could be said of the First World War. It has been estimated, for instance, that the Yale library has 34,000 titles on that conflict published before 1977 and more than 5,000 since.

What I propose to do in this chapter is to survey a few recent works.

Michael Howard, *The First World War* (Oxford University Press, 2002)

The author is, in fact, *Sir* Michael Howard. It is significant that Howard was knighted, when A. J. P. Taylor, for one, an infinitely more interesting historian—even with all his faults—never got close to that. Knighthood in Britain plays something of the same role that

---

This is based on a talk delivered at the Mises Institute, Auburn, Alabama, and published by the *Mises Daily* on April 19, 2004.

the Legion of Honor, founded by Napoleon, does in France. It rewards men who have spent their lives promoting the interests of the state. In this way it permanently skews the country's intellectual life towards the state and its beneficent wonderfulness.

It is a question worth considering in an idle moment whether there has ever been a military historian more boring than Michael Howard. His unending banalities contrast sharply with the works of two great past British historians of warfare, J. F. C. Fuller and Basil Liddell Hart, of whom Charles de Gaulle said he was a captain who taught generals.

Besides his knighthood, Howard has been showered with other honors. He has held prestigious chairs at King's College, London and at Yale, and the Chair of History of War and the Regius professorship of Modern History at Oxford. I understand, incidentally that at Yale he did not exactly overwhelm the history faculty with his immense learning and analytical skill.

In the foreword to his book, Howard writes that "it was the ruling circles in Imperial Germany who were ultimately responsible, both for the outbreak and for the continuance of the war," and regrets that he will not have space to argue this thesis.

That is truly a pity, since his thesis here is, shall we say, rather central to the whole issue of the First World War.

Some scatterbrain schoolboy mistakes: Sir Michael lists the Greeks and the Romanians (twice) as among the Slavic peoples of the Balkans, and Slavs as a nationality along with the Czechs and Slovaks. In addition, the First Balkan War of 1912 did not reduce Turkey to a "bridgehead around Adrianople." Rather, that city was included in an expanded Bulgaria; it was regained by Turkey in the Second Balkan War of 1913.

But these are errors that Oxford University Press presumably considers trivial, just as in the *Oxford History of the Twentieth Century*, co-edited by Michael Howard and published in 1998, we read of Auschwitz, that "approximately 4 million people were killed [there] in the Nazi 'Final Solution' to the 'Jewish problem' in Europe." That figure of four million has long since been discarded by every knowledgeable student of the Holocaust as too high by two or three million for Auschwitz alone.

Anti-German clichés abound in Howard's book. The German ruling elite—there is no mention of any British ruling elite—was

THE OTHER WAR THAT NEVER ENDS 187

characterized by "archaic militarism, vaulting ambition, and neurotic insecurity." Prussia had been created by its army—unlike, one supposes, France and Russia. He claims that German policy towards the civilian populations of the eastern territories they conquered "grimly foreshadowed their behavior in the Second [World War]," a statement for which Sir Michael provides no evidence and which is simply absurd.

There are occasional insights. Howard makes a telling point when he states that the potential for belligerent nationalism had been inculcated for a century by state education, assisted by conscription. In an increasingly secularized society, "the Nation ... acquired a quasi-religious significance." He is good on the Allied infringement of Greek neutrality—the landing of troops at Salonika—and on the secret treaties, with Italy and others, that divided up the anticipated spoils of war. He realizes that the Balfour Declaration endorsing Zionism was a betrayal of promises the British had made to the Arabs.

Yet, finally, Howard writes of the Versailles treaty that, "most of its provisions have stood the test of time. The new states it created survived, if within fluctuating borders, until the last decade of the century...." No hint that these new states underwent certain well-known wrenching vicissitudes in the 80 years from Versailles to the collapse of Soviet Communism, nor of the role of the Treaty in the rise of Nazism and the outbreak of the Second World War.

Fred Barnes, one of Rupert Murdoch's stable of neocon masterminds, reviewed Sir Michael's book in the *Weekly Standard* and concluded that "for someone who is just starting to explore the war, Howard's book is the place to begin."

No, it isn't, not at all. At the end of this chapter I will mention which of the new crop of books *is* the place to start.

Thomas Fleming, *The Illusion of Victory: America in World War I* (Basic Books, 2003)

I was not as fond as others were of Fleming's earlier work, *The New Dealers' War: FDR and the War within World War II*. Besides serious problems inherent in Fleming's style and approach, I could not agree with his conclusion that Harry Truman was the godsend who made good the damage caused by Roosevelt and the political genius who started America on the glorious road to a half-century of Cold War.

Fleming's level of reasoning on economic and social issues was already apparent in his earlier book, where he wrote:

> Henry Wallace was probably the most successful secretary of agriculture [in history]. He created an "ever normal granary" in which the government worked with farmers to keep prices reasonably high and provide the nation with protection against food shortages.

Clearly, Fleming's understanding of economics is on a par with that of your average U.S. Congressman.

As in the earlier work, many pages are devoted to the massive bungling of the government's war effort. Fleming frames these incidents as a kind of shocking exposé. He seems unaware that for the U.S. government, mismanagement on an appalling scale is simply Standard Operating Procedure. Earlier this month, the General Accounting Office reported that the Defense Department may have spent as much as $8 billion (sic) in fiscal 2003 reworking software "because of quality-related issues." After running through trillions of dollars, the Pentagon was so lacking in military cargo planes during the invasion of Iraq that it had to hire Russian aircraft to ferry tanks and other materiel. The Navy is now so short of money that it requires pilots to fly simulators rather than real jets to practice carrier landings, according to Vice Admiral Charles W. Moore, Jr., Deputy Chief of Naval Operations. All SOP—discreetly hidden from the people by the complicit media—for the American state.

Fleming goes on and on over well-trodden ground. There is much "human interest" material, most of it irrelevant. One item, though, I found interesting. The soldiers in the American Expeditionary Force were expected to refrain from fraternizing with French women. General Pershing sternly declared that his ideal for the young doughboys was "continence." At the same time, throughout his stay in France Pershing enjoyed the company of his French-Romanian mistress, an artist named Micheline Resco—another example of the Latin tag that Thomas Szasz likes to quote, "Quod licet jovi, non licet bovi": "what is permitted to Jove is not permitted to a cow."

The author repeats the legend of Clemenceau's "vicious wisecrack" that "there are 20 million Germans too many." Jean Stengers, of the University of Brussels, and others have shown this to be a myth. Unfortunately, it was widely believed in Germany, including by Adolf Hitler, and may well have contributed to his notion of what the French philosopher Louis Rougier called "zoological warfare."

It is to Fleming's credit that he severely criticizes Woodrow Wilson. But here he isn't nearly as informative or analytical as Walter Karp in his brilliant work, *The Politics of War*. Actually, my favorite description of Wilson's character is by Sigmund Freud, in the book he wrote together with William C. Bullitt, *Thomas Woodrow Wilson, Twenty-eighth President of the United States: A Psychological Study*. Here is Freud on Wilson at the Paris Peace Conference:

> He was rapidly nearing that psychic land from which few travelers return, the land in which facts are the products of wishes, in which friends betray, and in which a chair in an asylum may be the throne of God.

That is a classic example of the psycho-smear, as practiced by its unrivaled master.

But when it comes to the fundamentals of policy, Fleming characteristically takes a middle of the road position: he is in favor, for instance, of U.S. entry into the League of Nations with the qualifications proposed by Henry Cabot Lodge. *The Illusion of Victory*, like his book on Roosevelt's war, shows Fleming to be much less of a maverick and debunker than he likes to think.

Niall Ferguson, *The Pity of War: Explaining World War I* (Basic Books, 1999)

I have to confess that I am prejudiced against Niall Ferguson. In the first place, because he has made himself into a media "celebrity intellectual" to a degree unprecedented in recent times. But more because, a few years ago, I saw him on C-Span, on a panel sponsored by *The New Republic*. Ferguson was just becoming popular in the United States, and he obviously knew which side his bread was buttered on. He was all smiles and geniality, sitting next to that pompous fake Daniel Goldhagen, who was also being lionized by *The New Republic* people. I got the distinct impression that Ferguson was basically untrustworthy.

The Pity of War confirms my impression.

It is a gimmicky book, which largely accounts for the splash it made. What mainly drew attention was the author's claim that it might well have been a good idea for Britain to have stayed out of the war, which would have made it a continental instead of a world war. He tends to feel that if Britain—and America—had remained aloof, "the victorious Germans might have created a version of the European Union eight decades ahead of schedule." German war aims were relatively modest at the start, he believes, and the Germans offered to give Britain as well as Belgium guarantees to assure their neutrality. It was only once the war began and Britain joined in that an extravagant pan-German annexationist program materialized.

This sounds gimmicky to me. In the absence of the British Expeditionary Force and active Belgian resistance, it is likely that what remained of the Schlieffen Plan would have worked. In any case, absent British, and later American, presence on the Western Front, it is hard to see how a German victory in the war could have been avoided.

Not to worry, says Ferguson. Most likely that would simply have meant a more or less benevolent German hegemony on the continent.

But it is not at all clear why a triumphant Germany, having subdued Russia and France, would bother to keep any engagements it had made with England.

And there's another consideration. A more recent work of Ferguson's is *Empire: The Rise and Demise of the British World Order and the Lessons for Global Power.* There he argues that, when all is said and done, the British Empire and the "Pax Britannica" it undergirded represented a great boon for mankind. Leaving aside the validity of that claim, the question is what would have happened to this wonderful British Empire in the event of Germany's becoming the unquestioned European hegemon? The Kaiser and the rest of the German elite openly aimed at making Germany a *world* power. Many influential Germans spoke of establishing settler colonies in various parts of the world, including South America.

Ferguson blithely states that "German objectives, had Britain stayed out, would not in fact have posed a direct threat to the Empire: the reduction of Russian power in Eastern Europe"—I like that, "reduction"; think of the Treaty of Brest-Litovsk—"the creation of a Central European Customs Union and acquisition of French colonies—these were all goals which were complementary to British interests."

This is how you write path-breaking books: implausible speculation regarding historical counterfactuals.

On the stories of the Belgian atrocities, Ferguson makes use, as everyone must, of the 2001 work by John Horne and Alan Kramer, *German Atrocities, 1914: A History of Denial*. Citing the letters and diaries of German soldiers and other materials, the authors show that in the invasion of Belgium, German troops executed something over 5,500 Belgian civilians. These civilians were killed because of their suspected, but non-existent, role as *francs-tireurs* (guerrilla fighters) or in reprisals against Belgian townspeople and villagers in connection with such imagined guerrilla actions.

Ferguson states that the Belgian atrocity stories, long lampooned by revisionists, were "based on truth"; indeed, he claims that the stories were effective *because* they were based on truth.

He does concede that "the Entente press wildly exaggerated what went on in Belgium." But the press did that, not on its own account, but rather on the basis of the official British government report on the atrocities, known as the Bryce Report. Ferguson ignores the fact that what incensed the public wasn't merely the claim that Germans had executed civilians thought to be guerrillas, or simply committed reprisals because of perceived guerrilla activity. The truth about Belgium would hardly have created the firestorm of rage against the Germans that British propaganda aimed for. It was all the gruesome fabricated details contained in the Bryce report—the women raped *en masse*, the children with their hands cut off, the violated nuns and the Canadian soldiers crucified to barn doors—that made people's blood boil and proved German savagery. Thomas Fleming, to his credit, mentions that the *real* cases of people, including children, with their hands cut off occurred in *the Congo* beginning in the 1880s, at the behest of the Belgian king Leopold II. Because of their great extent and nearly incredible cruelty, it's *those* that deserve to be called "the Belgian atrocities."

Ferguson likewise ignores the facts regarding Tsarist *Russian* behavior on the eastern front, facts presented in the very work by Horne and Kramer he relies on. In their retreat in 1915, the Russians brutalized minority populations: Germans, Poles, Ruthenes and especially Jews. They deported at least 300,000 Lithuanians, 250,000 Latvians, 350,000 Jews, and three-quarters of a million Poles to the interior. As Horne and Kramer write: "The devastation caused by the Russian retreat of 1915 was probably greater than anything experienced by civilians in France and Belgium."

Ferguson tells us that the British sunk no ships without warning, "and no citizens of neutral countries were deliberately killed by the Royal Navy."

They would have been, however, had any neutral—in particular, the United States—insisted on its rights under international law and attempted to run the British hunger blockade.

There is no entry in Ferguson's book for Robert Lansing, the American Secretary of State. In his memoirs, Lansing openly and brazenly explains U.S. policy towards the illegal British blockade prior to America's entry in the war: "there was always in my mind the conviction that we would ultimately become an ally of Great Britain ... [once joining the British] we would presumably wish to adopt some of [their] policies and practices" aiming to "destroy the morale of the German people by an economic isolation, which would cause them to lack the very necessaries of life ... [in negotiating with the British] every word was submerged in verbiage. It was done with deliberate purpose. It ... left the questions unsettled, which was necessary in order to leave this country free to act and even act illegally when it entered the war."

While distorting the facts of the Belgian atrocities, Ferguson neglects to inform us that the illegal British hunger blockade led to the death of at least 100 times as many German civilians as civilians killed in Belgium.

Richard Gamble, *The War for Righteousness: Progressive Christianity, the Great War, and the Rise of the Messianic Nation* (ISI Press, 2003)

This highly important work was published by the ISI Press, which suggests that there are still some with Old Right tendencies in the Intercollegiate Studies Institute.

The theme of the book is how the "forward-looking clergy [progressive Protestants] embraced the war as a chance to achieve their broadly defined social gospel objectives." Thus, the situation Gamble describes is, in a sense, the opposite of the one today, when it is the leaders of "fundamentalist" Protestantism that are among the worst warmongers. In both cases, however, the main contribution of the clergy has been to translate a political conflict into apocalyptic spiritual terms.

Gamble traces the susceptibility of Americans to this view back to colonial Puritan New England. During the later eighteenth century and the Revolutionary War the conception was fixed of the United States as the brand-new nation, casting off the burdens of the past, instituting a *novus ordo seclorum*, a New Order of the Ages. The Americans were the new Chosen People, destined to lead the world to an age of reason and universal virtue.

By the end of the nineteenth century, progressive Protestants, often influenced by the theory of evolution, were preaching the successive remaking of the church, of American society, and finally of the whole world. Rejecting old-line Calvinism, they rejected also the Augustinian distinction between the City of God and the City of Man. The City of Man was to be *made into* the City of God, here on earth, through a commitment to a redefined, socially-activist Christianity. As Shailer Mathews, Dean of the University of Chicago School of Divinity, said: "As civilization develops, sin grows corporate. We sin socially by violating social rather than individualistic personal relations."

The progressive gospel was spread through the takeover of influential churches, the infiltration of prestigious seminaries and divinity schools (now offering courses in "Social Ethics" and "Christian Sociology"), the control of journals such as *Christian Century*, and, nationally, the creation of the forerunner of the National Council of Churches. At conferences sponsored by the progressive Christians, speakers included Theodore Roosevelt, William Howard Taft, and, naturally, Woodrow Wilson. Wilson claimed that the role of Christian youth was to ignore divisive "dogma" and instead to concentrate on the goal of making "the United States a mighty Christian nation, and to christianize the world!"

The vision of the progressive clergy was internationalized, as they looked to America to lead the world in accordance with God's will for human society. "Isolationism" was a selfish doctrine that had to be overcome. Many of them supported the war with Spain from this point of view. Among the supporters was Julia Ward Howe, composer of the "Battle Hymn of the Republic," who addressed progressive meetings. She reported on her vision of all mankind "advancing with one end in view, one foe to trample ... All of evil was gone from the earth ... Mankind was emancipated and ready to march forward in a new Era of human understanding ... the Era of perfect love."

Once the war in Europe began, and even more after America entered, "The Battle Hymn of the Republic" was continually cited and sung by the Christian progressives. A favorite line, of course, was "As He died to make men holy, let us die to make men free." The progressive Protestants saw World War I as a continuation of the great crusade for righteousness that was the American Civil War. As Gamble writes, "the fight for freedom had to be resumed, but this time it was to be carried to ends of the earth." Fittingly, there was a constant invocation of the hovering spirit of Abraham Lincoln.

The progressives quickly realized that President Woodrow Wilson was one of their own, flesh of their flesh. They eagerly took to his cant on the duty of national self-sacrifice and of America as the Suffering Servant. "A war of service is a thing in which it is a proud thing to die," Wilson declared, in another of his weird musings. The day was coming when the nations would realize that Old Glory was "the flag, not only of America, but of humanity." In 1915, addressing the Federal Council of Churches, Wilson asserted that America had been founded and had "its only object for existence" (sic) to lead humanity on the "high road" to universal justice.

Once the war was underway, the rhetoric of the progressive Christians grew increasingly blood-thirsty. One contingent became "militant pacifists," that is, men whose aim was world peace, but to be achieved whenever necessary by waging ongoing murderous war. As the butchery in Europe intensified, they attacked the notion of "a premature peace," an end to hostilities that would permit the continued existence of iniquitous regimes. A statement signed by over sixty eminent churchmen, including Harry Emerson Fosdick, Billy Sunday, and the president of Princeton, scorned the idea of "a premature peace:" "The just God, who withheld not his own Son from the cross, would not look with favor upon a people who put their fear of pain and death ... above the holy claims of righteousness and justice...."

On the day that national registration for the draft began, Wilson addressed a reunion of Confederate veterans. He told them that God had preserved the American Union in the Civil War so that the United States might be "an instrument in [His] hands ... to see that liberty is made secure for mankind." Regrettably, here, as before and ever after, the grandsons and great-grandsons of the valiant Confederate soldiers who resisted the North's invasion of their country took the side of their former mortal enemies. In a kind of Stockholm syndrome, of identifying with the aggressor, they identified with the Union and disproportionately supported and fought and died in its wars. That strange anomaly continues to this day.

When the time came for Congress to consider war against Germany, the people's representatives repeated the rhetoric and imagery of the progressive Protestants. One congressman stated that, "Christ gave his life upon the cross that mankind might gain the Kingdom of Heaven, while tonight we shall solemnly decree the sublimest sacrifice ever made by a nation for the salvation of humanity, the institution of world-wide liberty and freedom."

In the Second World War there was a nice sentimental propaganda song, "The White Cliffs of Dover," which went more or less like this:

> There'll be bluebirds over
> The White Cliffs of Dover,
> Tomorrow, just you wait and see.
>
> There'll be love and laughter
> And peace ever after,
> Tomorrow, when the world is free.

The poor deluded people ate that up, as they ate up the fantasies of the progressive Protestants during the Great War, as they swallow all the lies dished out to them to this day.

Of all people, H. G. Wells, the freethinker and prophet of evolution, who got religion during the war, became a favorite of the progressive clergy. Wells, who coined the phrase, "the war to end war," wrote that "the kingdom of God on earth is not a metaphor, not a mere spiritual state, not a dream ... it is the close and inevitable destiny of mankind." By the kingdom of God, it turned out, Wells meant his Fabian socialist utopia globalized, through total war against evil.

Incidentally, one of H. G. Wells's last books, published in 1944, is *Crux Ansata: An Indictment of the Roman Catholic Church*. Wells had been in charge of British propaganda during the war. The first chapter is titled, "Why Do We Not Bomb Rome?" Rome, he argued, was not only the center of Fascism, but "the seat of a Pope [Pius XII] ... who has been an open ally of the Nazi–Fascist–Shinto Axis since his enthronement." "*Why* do we not bomb Rome?... A thorough bombing (*à la* Berlin) of the Italian capital seems not simply desirable but necessary."

If the Allies had taken Wells's heartfelt advice, today tourists would be able to take photos of the ruins of St. Peter's just as they do of the ruins of the Kaiser Wilhelm Memorial Church in Berlin. *This* is the way this Fabian humanitarian ended up—screaming to have the city of Rome burned to the ground.

The progressive Protestants intertwined their warmongering with their social gospel. William Faunce, president of Brown, gloated that "the old petty individualism and laissez-faire" were dead: " 'Me' and 'mine' will be small words in a new world which has learned to say the great word 'our.' " The president of Union Theological Seminary warned that the churches had to abandon their "egoistic and other-worldly character," and "must cease to minister to selfishness by promising personal salvation"—blah, blah, blah.

I confess that the one drawback of Gamble's excellent book is having to slog through the endless high-minded drivel of these progressive Protestants.

In fact, the best introduction to the history of the World War I —and the best concise account of the war altogether—is T. Hunt Tooley's *The Western Front: Battle Ground and Home Front in the First World War*, discussed in the present volume.

CHAPTER 9

Starving a People into Submission

States throughout history have persisted in severely encumbering and even prohibiting international trade. Seldom, however, can the consequences of such an effort—the obvious immediate results as well as the likely long-range ones—have been as devastating as in the case of the Allied, really, the British, naval blockade, of Germany in the First World War. This hunger blockade belongs to the category of forgotten state atrocities of the twentieth century, of which there have been many. Who now remembers the tens of thousands of Biafrans starved to death during their war for independence through the policy of the Nigerian generals with the full support, naturally, of the government of Great Britain? Thus, C. Paul Vincent, a trained historian and currently library director at Keene State College in New Hampshire, deserves our gratitude for recalling it to memory in this scholarly and balanced study.

This review of C. Paul Vincent's *The Politics of Hunger: The Allied Blocade of Germany, 1915–1919* (Ohio University Press, 1985), slightly modified, first appeared in *The Review of Austrian Economics*, 1989.

Vincent tellingly recreates the atmosphere of jubilation that surrounded the outbreak of the war that was truly the fateful watershed of the twentieth century. While Germans were overcome by a mystical sense of community—as the economist Emil Lederer declared, now *Gesellschaft* (Society) had been transformed into *Gemeinschaft* (Community)—the British gave themselves over to their own patented form of cant. The socialist and positivist-utopian H. G. Wells gushed: "I find myself enthusiastic for this war against Prussian militarism.... Every sword that is drawn against Germany is a sword drawn for peace." Wells later coined the mendacious slogan, "the war to end war." As the conflict continued, the state-socialist current that had been building for decades overflowed into massive government intrusions into every facet of civil society, especially the economy. The German *Kriegssozialismus* that became a model for the Bolsheviks on their assumption of power is well known, but, as Vincent points out, "the British achieved control over their economy unequaled by any of the other belligerent states."

Everywhere state seizure of social power was accompanied and fostered by propaganda drives without parallel in history to that time. In this respect, the British were very much more successful than the Germans, and their masterly portrayal of the "Huns" as the diabolical enemies of civilization, perpetrators of every imaginable sort of "frightfulness,"[1] served to mask the single worst example of barbarism in the whole war, aside from the Armenian massacres. This was what Lord Patrick Devlin frankly calls "the starvation policy" directed against the civilians of the Central Powers, most particularly Germany,[2] the plan that aimed, as Winston Churchill, First Lord of the Admiralty in 1914 and one of the framers of the scheme, admitted, to "starve the whole population—men, women, and children, old and young, wounded and sound—into submission."[3]

The British policy was in contravention of international law on two major points.[4] First, in regard to the character of the blockade,

---

[1] Cf. H. C. Peterson, *Propaganda for War. The Campaign against American Neutrality, 1914–1917* (Norman, Okla.: University of Oklahoma Press, 1939), especially pp. 51–70, on propaganda regarding German atrocities.

[2] Patrick Devlin, *Too Proud to Fight: Woodrow Wilson's Neutrality* (New York: Oxford University Press, 1975), pp. 193–98.

[3] Cited in Peterson, *Propaganda*, p. 83.

[4] Cf. Devlin, *Too Proud to Fight*, pp. 158–67, 191–200; and Thomas A. Bailey and Paul B. Ryan, *The Lusitania Disaster: An Episode in Modern Warfare and Diplomacy* (New York: Free Press, 1975), pp. 27–33.

it violated the Declaration of Paris of 1856, which Britain itself had signed, and which, among other things, permitted "close" but not "distant" blockades. A belligerent was allowed to station ships near the three-mile limit to stop traffic with an enemy's ports; it was not allowed simply to declare large areas of the high seas comprising the approaches to the enemy's coast to be off-limits. This is what Britain did on November 3, 1914, when it announced, allegedly in response to the discovery of a German ship unloading mines off the English coast, that henceforth the whole of the North Sea was a military area, which would be mined and into which neutral ships proceeded "at their own peril." Similar measures in regard to the English Channel insured that neutral ships would be forced to put into British ports for sailing instructions or to take on British pilots. During this time they could easily be searched, obviating the requirement of searching them at sea.

This introduces the second question: that of contraband. Briefly, following the lead of the Hague Conference of 1907, the Declaration of London of 1909 considered food to be "conditional contraband," that is, subject to interception and capture only when intended for the use of the enemy's military forces. This was part of the painstaking effort, extending over generations, to strip war of its most savage aspects by establishing as sharp a distinction as possible between combatants and noncombatants. Among the corollaries of this was that food not intended for military use could legitimately be transported to a neutral port, even if it ultimately found its way to the enemy's territory. The House of Lords had refused its consent to the Declaration of London, which did not, consequently, come into full force. Still, as the U.S. government pointed out to the British at the start of the war, the Declaration's provisions were in keeping "with the generally recognized principles of international law." As an indication of this, the British Admiralty had incorporated the Declaration into its manuals.

The British quickly began to tighten the noose around Germany by unilaterally expanding the list of contraband and by putting pressure on neutrals (particularly the Netherlands, since Rotterdam was the focus of British concerns over the provisioning of the Germans) to acquiesce in its violations of the rules. In the case of the major neutral, the United States, no pressure was needed. With the exception of the isolated Secretary of State, William Jennings Bryan, who resigned in 1915, the American leaders were consistently, astonishingly sympathetic to the British point of view and their homicidal method—imposing famine on the whole civilian population of Germany.[5]

The Germans responded to the British attempt to starve them into submission by declaring the seas around the British Isles a "war zone," subject to U-boat attacks. Now the British openly announced their intention to impound any and all goods originating in or bound for Germany. Although the British measures were lent the air of reprisals for German actions, in reality the great plan was hatched and pursued independently of anything the enemy did or refrained from doing:

> The War Orders given by the Admiralty on 26 August [1914] were clear enough. All food consigned to Germany through neutral ports was to be captured and all food consigned to Rotterdam was to be presumed consigned to Germany.... The British were determined on the starvation policy, whether or not it was lawful.[6]

The effects of the blockade were soon being felt by the German

---

[5] The U.S. government's bias in favor of the Allied cause is well documented. Thus, even such an establishment historian as the late Thomas A. Bailey, in his *A Diplomatic History of the American People*, 9th ed. (Englewood Cliffs, N.J.: Prentice-Hall, 1974), p. 572, states: "The obvious explanation of America's surprising docility [in the face of British violations of neutrals' rights] is that the Wilson administration was sympathetic with the Allies from the beginning." The partisanship of Wilson, his advisor Colonel House, Secretary of State Robert Lansing, and, especially, the American ambassador to England, Walter Hines Page, is highlighted in Bailey's even-handed account of the entry of the United States into the war (pp. 562–95). The reader may find it an interesting exercise to compare Bailey's treatment with that from a newer generation of establishment authority, Robert H. Ferrell, *American Diplomacy: A History*, 3rd ed. (New York: Norton, 1975), pp. 456–74. Ferrell gives no hint of the administration's bias toward Britain. Of the notorious British propaganda document luridly detailing sickening but non-existent German atrocities in Belgium, he writes: "It is true that in the light of postwar investigation the veracity of some of the deeds instanced in the Bryce Report has come into question" (p. 462). (On the Bryce Report, see Peterson, *Propaganda*, pp. 53–58, and Phillip Knightley, *The First Casualty* (New York: Harcourt Brace Jovanovich, 1975), pp. 83–84.) Ferrell's account could itself pass muster as somewhat refined Entente propaganda. Lest American college students miss the moral of his story, Professor Ferrell ends with the assertion: "It was certainly in the interest of national security to go to war ... logic demanded entrance."

[6] Devlin, *Too Proud to Fight*, pp. 193, 195.

civilians. In June 1915, bread began to be rationed. "By 1916," Vincent states, "the German population was surviving on a meager diet of dark bread, slices of sausage without fat, an individual ration of three pounds of potatoes per week, and turnips," and that year the potato crop failed. The author's choice of telling quotations from eyewitnesses brings home to the reader the reality of a famine such as had not been experienced in Europe outside of Russia since Ireland's travail in the 1840s. As one German put it: "Soon the women who stood in the pallid queues before shops spoke more about their children's hunger than about the death of their husbands." An American correspondent in Berlin wrote:

> Once I set out for the purpose of finding in these food-lines a face that did not show the ravages of hunger.... Four long lines were inspected with the closest scrutiny. But among the 300 applicants for food there was not one who had had enough to eat for weeks. In the case of the youngest women and children the skin was drawn hard to the bones and bloodless. Eyes had fallen deeper into the sockets. From the lips all color was gone, and the tufts of hair which fell over the parchmented faces seemed dull and famished—a sign that the nervous vigor of the body was departing with the physical strength.

Vincent places the German decision in early 1917 to resume and expand submarine warfare against merchant shipping—which provided the Wilson administration with its final pretext for entering the war—in the framework of collapsing German morale. The German U-boat campaign proved unsuccessful and, in fact, by bringing the United States into the conflict, aggravated the famine. Wilson, the sainted idealist, "ensured that every loophole left open by the Allies for the potential reprovisioning of Germany was closed." Rations in Germany were reduced to about one thousand calories a day. By 1918, the mortality rate among civilians was 38 per cent higher than in 1913; tuberculosis was rampant, and, among children, so were rickets and edema. Yet, when the Germans surrendered in November 1918, the armistice terms, drawn up by Clemenceau, Foch, and Pétain, included the continuation of the blockade until a final peace treaty was ratified. In December 1918, the National Health Office in Berlin calculated that 763,000 persons had died as a result of the blockade by that time; the number added to this in the first months of 1919 is unknown.[7] In some respects, the armistice saw the intensification of the suffering, since the German Baltic coast was now effectively blockaded and German fishing rights in the Baltic annulled.

One of the most notable points in Vincent's account is how the perspective of "zoological" warfare, later associated with the Nazis, began to emerge from the maelstrom of ethnic hatred engendered by the war. In September 1918, one English journalist, in an article titled "The Huns of 1940," wrote hopefully of the tens of thousands of Germans now in the wombs of famished mothers who "are destined for a life of physical inferiority."[8] The famous, universally admired founder of the Boy Scouts, Robert Baden-Powell, naïvely expressed his satisfaction that "the German race is being ruined; though the birth rate, from the German point of view, may look satisfactory, the irreparable harm done is quite different and much more serious."

Against the genocidal wish-fantasies of such thinkers and the heartless vindictiveness of Entente politicians should be set the anguished reports from Germany by British journalists and, especially, army officers, as well as by the members of Herbert Hoover's American Relief Commission. Again and again they stressed, besides the barbarism of the continued blockade, the danger that famine might well drive the Germans to Bolshevism. Hoover was soon persuaded of the urgent need to end the blockade, but wrangling among the Allies, particularly French insistence that the German gold stock could not be used to pay for food, since it was earmarked for reparations, prevented action. In early March 1919, General Herbert Plumer, commander of the British Army of Occupation, informed Prime Minister David Lloyd George that his men were begging to be sent home: they could no longer stand the sight of "hordes of skinny and bloated children pawing over the offal" from the British camps. Finally, the Americans and British overpowered French objections, and at the end of March, the first food shipments began arriving in Hamburg. But it was only in July, 1919, after the formal German signature to the Treaty of Versailles, that the

---

[7] The British historian Arthur Bryant, writing in 1940, put the figure even higher, at 800,000 for the last two years of the blockade, "about fifty times more than were drowned by submarine attacks on British shipping." Cited in J. F. C. Fuller, *The Conduct of War, 1789–1961* (London: Eyre & Spottiswoode, 1961), p. 178.

[8] F. W. Wile, "The Huns of 1940," *Weekly Dispatch*, September 8, 1918.

Germans were permitted to import raw materials and export manufactured goods.

Herbert Hoover resumed his humanitarian efforts in the Second World War. In 1940 he warned of impending starvation in German-occupied Europe, in the Low Countries, Norway, and especially Poland. His efforts were stymied by Churchill, however. Hoover afterwards concluded that the Prime Minister "was a militarist of the extreme old school who held that the incidental starvation of women and children" was justified if it contributed to the earlier ending of the war by victory. Hoover's Polish Relief had been feeding some 200,000 persons daily. Hoover wrote that "when Churchill succeeded Chamberlain as Prime Minister in May, 1940, he soon stopped all permits of food relief to Poland." Churchill's cherished policy of inflicting famine on civilians was thus extended to "friendly" peoples. The Poles and the others would be permitted food when and if they rose up and drove out the Germans.[9] Another of Churchill's reckless, lethal fantasies.

To return to the hunger blockade of the First World War, besides its direct effects there are the probable indirect and much more damaging effects to consider. A German child who was ten years old in 1918 and who survived was twenty-two in 1930. Vincent raises the question of whether the suffering from hunger in the early, formative years help account to some degree for the enthusiasm of German youth for Nazism later on. Drawing on a 1971 article by Peter Loewenberg, he argues in the affirmative.[10] Loewenberg's work, however, is a specimen of psychohistory and his conclusions are explicitly founded on psychoanalytic doctrine. Although Vincent does not endorse them unreservedly, he leans toward explaining the later behavior of the generation of German children scarred by the war years in terms of an emotional or nervous impairment of rational thought. Thus, he refers to "the ominous amalgamation of

---

[9] Nicholson Baker, *Human Smoke*, pp. 220, 223.

[10] Peter Loewenberg, "The Psychohistorical Origins of the Nazi Youth Cohorts," *American Historical Review* 76, no. 5 (December 1971), pp. 1457–502. Loewenberg writes, for instance: "The war and postwar experiences of the small children and youth of World War I explicitly conditioned the nature and success of National Socialism. The new adults who became politically effective after 1929 and who filled the ranks of the SA [Storm Troops, Brown Shirts] and the other paramilitary party organizations ... were the children socialized in the First World War." (p. 1458)

twisted emotion and physical degradation, which was to presage considerable misery for Germany and the world" and which was produced in large part by the starvation policy.

But is such an approach necessary? It seems much more plausible to seek for the mediating connections between exposure to starvation and the other torments caused by the blockade and later fanatical and brutal German behavior in commonly intelligible—though, of course, not thereby justifiable—human attitudes generated by the early experiences. These would include hatred, deep-seated bitterness and resentment, and a disregard for the value of life of "others" because the value of one's own life and the lives of one's family, friends, and compatriots had been so ruthlessly disregarded. A starting point for such an analysis could be Theodore Abel's 1938 work, *Why Hitler Came into Power: An Answer Based on the Original Life Stories of Six Hundred of His Followers*. Loewenberg's conclusion after studying this work that "the most striking emotional affect expressed in the Abel autobiographies are the adult memories of intense hunger and privation from childhood."[11] An interpretation that would accord the hunger blockade its proper place in the rise of Nazi savagery has no particular need for a psychoanalytical or physiological underpinning.

Occasionally Vincent's views on issues marginal to his theme are distressingly stereotyped: he appears to accept an extreme Fischer school interpretation of guilt for the origin of the war as adhering to the German government alone, and, concerning the fortunes of the Weimar Republic, he states: "That Germany lost this opportunity is one of the tragedies of the twentieth century.... Too often the old socialists seemed almost terrified of socialization." The cliché that, if only heavy industry had been socialized in 1919, then German democracy could have been saved, was never very convincing. It is proving less so as research begins to suggest that it was precisely the Weimar system of massive state intervention in the labor markets and the advanced welfare state institutions (the most "progressive" of their time) that so weakened the German economy that it collapsed in the face of the Great Depression.[12] This collapse,

---

[11] Ibid., p. 1499.

[12] The debate among German economic historians on this question is discussed in Jürgen von Kruedener, "Die Überforderung der Weimarer Republik als Sozialstaat," *Geschichte und Gesellschaft* 11, no. 3 (1985), 358–76.

particularly the staggering unemployment that accompanied it, has long been considered by scholars to have been a major cause of the Nazi rise to power in 1930–33.

These are, however, negligible points in view of the service Vincent has performed both in reclaiming from oblivion past victims of a murderous state policy and in deepening our understanding of twentieth-century European history. There has recently occurred in the Federal Republic of Germany a "dispute of historians" over whether the Nazi slaughter of the European Jews should be viewed as "unique" or placed within the context of other mass murders, specifically the Stalinist atrocities against the Ukrainian peasantry.[13] Vincent's work suggests the possibility that the framework of the discussion ought to be widened more than any of the participants has so far proposed.

---

[13] *"Historikerstreit." Die Dokumentation der Kontroverse um die Einzigartigkeit der nationalsozialistischen Judenvernichtung* (Munich: Piper, 1987).

CHAPTER 10

John T. Flynn and the Apotheosis of Franklin Roosevelt

Albert Jay Nock, distinguished man of letters and philosophical anarchist, was an inspiration to thinkers as diverse as Murray Rothbard and Robert Nisbet, Frank Chodorov and Russell Kirk. A personal friend of the father of William F. Buckley, Jr., he was a kind of guru to the young Buckley as well. In April, 1945, Nock wrote a cheery letter to two of his friends, describing the death of Franklin Roosevelt as "the biggest public improvement that America has experienced since the passage of the Bill of Rights," and proposing a celebration luncheon at Luchow's.[1]

Today Nock's unabashed delight would be regarded as obscene, a sacrilege against the civic religion of the United States. Republican no less than Democratic leaders revere and invoke the memory

---

This essay, somewhat modified here, served as an introduction to the 50th anniversary edition of John T. Flynn's *The Roosevelt Myth*, published by Fox & Wilkes, 938 Howard St., San Francisco, 94103.

[1] Albert Jay Nock, *Letters from Albert Jay Nock, 1924–1945* (Caldwell, Id.: Caxton, 1949), p. 211.

of Franklin Roosevelt. His praises are sung from the *Wall Street Journal* to the *New York Times*, and herds of historians (the phrase is Mencken's) regularly announce that FDR was one of our truly "Great Presidents." Symbolic of his apotheosis was the dedication, in May, 1997, of the vast Franklin Delano Roosevelt Memorial in Washington, D.C. As the *Times* happily reported, it is "a memorial laced with a zest for the power of government." The current executors of that power had eagerly lent their plundered support, Congress voting $42.5 million, with bipartisan enthusiasm. Amid the hosannas that rose up everywhere in politics and the press, the few dissident voices were inaudible. The dominant credo is that, as an editor of the *Wall Street Journal* informed us, criticism of FDR is conceivable only from enemies "maddened by hatred of him."

Yet it is a fact that throughout his long presidency FDR was hotly opposed, even pilloried, by a host of intelligent, respected, and patriotic men and women. The most consistent of his adversaries formed a loose coalition known today as the Old Right.[2] There is little doubt that the best informed and most tenacious of the Old Right foes of Franklin Roosevelt was John T. Flynn.

When Flynn came to write his major study of the four-term president, he aptly titled it *The Roosevelt Myth*. Myths continue to abound concerning Roosevelt and his reign; one of the most convenient is that the antagonists of his New Deal were all "economic royalists," self-serving beneficiaries and moneyed defenders of the status quo. In Flynn's case, such an accusation is laughable. When he became a critic of the New Deal, Flynn enjoyed a well-established reputation as a progressive and a muckraker, with, as Bill Kauffman writes, "a taste for plutocrat blood."[3]

John Thomas Flynn was born in 1882 into a middle class Irish Catholic family in the suburbs of Washington, and educated first in public schools, then in the parochial schools of New York City. The debate that raged around 1900 on U.S. annexation of the Philippines seems to have exercised a formative influence on the young Flynn: all his life he remained an resolute opponent of Western, including

---

[2]Sheldon Richman, "New Deal Nemesis: The 'Old Right' Jeffersonians," *The Independent Review*, Fall 1996; and Justin Raimondo, *Reclaiming the American Right: The Lost Legacy of the Conservative Movement* (Burlingame, Cal.: Center for Libertarian Studies, 1993).

[3]Bill Kauffman, *America First! Its History, Culture, and Politics* (Amherst, N.Y.: Prometheus, 1995), p. 58.

American, imperialism. He studied law at Georgetown, but found journalism irresistible. After serving as editor on papers in New Haven and New York, he worked as a freelance writer exposing crooked financial dealings on Wall Street. In the early and mid-1930s, Flynn authored a series of books attacking the trusts and what he viewed as the misdeeds of the securities business. His *God's Gold: The Story of Rockefeller and His Times* (1932) became something of a classic.[4]

Flynn was not a strict libertarian nor was his thinking on economics notably sophisticated. He fully appreciated the productive dynamism of the private-property market economy. But in his progressive phase, he held that government had a crucial role to play in reining in the "excesses" of capitalism, by thwarting monopolies, protecting small investors, and undertaking moderate social reform. Yet he was never a socialist; to his mind, the hopes for a free and prosperous society lay in a truly competitive private-enterprise system.[5] Above all, Flynn always distrusted any close tie-in between the state and big business, at home or abroad. In 1934, he acted as chief researcher for the Nye committee of the U.S. Senate, which investigated the role of the New York banks and the munitions industry ("the Merchants of Death") in leading the United States into the First World War.

Flynn opposed the New Deal practically from the start. Instead of opening up the economy to competitive forces, Roosevelt seemed bent on cartelizing it, principally through the National Recovery Act (NRA), which Flynn regarded as a copy of Mussolini's Corporate State. As one failed New Deal program followed another, Flynn suspected that Roosevelt would try to divert attention to alleged foreign dangers, a recourse facilitated by world events. The sinking by the Japanese of an American gunboat, the *Panay*, which had been patrolling the Yangtze, precipitated an early crisis. Flynn asked why we had gunboats patrolling Chinese rivers in the first place—and found the answer in the fact that the *Panay* had been convoying tankers of the Standard Oil Company.[6] Incidents such as this, Flynn charged, were exploited by the administration "to churn up as much

---

[4] Michele Flynn Stenehjem, *An American First: John T. Flynn and the America First Committee* (New Rochelle, N.Y.: Arlington House, 1976), pp. 26–29.

[5] Ronald Radosh, *Prophets on the Right: Profiles of Conservative Critics of American Globalism* (New York: Simon and Schuster, 1975), pp. 197–201.

[6] Ibid., p. 205.

war spirit as possible." In 1938, he joined with the democratic socialist leader Norman Thomas and others to establish the Keep America Out of War Congress, composed mainly of pacifists and socialists.

In *Country Squire in the White House* (1940), Flynn set forth themes he would develop more fully in *The Roosevelt Myth*. He painted the Hudson Valley patrician as a dilettante with no principles of his own, a mere power-seeker with a genius for winning votes. Roosevelt had reneged on his promises of progressive reform and instead created a federal Leviathan based on the cynical policy of "tax and tax, spend and spend, elect and elect"—the formula which has since become the bedrock of American politics in our blessed two-party system. Characteristically, it was the government's intimate relationship with the armaments industry that came in for Flynn's sharpest censure.

Roosevelt, who always viewed any criticism of himself as a perversion of true democracy, was outraged. The President of the United States wrote a personal letter to a magazine editor declaring that Flynn "should be barred hereafter from the columns of any presentable daily paper, monthly magazine, or national quarterly."[7] Whether or not as a consequence of FDR's spite, *The New Republic* dropped the column by Flynn it had been publishing since 1933, a sign things were changing in the circles of left-liberalism. In the years to come, FDR would use the FBI, the IRS, and other agencies to spy on, harass, and intimidate his critics.[8] This—and his lying, his *constant lying*—more than any supposed mental affliction, explains the hatred that so many harbored for Franklin Roosevelt.

As FDR edged closer to war the need was felt for a mass-based anti-interventionist organization. In August, 1940, Flynn became one of the founders of the America First Committee and chairman of the New York City chapter. At its height, the America First Committee had over 800,000 card-carrying members, among them E. E. Cummings, Sinclair Lewis, Kathleen Norris, Alice Roosevelt Longworth, and Irene Castle. (The actress Lillian Gish served for a time on the national board, but was forced to resign when this led

---

[7] Ibid., pp. 204–05.

[8] See, for instance, Robert Dallek, *Franklin Roosevelt and American Foreign Policy, 1932–1945* (Oxford: Oxford University Press, 1979), pp. 289–90; and Richard Norton Smith, *The Colonel: The Life and Legend of Robert R. McCormick* (Boston: Houghton Mifflin, 1997), pp. 405–06, 424–28.

to her being blackballed—"blacklisted"? —in Hollywood and on Broadway.) Younger supporters of America First included John F. Kennedy, Sargeant Shriver, Gerald Ford, and Gore Vidal.[9]

America First was tapping into a deep vein: poll after poll showed that 80% of the people were against going to war with Germany. Soon the Committee was subjected to a relentless campaign of defamation. Its most popular speaker, Charles Lindbergh, was labeled the "no. 1 Nazi fellow traveler" in the United States by Harold Ickes, Secretary of the Interior and Roosevelt's chief hatchet man,[10] while Robert Sherwood, the president's speechwriter, dismissed the heroic aviator as "simply a Nazi."[11] The slur by the philosopher and socialist John Dewey, that the America First Committee was a "transmission belt" for Nazi propaganda, was echoed by scores of other interventionist hacks.[12] Self-appointed "antifascist" patriots in Hollywood and elsewhere depicted a vast (imaginary) network of Nazi agitators and saboteurs at work throughout the land, and linked these domestic Nazis to the "isolationists,""Hitler's conscious or unconscious allies."[13]

---

[9] Bill Kauffman, *America First!* On Lillian Gish, see Justus D. Doenecke, ed., *In Danger Undaunted: The Anti-Interventionist Movement of 1940–1941 as Revealed in the Papers of the America First Committee* (Stanford, Cal.: Hoover Institution Press, 1990), p. 14.

[10] Ickes, often taken to be a liberal, was probably the most blood-thirsty of Roosevelt's intimates. At a meeting of the Cabinet in July 1941—months before Pearl Harbor—he urged that one of the U.S. bombers given the Soviets "go to Siberia by way of Japan. It could set fire to Tokyo en route, by dropping a few incendiary bombs," the assumption being that the capital of Japan was built largely of paper and light wood. Nicholson Baker, *Human Smoke*, p. 370

[11] Wayne S. Cole, *Charles A. Lindbergh and the Battle Against American Intervention in World War II* (New York: Harcourt Brace Jovanovich, 1974), pp. 130, 147.

[12] Radosh, *Prophets on the Right*, p. 219.

[13] John Earl Haynes, *Red Scare or Red Menace? American communism and Anticommunism in the Cold War Era* (Chicago: Ivan R. Dee, 1996), pp. 17–36. In December, 1942—in the midst of the war—it was Roosevelt himself who shocked the Washington press corps by mockingly presenting John O'Donnell, the anti-interventionist columnist for the New York *Daily News*, with an Iron Cross for his services to the Reich. Graham J. White, *FDR and the Press* (Chicago: University of Chicago Press, 1979), pp. 44–45. The slurs continue to this day. Professor Harry Jaffa ("In Defense of Churchill," *Modern Age*, vol. 34, no. 3 (Spring 1992), p. 281) refers to "Charles Lindbergh and Fritz Kuhn [*Führer* of the pro-Nazi German-American Bund] standing together" in warning that participation in the war

Flynn termed the campaign a "witch hunt." He and his ideological comrades would remember the establishment's viciousness when the tables were briefly turned, during the episode known as "McCarthyism."

As the battle over intervention intensified, Flynn observed that Roosevelt was wrecking the constitutional balance in foreign affairs as he had domestically. When the President sent troops to occupy Iceland in July, 1941, Flynn assailed the unconstitutional act and the supine Congress that permitted it: Roosevelt "could not do this if the Congress of the United States had not been reduced to the state of a servile shadow" of what the Founders intended.[14] In the "Four Freedoms" declaration issued by Roosevelt and Churchill, in August, 1941, Flynn saw prefigured the globalist program for America: "the task is forever to be ours of policing the world, inflicting our ideologies and our wishes upon the world."[15]

Roosevelt needed the war and wanted the war, and the war came.

Immediately following Pearl Harbor the America First Committee dissolved itself, but Flynn did not cease his attacks. In 1944, he published *As We Go Marching*, an analysis of the nature of European fascism and the clear parallels to trends in the United States. "As we go marching to the salvation of the world," Flynn warned, government power expands, our economic and social life is militarized, and we are coming to resemble the very dictatorships we were fighting.[16] With the end of the war and the death of FDR, Flynn was ready for his summation of the career of the four-term president.

---

would "be mainly in the interest of the Jews." Professor Jaffa wishes to evoke the picture of Lindbergh next to Kuhn addressing an antiwar rally. Needless to say, it never happened. They "stood together" in the same sense that Professor Jaffa's ilk "stood together" with Stalin and his mass-killers in agitating for U.S. entry. Lindbergh did not maintain that it was "in the interest of Jews" for the United States to enter the war; on the contrary, he believed it would damage the status of Jews in America (Cole, *Charles A. Lindbergh*, pp. 157–85). The cause of Professor Jaffa's typically foolish diatribe is clearly his clammy fear that the voice of America First "is once again abroad in the land."

[14] Cole, *Roosevelt and the Isolationists*, p. 432.

[15] Ibid., p. 495.

[16] The continuing militarization of American life since 1933 is dealt with by Michael S. Sherry, *In the Shadow of War: The United States Since the 1930s* (New Haven, Conn.: Yale University Press, 1995).

It is fairly obvious that the routine judgment of American historians, that Roosevelt was a truly "Great President," has nothing objective about it. Historians, like everyone else, have their own personal values and political views. Like other academics they tend to be overwhelmingly on the left. Analyzing one recent poll, Robert Higgs notes: "Left-liberal historians worship political power, and idolize those who wield it most lavishly in the service of left-liberal causes."[17] Why should it be surprising, or even noteworthy, that they venerate Roosevelt and try to get a credulous public to do the same?

For a rather different view, the reader can now turn to *The Roosevelt Myth*, thankfully once more in print, which was and, after half a century, remains the major debunking of Franklin Roosevelt. "Polemical as only Flynn could be polemical,"[18] the work was turned down by every publisher the author approached. Flynn was desperate: "For the first time in my life I am peddling a book around like a fresh unknown.... I am at my wits' end." Finally, he met Devin Garrity, head of a small house in New York specializing in Irish and revisionist works, and the book appeared in 1948 under the imprint of Devin-Adair. It quickly became number two on the *New York Times* best-seller list.[19]

Taking every phase of his presidency in turn, Flynn is merciless in exposing Roosevelt as a failure, a liar, and a fraud. Two subsidiary myths which he demolishes are of particular interest today, since they are the main supports for FDR's supposed greatness: his roles in the Depression and in the Second World War.

The mantra, "Roosevelt cured the Depression," exasperated Flynn. (Now it is often replaced with the banal and much more cautious: "He gave the people hope.") Didn't anyone care about facts? he demanded. The "first" New Deal came and went, then came the "second" New Deal, in 1935 — and still the Depression, unlike every previous downturn, dragged on and on. Flynn pointed out that

---

[17] Robert Higgs, "No More 'Great Presidents'" *The Free Market*, vol. 15, no. 3 (March 1997). Higgs says everything that needs to be said on these politically-inspired surveys of historians, concluding: "God save us from great presidents."

[18] Justus D. Doenecke, *Not to the Swift: The Old Isolationists in the Cold War Era* (Lewisburg, Pa.: Bucknell University Press, 1979), pp. 97–98. This work is discussed in the present volume.

[19] Stenehjem, *An American First*, pp. 172–73.

in 1938 the number of persons unemployed totaled "11,800,000—*more than were unemployed when Roosevelt was elected in 1932*" (his italics). Flynn deals with the impotence of successive New Deal programs and the fulminations of the "planners" and "spenders" in his chapters on "The Forgotten Depression" and "The Dance of the Philosophers."

Recent scholarship has bolstered Flynn's analysis. In studying why the slump that started in 1929 became "the Great Depression," the longest-lasting in U.S. history, Robert Higgs identifies a critical factor: the exceptionally low rate of private investment. A chief cause of this failure to invest and create productive jobs, Higgs finds, was "regime uncertainty." For the first time in our history, investors were seriously worried over the security of property rights in America. There had been an

> unparalleled outpouring of business-threatening laws, regulations, and court decisions, the oft-stated hostility of President Roosevelt and his lieutenants toward investors as a class, and the character of the antibusiness zealots who composed the strategists and administrators of the New Deal from 1935 to 1941.[20]

The comfortable mythology has it that businessmen hated Roosevelt because he was "a traitor to his class." The truth is that they feared him as a menace to the private property system, and they restricted their investments accordingly.

On FDR's role before and after our entry into World War II Flynn is scathing. When he wrote his book, Thomas A. Bailey, diplomatic historian at Stanford, had already published the defense of Roosevelt's pro-war policy that has now become standard. Casually conceding the whole revisionist indictment by Charles Beard and others, Bailey wrote that Roosevelt had indeed deceived the American people before Pearl Harbor, but he did it as a physician lies to a patient, for his own good. The people ("the masses," in Bailey's statement) are too short-sighted; statesmen must deceive

---

[20] Robert Higgs, "Regime Uncertainty: Why the Great Depression Lasted So Long and Why Prosperity Resumed After the War," *The Independent Review*, (Spring 1997), p. 586. See also the chapter on the New Deal in Higgs's indispensable work, *Crisis and Leviathan: Critical Episodes in the Growth of American Government* (New York: Oxford University Press, 1987), pp. 159–95.

them, to further "the masses' " own long-run interests. That is what FDR "had to do, and who shall say that posterity will not thank him for it?"[21]

But Flynn asked: "If Roosevelt had the right to do this, to whom is the right denied?" In 1948, Flynn was speaking for the "patients," the lied to, the duped and manipulated "masses," those once known as the free and sovereign citizens of the American Republic. Today, the conventional wisdom is all on the side of the lying Roosevelt and against the people he deceived.

On another subject, also, standards have changed. In our own enlightened times, it is considered entirely in the natural order of things that the United States should have emerged triumphant from the costliest and second-bloodiest war in our history and then been instantly plunged into another struggle against a more powerful foe. Yet in 1948, Winston Churchill himself admitted that: "we have still not found Peace or Security, and ... we lie in the grip of even worse perils than those we have surmounted."[22] A half century ago, this suggested, reasonably enough, that something had gone seriously wrong in the political conduct of the war.

In accounting for the sorry state of the postwar world, Flynn focused on Roosevelt's failures: "Our government put into Stalin's hands the means of seizing a great slab of the continent of Europe, then stood aside while he took it and finally acquiesced in his conquests." Forty years later, Robert Nisbet reinforced Flynn's case, laying out in detail FDR's fatuousness in looking on Stalin—*Stalin*—as a friend and fellow progressive, his main ally in constructing the New World Order.[23] These facts have, however, made little impression on the herds of historians. It seems that there is no degrading inanity, no catastrophic blunder that is not permitted a truly "Great President."

Franklin Roosevelt's impact on America was measureless. Flynn's account—composed in his trademark fighting-Irish style—is still the best analysis of why it was so deeply destructive.

---

[21]Thomas A. Bailey, *The Man in the Street: The Impact of American Public Opinion on Foreign Policy* (New York: Macmillan, 1948), p. 13.

[22]Winston S. Churchill, *The Gathering Storm* (Boston: Houghton Mifflin, 1948), p. v. See the chapter on "Rethinking Churchill," in the present volume.

[23]Robert Nisbet, *Roosevelt and Stalin: The Failed Courtship* (Washington, D.C.: Regnery, 1988).

In the years that followed, Flynn became the intellectual mainstay of the Old Right, shedding the remnants of his old-line progressivism and growing more clearly constitutionalist and anti-statist. This was the Flynn of *The Road Ahead*, another bestseller, which reached a printing of 4,000,000 in the *Reader's Digest* condensation. The road Flynn warned that we were following was the path of Fabian socialism towards omnipotent government.

As the new president, Harry Truman, engaged the United States in yet another crusade, Flynn sided with what remained of the anti-interventionist movement, which looked to Senator Robert Taft as its leader. Opposed to open-ended American commitments everywhere, suspicious of foreign aid programs that entailed underwriting the status quo in a rapidly changing world, these conservatives became, once again, the target of interventionist slanders. According to Truman, Republicans who opposed his foreign policy were "Kremlin assets," the sort of miscreants who would shoot "our soldiers in the back in a hot war."[24] Once again, the establishment press echoed administration lies.

All of this has been forgotten now, along with the prewar campaign of defamation of patriotic Americans as "Nazis." All that remains in the popular memory is the perpetually rehashed tale of a time of terror known as the Age of McCarthyism. Flynn was a fervent supporter of Joseph McCarthy, and in several works he examined the influence of Communists and Communist sympathizers on U.S. foreign policy, especially on China.[25] While it is clear that Flynn basically misunderstood the Chinese revolution, on other points he was closer to the truth than McCarthy's enemies, then and now. Owen Lattimore, for instance, was not the mild-mannered, ivory-tower scholar of left-liberal mythology, but a dedicated apologist for Stalin, for the purge-trials and the Gulag. With the continuing release of documents from the 1930s and '40s, from U.S. and Russian archives, the received wisdom regarding the "McCarthyite terror" is due for revision.[26]

---

[24]Doenecke, *Not to the Swift*, p. 216.

[25]E.g., *While You Slept: Our Tragedy in Asia and Who Made It* (1951) and *The Lattimore Story* (1953).

[26]See, for instance, M. Stanton Evans, "McCarthyism: Waging the Cold War in America," *Human Events*, May 30, 1997, pp. 51–58.

In the watershed campaign for the Republican presidential nomination in 1952, Flynn was an ardent supporter of Robert Taft. Eisenhower he saw as simply a front man for the Eastern Republican establishment, centered in Wall Street, that had foisted Willkie and Dewey on the party; he felt the same way about Eisenhower's running mate, Senator Richard M. Nixon.

Flynn continued to oppose globalism to the end. He contended against American meddling in the Middle East; and when Senator McCarthy—true to his own internationalist bent—supported the British–French–Israeli attack on Egypt in 1956, Flynn broke with him. Growing American involvement in Indochina under Eisenhower and John Foster Dulles incensed Flynn. He asked pointedly, "I would like to know who in Asia is going to cross the Pacific and attack us." At the time of the French debacle at Điện Biên Phủ, Flynn called on Eisenhower to make it clear that "we're not going to get involved in any kind of war in Indo-China, hot or lukewarm, all-out or part-way."[27]

A constant target of Flynn's was the "bipartisan foreign policy," a hoax that has functioned to deprive Americans of any choice on questions of peace or war for many decades. As a central source of this ruse he identified the Council on Foreign Relations, noting that both Dean Acheson and John Foster Dulles—Secretaries of State from nominally opposed parties—as well as most of the other makers of U.S. foreign policy were members of the New York organization. Palpably a front for big business interests, the Council's goal was a radical transformation of the attitudes of the American people, their conversion to the dogma that our security required that we "police the whole world, fight the battles of the whole world, make every country in the world like the United States."[28]

Flynn's highlighting of the influence of big business on American foreign policy has inevitably led some writers to link his outlook to Marxism. Nothing could be more wrongheaded. Flailing capitalists for using their links to the state to further their own sinister interests—*especially* their overseas interests—has been a cornerstone of classical liberalism from at least the time of Turgot, Adam Smith, and Jeremy Bentham.

---

[27]Doenecke, *Not to the Swift*, pp. 241, 243; Radosh, *Prophets on the Right*, p. 261.
[28]Radosh, *Prophets on the Right*, p. 258.

In 1956 occurred a small event that, like Flynn's firing from *The New Republic* in 1938, symbolized the passing of an era in American politics. As Flynn had earlier been dismissed because his anti-war views were inconsistent with the new turn on the left, so now he ran into opposition from a nascent "New Right." William F. Buckley, Jr., nurtured on the American anti-statism of Albert Jay Nock and Frank Chodorov, had fallen in with a crowd of ex-Stalinists, ex-Trotskyists, and conservative European émigrés. His position now was that "we have to accept Big Government for the duration—for neither an offensive nor a defensive war can be waged … except through the instrument of a totalitarian bureaucracy within our shores." The anti-Communist crusade required high taxes for vast armies and navies, even "war production boards and the attendant centralization of power in Washington."[29]

As editor of *National Review*, Buckley commissioned an article from Flynn. Flynn turned in a gruff critique of the hypertrophic growth of the central government under Republican as well as Democratic administrations, which concluded: "There has been, since Roosevelt's regime, no plan whatever for restoring the American Republic in its constitutional form."[30] This was not something that Buckley, as committed to global meddling and as indifferent to American constitutionalism as any New Dealer, could accept. The manuscript was returned, ending Flynn's connection with what now passed for the conservative movement in America.

Gregory Pavlik, editor of this fine edition of Flynn's essays, summed it up well: "When Flynn died in 1964 he was an outcast from both the then-fashionable varieties of liberalism and conservatism. His life was a testament to his character—he refused to compromise his deepest convictions for the affection of trendy demagogues of any political stripe."[31]

---

[29] William F. Buckley, Jr., "A Young Republican's View," *Commonweal*, January 25, 1952, quoted in Murray N. Rothbard, *The Betrayal of the American Right*, p. 159.

[30] The essay is published for the first time in John T. Flynn, *Forgotten Lessons: Selected Essays*, Gregory P. Pavlik, ed. (Irvington-on-Hudson, N.Y.: Foundation for Economic Education, 1996), pp. 129–34.

[31] Ibid., p. 4.

Chapter 11

On the Brink of World War II

Justus Doenecke, professor of history at the University of South Florida, has made a distinguished career of researching the history of American "isolationism" before and after World War II. His latest book, *Storm on the Horizon: The Challenge to American Intervention, 1939–1941* (Lanham, Md.: Rowman and Littlefield, 2000), is marked by his unsurpassed familiarity with the relevant archives—reflected in the 170 pages of endnotes—and by his rare and refreshing objectivity. The work has already won the annual book award of the Herbert Hoover Presidential Library Association.

Doenecke begins with the inevitable terminological issue. He eschews referring to the protagonists of *Storm on the Horizon* as *isolationists*, the term preferred by their interventionist adversaries. This rhetorically powerful argument by epithet has been deployed from 1898 (against the opponents of the war with Spain) to the present. Today, simply uttering the word itself is probably decisive

---

This piece on Justus Doenecke's *Storm on the Horizon*, here slightly modified, first appeared in *The Independent Review*, Spring, 2002.

for most Americans on questions of foreign policy. In its place, Doenecke prefers the less-loaded terms *anti-interventionist* and *non-interventionist*, though it is doubtful that such a semantic decontamination could ever be effected.

As our author makes amply clear, there were "many mansions" in the anti-war movement, from Father Charles Coughlin and his magazine *Social Justice* to the Communist Party (until June 22, 1941, that is, when the CPUSA and it many sympathizers turned on a dime and became fanatically *pro*-war). Very sensibly, however, Doenecke pays the most attention to the pacifist and, above all, the liberal and conservative opponents of war, most of whom were associated in one way or another with the America First Committee (AFC), founded in September 1940.

During its brief existence and ever after, the AFC was and has been subjected to mindless slurs. A recent example occurred in connection with Princeton University's unsealing of many of the papers of Charles Lindbergh, the Committee's most prominent speaker, and of his wife Anne Morrow Lindbergh. In a report for the Associated Press (March 30, 2001), Linda A. Johnson informs us that "Lindbergh gave numerous speeches at the time denouncing President Franklin D. Roosevelt and Jews as 'warmongers.'" As concerns the Jews, this statement is a lie or, more likely, the product of a slovenly scribbler who could not be bothered to ascertain the easily accessible truth (see Berg 1998, pp. 425–27). Lindbergh gave only a single, famous (or notorious) speech mentioning the Jews, in Des Moines, in October 1941. There he identified them not as "warmongers" but as, along with the Roosevelt administration and the British government, one of the main forces agitating for war with Germany but strongly cautioning that this policy was detrimental to the interests of Jewish Americans.

It is noteworthy that among the hundreds of letters Princeton made public were expressions of support for Lindbergh's antiwar stance from well-known writers such as W. H. Auden and, rather lower down the literary line (although she won the Nobel Prize for Literature in 1938), Pearl Buck. Readers surprised by the appearance of these names in this context would profit from consulting Bill Kauffman's brilliant *America First! Its History, Culture, and Politics* (1995). As Kauffman shows, many of the celebrities of the American cultural scene—outside of Manhattan and Hollywood—strongly sympathized with the AFC: Sherwood Anderson, E. E. Cummings, Theodore Dreiser, Edgar Lee Masters, Henry Miller, Sinclair Lewis, Kathleen Norris, Frank Lloyd Wright, Charles Beard, and H. L. Mencken, among others. The total membership of the AFC exceeded 800,000, and it had millions of fellow travelers.

Storm on the Horizon proceeds by examining in detail the various episodes of the war abroad and the controversies they generated at home, beginning with the German invasion of Poland and the "Phony War" on the western front, and ending with the last, futile negotiations with the Japanese envoys and the attack on Pearl Harbor. Doenecke deals with every significant issue of American foreign or military policy in this period. Many of these issues were new to me—for instance, the debates over a possible loan to Finland after the Soviet attack in November 1939 and over the fortification of Guam. Also indicative of the richness of the book are the frequent fascinating tidbits Doenecke serves up; for example, American gunboats were still patrolling the Yangtze as late as 1940 (three years after the *Panay* incident), presumably still in the interest of Standard Oil. Also revealed is that the two principal anti-war papers, the *Chicago Tribune* and the New York *Daily News*, supported Dewey against Taft for the Republican presidential nomination in 1940 (pp. 158–59).

The non-interventionists lost the battle for the Republican nomination, as they were to lose all the battles in their short-lived campaign. The winner, Wendell Willkie, "a utilities lawyer and Wall Street magnate who had been a Democrat all but four years of his life ... came into the convention with only a handful of delegates" (p. 159). However, he enjoyed the fervent support of Henry Luce's magazines, *Life*, *Time*, and *Fortune* (the *Chicago Tribune* irreverently wondered why Luce didn't add *Infinity* to his stable), as well as, above all, the support of the *New York Herald-Tribune* and with it Wall Street and the rest of the eastern Republican establishment whose agent it was. Willkie won on the sixth ballot. He had already chided Roosevelt for tardiness in aiding the Allies and denounced other Republican leaders as "isolationists." With Willkie as the nominee, foreign policy, the one crucial issue facing the nation, was taken off the table—as is customary in American elections—much to the delight of the British intelligence operatives working to embroil the United States in yet another world war (see Mahl 1998, 155–76).

A major landmark on the road to war was the transfer to Britain of some fifty naval destroyers in return for long-term leases on bases stretching from Newfoundland to British Guiana. The deal was effected by presidential decree and sharply criticized by most non-interventionists as contrary to U.S. and international law, whereas a few jingoists such as Colonel McCormick of the Chicago Tribune reveled in the expansion of American power. It contributed to the formation in September 1940 of the Tripartite Pact of Japan, Germany, and Italy. In turn, this agreement was misinterpreted in Washington as directed *aggressively* against the United States, rather than as intended *defensively* to forestall an American attack on any of the signatories (pp. 125–28). The Pact permitted Roosevelt to claim that "the hostilities in Europe, in Africa, and in Asia are all parts of a single world conflict" (p. 310). Henceforth, this "fundamental proposition," specious as it was, would guide U.S. policy.

Emboldened by his reelection, Roosevelt proposed the Lend-Lease Bill (H.R. 1776), one of the greatest extensions of presidential power in American history, which became law in March 1941. Although the AFC opposed Lend-Lease, it was faced with a quandary, as some anti-interventionists pointed out at the time. By supporting aid to Britain "short of war," it had opened the door to the incremental steps toward war that Roosevelt was taking and representing as his untiring struggle for peace.

Today Roosevelt's record of continual deception of the American people is unambiguous. In that sense, the old revisionists such as Charles Beard have been completely vindicated. Pro-Roosevelt historians—at least those who do not praise him outright for his noble lies—have had to resort to euphemism. Thus, Doenecke cites Warren F. Kimball, who is shocked—*shocked*—by FDR's "lack of candor" in leading the nation to war. Doenecke is much more straightforward. He notes, for example, the true role of the "neutrality patrol" that the President established in the western Atlantic in May 1941: "By flashing locations of German U-boats, the patrol would alert British merchantmen to veer away while inviting British cruisers and destroyers to attack" (p. 178). "From later March through May 1941, the president told intimates like Harold Ickes and Henry Morgenthau that he hoped an incident on the high seas might result" in providing an excuse for U.S. convoys or "possibly even a state of war with Germany" (p. 181). Still, some confirmed revisionists may conclude that Doenecke does not give due weight to FDR's colossal duplicity. Thus, although he mentions Roosevelt's meeting with George VI in Hyde Park in June 1939 (p. 125), he is silent on the President's promise to the British monarch—before the war even began—of full U.S. support in any military conflict with Germany (Wheeler-Bennett 1958, pp. 390–92).

The German invasion of Russia in June 1941 seemed to strengthen the anti-interventionist case, in two ways. On the one hand, it pulled the rug out from under those who had argued (as some still argue) for the infinite moral superiority of the anti-Hitler coalition. Even the tabloid New York *Daily News* was able to perceive a truth that has somehow escaped practically all current commentators: "The Soviets' Christian victims have far outnumbered the Nazis' Jewish victims" (p. 212). On the other hand, with the first German reverses in December, doubt was cast on the notion that U.S. participation in the war was required to foil a Nazi victory. As Doenecke observes, "The tide of battle, however, had swung in the Soviets' favor long before American aid had arrived in quantity" (p. 225). Taft and others had remarked that if Hitler could not conquer Britain, how was he supposed to be able to attack the United States (p. 115)? Now that the Wehrmacht was confronting the Red Army, non-interventionists could reasonably question the fantasy that Hitler was on the verge of conquering the world.

Still, hysterical scenarios from Washington and the pro-war press continued to highlight the "invasion routes" that the Germans and occasionally the Japanese might take to the conquest of the United States, via the Caribbean, the Aleutians, and Alaska, or from West Africa to Brazil and thence, somehow, to New Orleans and Miami. This last scenario was the most frequently bruited about. Anti-administration spokesmen pointed out that even if a German expeditionary force were somehow able to cross the Sahara to occupy West Africa and then pass over the Atlantic to Brazil, it would still be as far from the United States as it had been in Europe. And how was a modern mechanized army to traverse the jungles and mountains of South and Central America to invade the United States (p. 135)? Roosevelt fed the hysteria by claiming that he possessed a "secret map" showing Nazi plans to conquer South and Central America, as well as secret documents proving that Hitler planned to supplant all existing religions with a Nazi Church (p. 266). Needless to say, these statements were further falsehoods.

Another landmark on the road to war was the Atlantic Charter meeting between FDR and Churchill off the Newfoundland coast in August 1941. Churchill reported to his cabinet: the President had confided that "he would wage war, but not declare it, and that he would become more and more provocative.... Everything was to be done to force an 'incident'" (pp. 239–40). A month later, FDR did provoke the "incident" involving the U.S. destroyer *Greer*, which he used as a pretext for his order to "shoot on sight" any German or Italian vessels in the three-quarters of the North Atlantic that, as Doenecke states, now comprised our "defensive waters." The AFC accused FDR of initiating "an undeclared war, in plain violation of the Constitution." The public did not care very much and the President not at all. A few days later, American ships and planes began escorting convoys carrying munitions of war to Britain (pp. 259–61). Attacks on U.S. warships multiplied as Congress voted to arm American merchant ships, depriving them of any immunity as neutrals, and to permit U.S. naval vessels to enter the previously off-limits "combat zones." What prevented a war from breaking out was Hitler's resolve to keep the United States neutral until he was ready for the American onslaught.

By this time, Herbert Hoover was privately warning that FDR and his people were "doing everything they can to get us into war through the Japanese back door" (p. 317). In response to Japanese advances in Indochina, Roosevelt, together with Churchill, froze all Japanese assets, effectively imposing an embargo on oil shipments and starting the clock on the final stranding of the Imperial Japanese Navy. Edwin M. Borchard, Yale Law professor and authority on international law, commented: "While threatening Japan with dire consequences if she touches the Netherlands East Indies, our embargoes force her to look in that direction" (p. 306). Glimpsing the future that America's rulers had in store for the Republic, Borchard noted, "Apparently we are getting to the point where no change can be made in the world's political control without offense to the United States" (p. 308).

One of the many merits of *Storm on the Horizon* is that it exhibits the contrast between the Old Right and the later conservative movement that took shape in the mid-1950s as a global anti-Communist crusade. (On the earlier movement, see the excellent study by Sheldon Richman [1996].) One important difference concerns the conservatives' attitudes toward Western imperialism, particularly in East Asia. William Henry Chamberlin criticized Roosevelt's evident intention to sacrifice American lives in order to keep the Dutch in the East Indies and the British in Singapore (p. 290). John T. Flynn ridiculed the notion of going to war against Japan over the Philippines, since such a conflict would, in reality, be in the service of only a few dozen U.S. corporations (p. 299). Unlike later conservatives, who were ready to portray any anti-Communist despot (for example, Syngman Rhee) as practically a Jeffersonian democrat, the non-interventionists saw Chiang Kai-shek for what he was, an autocrat and a gangster (p. 287).

The anti-interventionists were a courageous bunch, and they paid a price for their scruples. Harry Elmer Barnes was purged from the *New York World-Telegram*, Oswald Garrison Villard from *The Nation*, and Flynn from *The New Republic*. The *Baltimore Sun* even had the nerve to fire H. L. Mencken, that paper's sole claim to fame in its 164-year history. Universities banned antiwar speakers from their campuses, and local officials tried to prevent the AFC from holding rallies (p. 275). In and out of the administration, interventionists defamed their opponents as mouthpieces of the Nazis, cogs in the Nazi propaganda machine, or, at best, "unwitting" tools of fascism. Roosevelt's Secretary of the Interior, Harold Ickes—a notable bottom feeder—called the old liberal Oswald Garrison Villard and the democratic socialist Norman Thomas allies of Hitler (p. 271). The influential Friends of Democracy, before and during the war, slandered non-interventionists such as Robert Taft for being "very closely" tied to the Axis line. This organization won the gushing plaudits of the ever-gushing Eleanor Roosevelt (Ribuffo 1983, p. 189). Egged on by Roosevelt, the FBI "began to tap the telephones and open the mail of vocal opponents of FDR's foreign policy and to monitor anti-intervention rallies." It "instituted surveillance of several of the president's prominent congressional critics," including Senators Burton K. Wheeler and Gerald Nye. "The White House and the Justice Department also leaked to sympathetic journalists information from FBI files that was thought to be embarrassing to anti-interventionists" (Haynes 1996, pp. 28–29).

Left-liberal intellectuals, academic and otherwise, never cease bemoaning a time of terror in America known as the Age of McCarthyism. In so doing, they lack what might be termed the dialectical approach. For many conservatives who supported Senator McCarthy in the early 1950s, it was essentially payback time for the torrent of slanders they had endured before and during World War II. Post-war conservatives took deep satisfaction in pointing out the Communist leanings and connections of those who had libeled them as mouthpieces for Hitler. Unlike the anti-war leaders, who were never "Nazis," the targets of McCarthyism had often been abject apologists for Stalin, and some of them actual Soviet agents.

Once or twice, Doenecke himself inadvertently and somewhat oddly comes close to echoing these interventionist charges. In June 1940, Congressional interventionists passed a resolution allegedly reaffirming the Monroe Doctrine: it proclaimed the non-admissibility of any transfer of sovereignty within the Western Hemisphere from one nation to another—for example, of the Dutch West Indies to Germany. The German diplomatic response denied any wish to occupy such territories, but observed in passing that the Monroe Doctrine could claim validity only under the condition that the United States refrain from interference in European affairs. Doenecke states that "several anti-interventionists adopted Foreign Minister Joachim von Ribbentrop's logic of two separate spheres" (p. 121). What the anti-interventionists adopted, however, was not Ribbentrop's logic, but the clear meaning of the Monroe Doctrine itself as expressed when it was first announced.

If *Storm on the Horizon* has any fault, it would mainly concern Doenecke's technique of proceeding from one event to the next, canvassing a few anti-interventionist voices involved in each in its turn. Though he insists on the importance of the underlying ideologies of the non-interventionists, some may find that his procedure militates against the presentation of a coherent account. Moreover, it is arguable that he might have paid more sustained attention to the views of Senator Taft, John T. Flynn, Felix Morley, Father James Gillis (editor of *The Catholic World*), and the international law experts Edwin M. Borchard and John Bassett Moore, and less to those of Hugh Johnson, Lawrence Dennis, William Randolph Hearst, and *Social Justice*.

Nonetheless, *Storm on the Horizon* is a work of outstanding scholarship. Students of the greatest anti-war movement in American history, revisionists and non-revisionists alike, are permanently in Justus Doenecke's debt.

Bibliography

Berg, A. Scott. 1998. *Lindbergh.* New York: G. P. Putnam's Sons, 1998.

Haynes, John E. 1996. *Red Scare or Red Menace: American Communism and Anticommunism in the Cold War Era.* Chicago: Ivan R. Dee, 1990.

Kauffman, Bill. 1995. *America First! Its History, Culture, and Politics.* Amherst, N.Y.: Prometheus, 1995.

Mahl, Thomas E. 1998. *Desperate Deception: British Covert Operations in the United States, 1939–44.* Washington, D.C.: Brassey's, 1998.

Ribuffo, Leo P. 1983. *The Old Christian Right: The Protestant Far Right from the Great Depression to the Cold War.* Philadelphia: Temple University Press, 1988.

Richman, Sheldon. 1996. "New Deal Nemesis: The 'Old Right' Jeffersonians." *The Independent Review* 1 (Fall), pp. 201–48.

Wheeler-Bennett, John W. 1958. *King George VI: His Life and Reign.* New York: St. Martin's, 1958.

White, Graham J. 1979. *FDR and the Press.* Chicago: University of Chicago Press, 1979.

Chapter 12

The Great War Retold

These are boom times for histories of World War I, which, like its sequel, though to a lesser degree, seems to be the war that never ends. Works keep appearing on issues once considered settled, such as the "Belgian atrocities" and the reputation of commanders such as Douglas Haig. Cambridge University Press recently published a collection of more than 500 pages on one of the most exhaustively examined subjects in the whole history of historical writing, the origins of World War I. In the past few years, at least six general works, by both academic and popular historians, have appeared in English. *The Western Front: Battle Ground and Home Front in the First World War* (New York: Palgrave, Macmillan, 2003) by T. Hunt Tooley, who teaches at Austin College in Texas, falls into the academic category, and for such a short volume (305 pages) it offers a very great deal indeed.

Tooley traces the roots of the world-historical catastrophe of 1914–18 to the Franco-Prussian War, which, though it achieved German unification in 1871, understandably fostered an enduring

---

This discussion, here slightly modified, of T. Hunt Tooley's *The Western Front* was first published in *The Independent Review*, Winter, 2005.

resentment in France, "a country that was accustomed to humiliating others during 400 years of warmaking and aggression" (p. 5). The German Chancellor Bismarck sought to ensure the Second Reich's security through defensive treaties with the remaining continental powers (the ones with Austria-Hungary and Italy constituted the Triple Alliance). Under the new (and last) Kaiser, Wilhelm II, however, the treaty with Russia was permitted to lapse, freeing Russia to ally with France. The British perceived the overambitious Wilhelm's extensive naval program as a mortal threat; starting in 1904, they developed an *Entente cordiale* (cordial understanding) with France, which was enlarged in 1907 to include Russia. Now the Germans had good reason to fear a massive *Einkreisung* (encirclement).

A series of diplomatic crises increased tensions, aggravated by the two Balkan wars of 1912–13, from which a strong Serbia emerged, evidently aiming at the disintegration of the Habsburg monarchy. With Russia acting as Serbia's mentor and growing in power every year, military men in Vienna and Berlin reflected that if the great conflict was destined to come, then better sooner than later.

Tooley lays out this background clearly and faultlessly, but he points out that the period preceding the war was by no means one of unalloyed hostility among the European nations. Cooperation was also apparent, formally, through the Hague agreements of 1899 and 1907, encouraging arbitration of disputes and the amelioration of warfare, and, more importantly, through the vast informal network of international commerce, undergirded by what Tooley calls the "unique advantage" of the international gold standard (p. 8). It was a time of remarkable prosperity and rising living standards, which, one may add, provoked the revisionist crisis in Marxist thought. Offsetting these gains were the steady growth of state apparatuses and the rise of protectionism and neomercantilism, providing a pretext for colonial expansion. In turn, the quest for colonies and spheres of influence fueled the spirit of militant rivalry among the powers.

Tooley deals deftly with the intellectual and cultural currents of prewar Europe. Contributing to the proneness to violence were a bastardized Nietzschianism and the anarchosyndicalism of Georges Sorel, but most of all Social Darwinism—really, just Darwinism—which taught the eternal conflict among the races and tribes of the human as of other species. The press and popular fiction, especially "boys' fiction," glorified the derring-do of war, while avoiding any graphic, off-putting descriptions of what combat actually inflicts on men, much as the U.S. media do today.

Archduke Franz Ferdinand's assassination in Sarajevo by a Bosnian Serb set "the stone rolling down the hill," as the German Chancellor Bethman Hollweg bleakly put it. Mobilizations and ultimatums quickly followed, and in a few days the giant conscript armies of the continental powers were in motion.

In democratic Great Britain, a commitment to France had been hidden from the public, from Parliament, and even from almost all of the Cabinet. The German declaration of war on Russia and France placed the Asquith government in a grave quandary, but, as Tooley writes, "the first German footfall in Belgium salvaged the situation" (p. 39). Now Foreign Secretary Edward Grey could deceitfully claim that England was joining its Entente partners simply to defend Belgian neutrality.

The war was greeted as a cleansing, purifying moment, at least by most of the urban masses, whose enthusiasm easily outweighed the rural population's resigned passivity. As Tooley states, untold millions were infused with a sense of "community"; they had finally found a purpose in their lives, "even perhaps a kind of salvation" (p. 43). Thus, back in 1914 the same dismal motivation was at work that Chris Hedges documents for more recent conflicts in his *War Is a Force That Gives Us Meaning* (New York: Public Affairs, 2002).

Especially ecstatic were the intellectuals, who viewed the war as a triumph of "idealism" over the selfish individualism and crass materialism of "the trading and shopkeeping spirit" (p. 43), i.e., free market capitalism. The poet Rupert Brooke (who was to die a year later) spoke for many of them on both sides when he wrote: "Now, God be thanked Who has matched us with His hour, / And caught our youth, and wakened us from sleeping...." Socialist parties, except in Russia and later Italy, added their eager support to the bloodletting, as did even renowned anarchists like Benjamin Tucker and Peter Kropotkin.

The German strategy in the event of war on two fronts, the famous Schlieffen plan, foolishly assumed the infallibility of its execution and ignored the factors that doomed it: active Belgian resistance, the rapid Russian mobilization, and the landing of the British Expeditionary Force (those mercenaries who, as another poet, A. E. Housman, wrote, "saved the sum of things for pay"). Tooley highlights the sometimes critical role of individual character here and at other points. The vacillating German commander Helmut von Moltke botched the invasion, suffered a nervous breakdown, and was demoted.

Though many battles have been billed as turning points in history, the first battle of the Marne actually was. The German Army cracked its head against the wall of "French decadence," some twenty-five miles north of Paris. The Germans pulled back, and the ensuing consolidation of the battle lines formed the Western front, which would not move more than a few dozen miles in either direction for the next three and a half years.

The author explains how advanced military technology—machine guns, grenades, poison gas, flamethrowers, and, above all, improved heavy artillery—soon began to take a toll no one could have imagined. The interplay of military hardware and evolving tactics is set forth plainly and intelligibly, even for those who, like me, had little or no previous knowledge of how armies operate in battle.

In 1916, "the butcher's bill," as Robert Graves called it, came due at Verdun and at the Somme. Ill-educated neoconservatives who in 2002–2003 derided France as a nation of cowards seem never to have heard of Verdun, where a half-million French casualties were the price of keeping the Germans at bay. On the first day of the battle of the Somme, the brainchild of Field Marshal Haig, the British lost more men than on any other single day in the history of the Empire, more than in acquiring India and Canada combined. Tooley's description of both murderous, months-long battles, as of all the major fighting on the front, is masterly.

The author states that his main theme is "the relationship between the battle front and the home fronts" (p. 1), and the interplay between the two is sustained throughout the book.

The dichotomy of a militarized Germany and a liberal West, Tooley shows, is seriously overdrawn. To be sure, the Germans pioneered and practiced "war socialism" most methodically (today in the Federal Republic, the man in charge, Walter Rathenau, is, predictably, honored as a great liberal). In Britain, France, and later the United States, proponents of centralization and planning cheerfully exploited the occasion to extend state activism into every corner of the economy.

The quickly escalating costs of the war led to unprecedented taxation and a vast redistribution of wealth, basically from the middle classes to the recipients of government funds: contractors and workers in war industries, subsidized industrialists and farmers, and, most of all, financiers. The deluded patriots who purchased government war bonds were crippled by inflation, now "introduced [to] the twentieth century ... as a way of life" (p. 113). Tooley cites Murray Rothbard on one of the hidden detriments of the war: it initiated the inflationary business cycle that led to the Great Depression.

Freedom of expression was beaten down everywhere. Many readers will be familiar with the outlines of the story as regards the United States, but Tooley fills in revealing details of the national ignominy: for example, the U.S. Attorney-General's imprisonment of Americans for even discussing whether conscription was unconstitutional or for recalling that Wilson had won the 1916 election on the slogan "He kept us out of war," as well as the action of groups of Boy Scouts stealing and destroying bundles of German-American newspapers that the alert lads intuited were fomenting treason and insurrection. In some countries, the suppression was worse. Australia, we learn, prohibited the teaching and use of the German language, incarcerated 4,500 citizens of German descent, and expropriated and deported those broadly defined as "enemy aliens." The aggrandizement of state power in the combatant countries reached, Tooley notes, a kind of *reductio ad absurdum* in what was probably the war's worst result: the establishment of a terrorist totalitarian regime by the Bolsheviks in Russia.

U.S. entry had been virtually determined in the wake of the sinking of the *Lusitania*, when the terminally anglophiliac Wilson administration declared that the Germans would be held "strictly accountable" for the loss of any Americans' lives through U-boat action, even when those Americans were traveling on armed British merchant ships carrying munitions of war. Wilson's "neutrality" was, in Tooley's term, seriously "lopsided" (p. 81) because the administration declined to challenge the British over their hunger blockade—"ruthless ... inexorable" (pp. 81–82), as well as illegal by the standards of international law—which was aimed at starving the whole German civilian population into submission.

British propaganda was, as always, topnotch. Its high point was the mendacious Bryce report on the "Belgian atrocities." Of course, the Germans had behaved harshly in Belgium (as the Russians had in the East), but it was the report's "bizarre and clinical sadism" (p. 128) that set American blood boiling, at least the blue blood of the East Coast Anglo elite. After the desperate Germans announced unrestricted submarine warfare, Wilson asked Congress for a declaration of war, not just to call Germany to account for supposed violations of U.S. rights, but to "make the world safe for democracy." Warmongering clergymen—supposedly humble followers of the Prince of Peace—manipulated public opinion on behalf of Wilson's open-ended crusade. This sellout is detailed in another recent work, Richard Gamble's excellent study *The War for Righteousness: Progressive Christianity, the Great War, and the Rise of the Messianic Nation*, discussed in this volume.

The Bolshevik *coup d'état* of November 1917 led to an armistice in the East, and the Germans launched their final, all-out push on the Western front. The Ludendorff offensive made some initial breakthroughs but petered out for lack of materiel and reserves, as Erich Maria Remarque describes in the last pages of *All Quiet on the Western Front*. By the summer of 1918, the American expeditionary force under General John G. Pershing amounted to two million men, many of them keen to make the whole world safe for democracy. Their Meuse-Argonne offensive, which began in September, helped convince the Germans that the time had come for an armistice. At the eleventh hour of the eleventh day of November, the guns fell silent on the Western Front.

At the Paris Conference of 1919, face to face with the seasoned and crafty politicians of the other victorious powers, Wilson, in Tooley's apt phrase, resembled "the parson showing up at a high-stakes poker game" (p. 252). It was a game at which the Princeton professor was pathetically inept. Fearing a Bolshevik revolution that might engulf Central Europe, "the Allies imposed as punitive a treaty as they dared upon the Germans" (p. 252). A century earlier, after the Napoleonic wars, the aristocrats at the Congress of Vienna fashioned a viable *system* that avoided general war for another hundred years. At Paris in 1919, the diplomats, now answerable to their democratic constituencies, set the stage for a virtually inevitable future conflict. Tooley very correctly places the word *peace*, as in the Versailles "Peace" Treaty, in ironic quotes.

On the overall consequences of the war, the author utilizes Robert Higgs's conceptual framework in his seminal *Crisis and Leviathan: Critical Episodes in the Growth of American Government*. In U.S. history, crises, most often wars, have resulted in a great expansion of state power. Once the crisis is over, the state and its budgets, deficits, functionaries, and regulations are cut back to more normal levels, but never to what they were before, and they go on from there. Ideology, the underlying political mentality of the people, is also permanently skewed in a state-receptive direction. As Tooley sums up, "If the twentieth century became the century of managerial control, of the prioritizing of group goals and group efficiency over the autonomies of individuals, families, and regions, then we will find in World War I the accelerator of processes which were emerging before then" (p. 267).

I have touched on only some of the main features of Tooley's book. Amazingly for such a concise work, it contains a great deal more. The only fault I can find is its somewhat misleading title. *The Western Front* is by no means merely an account of the war in the West. In my opinion, it is the best introduction we have to the history of the Great War altogether.

Index

A
ABC of Communism, The, 147
Abel, Theodore, 204
Acheson, Dean, 117, 217
Adenauer, Konrad, 159
Alienation and the Soviet Economy, 169
All Quiet on the Western Front, 234
Ambrose, Stephen, 123
America First Committee, 210, 211, 220
America First!, 220
America's Second Crusade, 163
anarcho-capitalism, ix
Anderson, Sherwood, 221
Anglo-American Sozialpolitik, 77
Anscombe, G. E. M., 138
Apis, 10
Arnold, Henry, 133
Artamonov, Colonel, 10
As We Go Marching, 212
Asquith, Prime Minister, 15, 64
Auden, W. H., 220
Attlee, Clement, 98

B
Back Door to War, 163
Baden-Powell, Robert, 202
Bailey, Thomas A., 75, 214
Baldwin, Hanson, 81

Baltimore Sun, 225
Barnes, Fred, 187
Barnes, Harry Elmer, 225
Baruch, Bernard, 35, 127
Bases-for-Destroyers deal, 73
Bataan death march, 133
Bauer, Peter, 128, 183
Beard, Charles, 121, 180, 214, 221, 22
Beesly, Patrick, 67
Ben-Moshe, Tuvia, 81
Beneš, Eduard, 48, 95
Bentham, Jeremy, 217
Berlin, Isaiah, 82
Beveridge, William, 56, 64, 99
Bismarck, Otto von, 5, 61
Black Hand, 10
Black, Hugo, 126
Boothby, Robert, 97
Borchard, Edwin M., 28, 224, 226
Bright, John, viii
Brooke, Rupert, 231
Brown, John, viii
Brüning, Heinrich, 51
Bryan, William Jennings, 22, 27, 199
Bryce Report, 26
Buchanan, Pat, 157
Buck, Pearl, 220
Buckley, William F., Jr., 54, 207, 218

Bukharin, Nikolai, 147, 170, 171
Bullitt, William C., 189
Burleson, Albert, 39
Bush, George, 136
butcher's bill, 232
Butler, Nicholas Murray, 39
Butler, R. A., 100
Byrnes, James F., 139

C

Carnegie, Andrew, 181
Castle, Irene, 210
Catholic World, The, 141, 226
Chamberlin, Stephen J., 111
Chamberlin, William Henry, 163, 225
Charmley, John, 73, 97
Chiang Kai-shek, 225
Chicago Tribune, 115, 221, 222
Chodorov, Frank, ix, 207, 218
Churchill, Winston
   Anglo-American Sozialpolitik, 77
   British Empire, 57
   carpet bombing, 90
   cradle to the grave, 99
   crimes and atrocities of the victors, 93
   Fascismo's triumphant struggle, 56
   forced repatriation, 93
   founder of the welfare state, 53
   fundamental and fatal mistake, 80
   German threat, 70, 86
   Grand Alliance, 70, 105
   hunger blockade, 66
   Iron Curtain speech, 98
   lost religious faith, 59
   love of war, 58
   modern mythology of, 69
   nature of man, 62
   opportunist, 55
   organisation of human society, 62
   perfect hustling political entrepreneur, 63
   plagiarized Clemenceau, 55
   Princip, Gavrilo, 11
   provocation, the back door to war, 78
   rabid for war, 16
   racism, 59
   rhetorical skill, 57
   Roosevelt, secret communications with, 73
   Savrola, 59
   sinking of the Lusitania, 66, 67
   slave labor reparations, 95
   soft underbelly strategy, 83
   Solzhenitsyn, Alexander, 94
   starve the population, 24
   Tito, Churchill's protégé, 94
   Twain, Mark, 60
   two principles, 56
   unconditional support to Stalin, 57
   war correspondent, 60
   welfare-warfare state, 53
   Zionist, 70
Clark, Champ, 40
Clark, Tom, 123, 126
Clausewitz, Carl von, 80
Clay, Lucius, 111
Clemenceau, Georges, 46
Clifford, Clark, 129
Clinton, Bill, 132
Cobden, Richard, vii, viii, 17, 178, 184
Cohn-Bendit, Daniel and Gabriel, 172
Colin Powell and the Power Elite, 157
Committee on Public Information, 39
Communist Manifesto, The, 172
Conquest of the United States by Spain, The, ix, 181
Constant, Benjamin, 151
Coughlin, Charles, 220
Council on Foreign Relations, 217
Country Squire in the White House, 210
Cowen, Tyler, 182
Craig, Gordon, 71
Craigie, Robert, 78
Creel, George, 39
Crisis and Leviathan, 34, 235

INDEX

Criticòn, 160
Crux Ansata, 196
Cummings, E. E., 210, 221
Czechoslovakia, creation of, 47

D
Daily News, 221, 223
Davies, Norman, 80
Debs, Eugene V., 38, 39, 41, 42
Declaration of London, 23
Declaration of Paris, 24
Dennis, Lawrence, 226
development aid, harmful effects, 128
Devlin, Patrick, 198
Dewey, John, 34, 211
Dewey, Thomas E., 119
Die Zeit, 161
Dimitrievic, Colonel Dragutin, 10
Doenecke, Justus D., 114, 219–226
Donovan, William, 76
Douglas, William O., 126
Dreiser, Theodore, 221
Dulles, John Foster, 217
Durant, William, 31

E
Eden, Anthony, 78, 80
Eighteenth Brumaire of Louis Bonaparte, The, 167
Eisenhower, Dwight D., 87, 100, 112, 130–131, 137, 217,
Empire, 190
Engels
   Bolshevik leaders, avid students of, 144
   bourgeois freedom and jurisprudence, 150
   equal labor liability, 172
   foreign policy of the International, 173
   seizure of the means of production, 145
Erdmann, Karl Dietrich, 15
Eshkol, Levi, 159
Espionage Act of 1917, 38

Ethnic America, 158
European Recovery Act, 111

F
Falaba, 25
Faunce, William, 196
Fay, Sidney, 3, 12, 65
Federal Trade Commission, 36
Ferdinand, Franz, 4, 10, 11
Ferguson, Niall, 189
Firmage, Edwin B., 120
First World War, The, 185
Fischer school, and Hitler's Germany, 4
Fischer, Fritz, 3–4, 14–15, 204
Fischer, Sir John, 16
Fisher, Warren, 86
Fleming, Thomas, 187, 191
Flynn, John T., 208, 225, 226
Ford, Gerald, 211
foreign aid, harmful effects, 128
Foreign Policy for America, A, 180
Forever Flowing, 152
Forrestal, James, 107, 139
Fortune, 221
Frankfurter Allgemeine, 160
Frankfurter, Felix, 126
Frederick II, King of Prussia, vii
Freud, Sigmund, 189
Fuller, J. F. C., 55, 141, 186

G
Gaddis, John Lewis, 112
Gamble, Richard, 192, 234
Garrity, Devin, 213
Gaulle, Charles de, 186
George VI (king), 73, 223
German Atrocities, 191
Gillis, James, 141, 226
Gingrich, Newt, 54
Gish, Lillian, 210, 211
Gladstone, William, Prime Minister, viii
glasnost, 147, 153
God's Gold, 209

Godkin, E. L., ix
Goebbels, Josef, 22
Goeben, 65
Goldhagen Debate, 162
Goldhagen, Daniel Jonah, 160, 189
Goldwater, Barry, 120
Gompers, Samuel, 37
Gorbachev, Mikhail, 147, 149, 150, 153, 155, 183
Gordon, Sarah, 161
Grab for World Power, 3
Grand Alliance, 70, 105
Graves, Robert, 232
Greenleaf, W. H., 99
Gregory, Thomas W., 38
Grew, Joseph, 78, 139
Grey, Foreign Secretary Edward, 15, 22, 231
Griff nach der Weltmacht, 3
Grossman, Vladimir, 152
Groves, Leslie, 133
Gulag Archipelago, The, 94

H

Habermas, Jürgen, 162
Habsburg, 6, 8, 11, 47, 230
Hague Tribunal, 25
Haig, Douglas, 229
Harding, Warren, 42
Harriman, Averell, 111, 115
Harris, Arthur, 90
Hart, Basil Liddell, 186
Hartwig, Nicholas, 7, 9
Hayek, August von, 56
Hearst, William Randolph, 226
Hedges, Chris, 231
Heller, Mikhail, 162
Herald Tribune, 115
Heydrich, Reinhard, 96
Higgs, Robert, 34, 103, 213, 214, 234
High Cost of Vengeance, The, 163
Hiroshima and Nagasaki, 134
historical revisionism, vii, x
Hitchens, Christopher, 54

Hitler, Adolf
  20 million Germans too many, 189
  anti-Hitler coalition, 223
  anti-Nazi Germans, 82, 86
  attack the United States, 223
  Churchill as adversary, 55, 57, 59, 69, 73
  conquered the world, 140
  Harriman's Hitler card, 112
  Hitler, Germans, and the Jewish Question, 161
  Hitler's Willing Executioners, 160
  Ickes, Harold, 225
  inveigaling US to enter the war, 78
  message from Roosevelt to Churchill, 75
  might makes right, 163
  moral postulate, 80
  mouthpieces, 226
  off-limits critical theses, 74
  peace overtures, 73
  prevention of, 1
  Red Hitler, 107
  Roosevelt, falsehoods, 223
  specter of Prussianism, 85
  Why Hitler Came into Power, 204
  zoological warfare, 189
Hitler, Germans, and the Jewish Question, 161
Hitler's Willing Executioners, 160
Hohenzollerns, Prussian, 1
Hollweg, Chancellor Bethmann, 11, 15, 16, 230
Holmes, Jr., Oliver Wendell, 39
Homo sovieticus, 148
Hoover, Herbert, 36, 139, 203, 219, 224
Hopkins, Harry, 21, 75
Horne, John, 191
House, Colonel Edward Mandell, 8, 20, 24, 30–31, 43
Housman, A. E., 232
Howard, Michael, 185
Howe, Irving, 165–176
Howe, Julia Ward, 193

INDEX 241

Human Events, 141

I
Ickes, Harold, 211, 222, 225
Illusion of Victory, The, 187, 189
Income Tax Amendment of 1913, 36
Industrial Workers of the World, 37
Infinity, 221
Intercollegiate Society of
    Individualists, x
Intercollegiate Studies Institute, x
International Court of Justice, 25
ISI, x
Isolationism Reconfigured, 181
Ivins, Molly, 157

J
J. P. Morgan, House of, 25
Jackson, Robert H., 131
Jacobson, Eddie, 129
Jaffa, Harry, 52, 79
James, Robert Rhodes, 60
jobbers' war, viii
Johnson, Hugh, 226
Johnson, Linda A., 220
Johnson, Lyndon, 182
Joll, James, 13
Josef, Franz, (emperor king), 7, 10

K
Kai-shek, Chiang, 225
Karp, Walter, 19, 42, 189
Kauffman, Bill, 208, 220
Kennan, George, 108
Kennedy, John F., 211
Kennedy, Joseph, 74
Kent, Tyler, 72
Khrushchev, Nikita, 155
Kimball, Warren F., 222
Kirk, Russell, 207
Kitchin, Claude, 33
Klugman, James, 84
Knightley, Philip, 22
Korda, Alexander, 76
Kramer, Alan, 191

Kristallnacht, 161
Kropotkin, Peter, 231
Kuehnelt-Leddihn, Erik von, 93

L
La Follette, Robert, 31, 32, 180
Lafore, Laurence, 6
Lage, William Pooter, 28
Lamb, Richard, 78
Landry, Robert B., 112
Langdon, John W., 15
Lansing, Robert, 29, 192
Lattimore, Owen, 155, 216
Lawrence, David, 142
League of Nations, 41, 43, 189
Leahy, William D., 137
Lederer, Emil, 198
Lee, Arthur, 16
LeMay, Curtis, 132
Lend-Lease Agreement, 73
Lend-Lease Bill, 222
Lenin
    abolition of rights, 150
    confronts Imperial Russian Army, 2
    contingent revolution, 173
    economic ignorance, 171
    labor camps, 152
    labor draft, 149
    Marxism, as understood by, 144
    opportunities of war, 34
    policy follows power, 170
    revolutionary terror, 150, 173
    skills to run a national economy, 147
    State and Revolution, 147
Lever Act, 35
Lewis, C. S., 149
Lewis, Sinclair, 210, 221
Liggio, Leonard, x
Lindbergh, Anne Morrow, 220
Lindbergh, Charles, 211, 220
Lindemann, Frederick, 87, 88, 90
Link, Arthur S., 19
Lippmann, Walter, 34
Literature and Revolution, 148
Lloyd George, David, 46, 50, 61, 202

Lodge, Henry Cabot, Jr., 109, 189
Loewenberg, Peter, 203
Longworth, Alice Roosevelt, 210
Luce, Henry, 115, 221
Lusitania, 26–27, 29, 67, 181, 233

M

MacArthur, Douglas, 117
MacDonough, Giles, 96
Machajski, Waclaw, 146, 168
Maclean, Fitzroy, 85
Madison, James, 122, 180
Maria Theresa, Empress, vii
Marshall, George, 110, 111
Marx, Marxism
  Bolshevik view, 144
  bourgeois ideology, 151
  conceptual pathway to power, 146
  Eighteenth Brumaire of Louis Bonaparte, The, 167
  foreign policy, 173
  guilt, 150
  People's State of Marx, 168
  right to coerce, 172
  Trosky view, 148, 174
  view of market processes, 145
Masaryk, Thomas, 48
Masters, Edgar Lee, 221
Maurer, Robert, 164
McCarthy, Joseph, 216, 217
McCarthyism, 40, 154, 212, 216, 226
McCormick, Robert R., 115, 221
McCullough, David, 123, 126
McDougall, Walter A.
  America as Promised Land, 179
  Anti-Imperialist League, 181
  global meddling, 180–184
  isolationism, 178, 179
  Promised Land, Crusader State, 177
  U.S. foreign policy, 177
  unilateralism, 179
McNutt, Paul V., 134
Mencken, H.L., ix, 221, 225
Mercader, Ramón, 166
military Keynesianism, 116

Miller, Henry, 221
Mises, Ludwig von, 1, 59, 98, 144
Molinari, Gustave de, ix
Moltke, Helmut, 14, 232
Monckton, Walter, 100
Mond, Robert, 70
Monroe Doctrine, 32, 177, 180, 226,
Monroe, James, 180
Moore, John Bassett, 25, 226
Moore, Jr., Charles W., 188
Morgenthau Plan, 87, 88, 163
Morgenthau, Hans, 122
Morgenthau, Henry, 222
Morley, Felix, 141, 226
Morley, Lord John, 17
Murdoch, Rupert, 187
Mussolini, Benito, 56
Myth of a Guilty Nation, The, ix

N

Nagasaki and Hiroshima, 134
Napoleon, 16, 186
Nation, The, 115, 225
National Defense Act, 34
National Geographic, 155
National Security Council, 116
NATO, 116, 131
Nekrich, Aleksandr M., 162
neocon, x
New Deal
  assertions of state sovereignty, 40
  Flynn, John Thomas, opposition, 209
  New Deal Brain Trust, 35
  property rights, 214
  Roosevelt Myth, The, 208
  scions of, 54
  successive New Deals, 213
New Dealers' War, The, 187
New Republic, The, 34, 115, 189, 210, 218, 225
New Right, x, 218
New Soviet Man, 148
New World Order, 46, 55, 82, 215
New York Herald-Tribune, 221

INDEX

New York Times
  best-seller list, 213
  Churchill revelations, 77
  claim unlimited presidential
    authority, 126
  Duranty, Walter, 154
  echo government's slanders, 115
  echoed government slander, 115
  mouthpiece of the powers, 38
  Roosevelt, Franklin, 208
  Rosenthal, Abe, 160
  Truman and presidential power, 126
New York Times Book Review, 74
New York World-Telegram, 225
Nicholas II, 13
Niles, David K., 129
Nisbet, Robert, 207, 215
Nixon, Richard M., 217
Nock, Albert Jay, ix, 207, 218
Nolte, Ernst, 161, 164
Nomad, Max, 168
Nordlinger, Eric, 181
Norris, Kathleen, 210, 221
North Atlantic Treaty Organization, 116
Nuremberg Trials, 97, 131
Nye, Gerald 225

O

On Compromise, 17
Operation Keelhaul, 132
Oxford History of the Twentieth Century, 186

P

Page, Walter Hines, 28
Paléologue, Maurice, 13
Palmer, A. Mitchell, 41
Pašic, Nicolas, 9
Paterson, Cissy, 115
Pavlik, Gregory, 217
peacetime sedition act, 41
Pendergast, Tom, 132
Pershing, John G., 234
Philip Dru: Administrator, 21, 31

Pity of War, The, 189
Plumer, Herbert, 202
Poincaré, Raymond, 7
Polanyi, Michael, 144
Political Writings, vii
Politics of War, The, 189
Ponting, Clive, 60, 72
Porter, Bruce, 40
Powell, Enoch, 100
Preobrazhensky, Evgeny, 147
Princip, Gavrilo, 11
Prinz Eugen, 78
Promised Land, Crusader State, 177, 181, 183

Q

Quayle, Dan, 54

R

Raimondo, Justin, 158
Rathenau, Walter, 232
Reader's Digest, 216
Regnery, Henry, 163
Reichstag elections and Hitler, 1
Reign of Terror, 149, 150
Remarque, Erich Maria, 234
Resco, Micheline, 188
revisionism, vii, ix, x, 30, 163
Rhee, Syngman, 117
Richardson, Robert C., 114
Riezler, Kurt, 11
Road Ahead, The, 216
Road to Serfdom, The, 56
Roberts, Paul Craig, 144, 169–170
Rockwell, Lew, x
Room 40, 67
Roosevelt, Eleanor, 129, 130, 225
Roosevelt, Elliott, 134
Roosevelt, Franklin
  accomplice for Joseph Kennedy, 75
  accomplice to Churchill, 75
  Albert Jay Nock, on news of
    Roosevelt's death, 207
  Anglo-American Sozialpolitik, 77
  apotheosis of, 207, 208

Roosevelt, Franklin *(cont.)*
   debunking of, 213
   despised for lying, 210
   Harry Hopkins, 21
   John T. Flynn, foe of, 208
   on delarations of war, 120
   Stalin as a fellow progressive, 82
   veneration of, 104
   Wilsonian revolution, 37
   Zionism, 128
Roosevelt Myth, The, 210, 213
Rothbard, Murray, x, 37, 69, 207, 233
Rougier, Louis, 189
Rousseau, Jean-Jacques, 149
Runciman, Walter, 67

S

Safire, William, 54, 157
Sakharov, Andrei, 155
Salisbury, Lord, British Prime Minister, 23
Savrola, 59
Sawyer, Charles, 125
Sazonov
   Erdmann, Karl Dietrich comment, 15
   on abandoning Serbia, 12
   on reading the Serbian ultimatum, 12
   our Fathers warned us of such men, 17
   Portalès presents declaration of war, 14
   the European War, 14
   writing to Hartwig, 7, 9, 10
Schlieffen Plan, 14, 16, 190, 231
Schmidt, Helmut, 161
Schumpeter, Joseph, 91
Schurz, Carl, 181
Screening History, 76
Sedition Act, 38, 41
Serge, Victor, 170
Shachtman, Max, 168
Sherwood, Robert, 211
Shriver, Sargeant, 211

Smith, Adam, 217
Social Justice, 220, 226
Solzhenitsyn, Alexander, 94, 152, 153
Sorel, Georges, 230
Sowell, Thomas, 158
Spaight, J. M., 90
Spencer, Herbert, viii
Spirit of '76, The, 38
Spooner, Lysander, viii
Spring-Rice, Cecil, 22, 24
Stalin apologists
   Duranty, Walter, 154
   Laski, Harold, 154
   Lattimore, Owen, 155, 216
   Sartre, Jean-Paul, 154
   Shaw, George Bernard, 154
   Webb, Sidney and Beatrice, 154
Stalin, Josef
   Churchill view, 57, 81, 85
   death tolls, comparative, 153
   Franklin Roosevelt's fatuousness, 82, 215
   free elections, 105
   Gorbachev indictment, 155
   Greece, 106
   intellectual affection for, x
   Lattimore, Owen, 216
   legacy, 163
   Marshall Plan, 110
   morality, 80
   personality cult, 150
   purpose of war, 80
   Red Terror, 149
   repatriation, 94
   Sakharov indictment, 155
   Taft, 115
   targets of McCarthyism, 226
   Trosky, 166, 173, 174, 176
   Truman view, 105, 113
   Turkey, 106
State and Revolution, 147
Stengers, Jean, 189
Stephenson, William, 76
Stern, Fritz, 4
Stimson, Henry, 68, 139

INDEX

Stone, Norman, 8
Storm on the Horizon, 219, 221, 224, 226
Stürmer, Michael, 159
Sumner, William Graham, ix, 181
surrender, unconditional, 87, 105, 139, 140, 141
Sussex, 28
Szasz, Thomas, 188
Szilard, Leo, 142

T

Taft, Robert, 97, 108, 124, 216, 217, 225
Taft, William Howard 19, 193
Tamas, Gaspar, 97, 158
Tansill, Charles Callan, 68, 163
Taylor, A. J. P., 69, 185
That Hideous Strength, 101
Thatcher, Margaret, 65, 183
The Nation, ix
Thomas, Norman, 210, 225
Tito, Josip Broz, 84–85, 94–95
Tocqueville, Alexis de, 143
Treaty of Versailles, 2, 50
Triple Alliance, 5, 6, 230
Triple Entente, 6
Trosky, Leon
  better never born, 176
  bureaucratic collectivism, 169
  economic ignorance, 171
  fear of capitalism restored, 169
  forced labor, 172
  historical materialism, 172, 173
  Howe's criticism, 166, 167
  ice axe to the head, 166
  industrial worker-slave armies, 175
  intellectual, 165
  Literature and Revolution, 148
  lost to Stalin, 166
  reconstruct society, 148
  revolution contingent on Lenin, 173
  rule of state functionaries, 168
  show trials, 166
  socialist rights, 174
  That Hideous Strength, 149
  war communism, 170

Truman, Harry S.
  claim unlimited presidential authority, 119, 126
  Cold War containment, 108
  exercise of dictatorial power, 124
  Fair Deal, 127
  feelings toward Stalin, 105
  from unpopular to near great, 103
  Greece and Turkey, 107
  Hiroshima and Nagasaki, 134
  international Communism, as palliative, 105
  Korean war, 117
  Marshall Plan, 110
  military Keynesianism, 116
  NATO, 116, 131
  non-existence of Soviet war plans, 113
  Operation Keelhaul, 132
  price and wage controls, 125, 127
  Truman Doctrine, 108
  unconditional, surrender, 87, 105, 139, 140, 141
  Zionism, 128
Tooley, T. Hunt, 196, 229–235,
Truman, Margaret, 130
Tucker, Benjamin, 231
Tugwell, Rexford, 35
Twain, Mark, 60

U

U.S. Aid to the Developing World, 182
U.S. News and World Report, 142
unconditional, surrender, 87, 105, 139, 140, 141
United Nations Participation Act of 1945, 121
Utley, Freda, 163
Utopia in Power, 162

V

Vandenberg, Arthur, 107
Vansittart, Robert, 86
Vidal, Gore, 76, 211
Villard, Oswald Garrison, 225

Vincent, C. Paul, 197
Vinson, Fred, 126

W
Waley-Cohn, Robert, 70
Wall Street Journal, 25, 54, 208
Wallace, Henry, 188
War Finance Corporation, 37
War for Righteousness, The, 192, 234
War Industries Board, 35
War Is a Force That Gives Us Meaning, 231
Warren, Earl, 120
Washington Times–Herald, 115
Washington, George, 32
Weaver, Richard, 142
Webb, Beatrice, 62, 64, 154
Webb, Sidney, 64
Wedemeyer, Albert C., 84
Weekly Standard, 187
Weizsäcker, Richard von, 160
Welles, Sumner, 129
Wells, H. G., 195, 196, 198
Western Front, The, 196, 229
What Is to Be Done?, 144
Wheeler-Bennett, John, 73, 223
Wheeler, Burton K., 225
White, Edward D., 22
Why Hitler Came into Power, 204
Wilhelm II, Kaiser, 5, 11, 230
Will, George, 183
Willkie, Wendell, 221
Wilson, Woodrow
  absurd Wilsonian principle, 25
  alter ego Edward Mandell House, 20, 21
  anti-John Quincy Adams, 32
  bellicose interventionism, 19
  Four Principles speech, 44
  Fourteen Points speech, 43
  House, Colonel Edward, confidant, 8
  idealist or power-hungry, 18
  keeper of the flame, Walter Karp, 19
  leadership of, 2
  peace without victory, 52
  second personality, 17
  Starving a People into Submission, 44
  Wilson's war, 40
  Wilsonian Revolution in government, 33
Wolffsohn, Michael, 164
Woods, Tom, x
Wormuth, Francis D., 120
Wright, Frank Lloyd, 221

Y
Youngstown Sheet & Tube Co. v. Sawyer, 126

Z
Zayas, Alfred de, 160
Zimmermann, Alfred, 32
Zinoviev, Lilina, 148
Zionism, 70, 128, 187
Zitelmann, Rainer, 160

About the Author

Ralph Raico is professor of European history at Buffalo State College and a specialist on the history of liberty, the liberal tradition in Europe, and the relationship between war and the rise of the state. He is the recipient of the 2000 Gary G. Schlarbaum Prize for Lifetime Achievement in the Cause of Liberty. The author is grateful to the Independent Institute for permission to reprint some of the essays in this work.

Printed in Great Britain
by Amazon